R
in
New Mexico

Religion in Modern New Mexico

EDITED BY

Ferenc M. Szasz

and Richard W. Etulain

Published in cooperation with the
UNIVERSITY OF NEW MEXICO CENTER FOR THE AMERICAN WEST

UNIVERSITY OF NEW MEXICO PRESS
Albuquerque

Library of Congress Cataloging-in-Publication Data

Religion in modern New Mexico / edited by Ferenc M. Szasz and Richard W. Etulain. — 1st ed.
　　　　p.　　cm.
"Published in cooperation with the University of New Mexico Center for the American West."
Essays first presented at a conference held at the University of New Mexico on September 11, 1993.
Includes bibliographical references and index.
ISBN 0-8263-1766-9
1. New Mexico—Religion—Congresses.
2. New Mexico—Church history—Congresses.
I. Szasz, Ferenc Morton, 1940-　.
II. Etulain, Richard W. (Richard Wayne), 1938-　.
III. University of New Mexico. Center for the American West.
BL2527.N6R45 1997
200'.9789—dc20　96-9995
CIP

© 1997 by the University of New Mexico Press
All rights reserved.
First edition

Contents

Introduction   vii

1. Roman Catholicism in Modern New Mexico
   A Commitment to Survive
   Carol Jensen   1

2. Protestantism in Modern New Mexico
   Randi Jones Walker   27

3. The Religious Culture of the Jews in Modern New Mexico
   Henry J. Tobias   63

4. Competition for the Native American Soul
   The Search for Religious Freedom in Twentieth-Century New Mexico
   Kathleen Egan Chamberlain   81

5. Mormons in Twentieth-Century New Mexico
   Leonard J. Arrington   101

6. A Rhetorical Approach to Protestant Evangelism
   in Twentieth-Century New Mexico
   Janice E. Schuetz   125

7. Boomer Dharma
*The Evolution of Alternative Spiritual Communities
in Modern New Mexico*
Stephen Fox   145

8. The United States and New Mexico
A Twentieth-Century Comparative Religious History
Ferenc M. Szasz   171

For Further Reading
An Annotated Bibliography
Daniel R. Carnett and John J. Griffin
197

Index
211

Contributors
219

Introduction

IN RECENT YEARS THE STUDY OF WESTERN AMERICAN HISTORY has evolved into a fiercely contested battleground. A cadre of "New Western Historians" has focused on "race, class, and gender" as a chief means of unlocking the secrets of the past. In numerous books and articles, they have accused more traditional western historians of an overemphasis on "triumphant expansionism," plus a blindness to the hardships that the western movement inflicted upon Native peoples and upon the land. In reply, the traditionalists have criticized their opponents' "negativity," accusing them of assuming a "moral superiority" that rests solely on the fact that they were born later in time.

In spite of often heated rhetoric, the traditionalists and the "new" western scholars have more in common than they are likely to admit. Foremost among their shared assumptions is a conspicuous lack of interest in the religious history of the American West.

To marginalize the religious aspect of western history, however, is to overlook an essential component of human experience. In addition to providing a faith perspective on life's ultimate questions, organized religion has often overlapped with western schooling, social mores, health care, ideas of justice, and even politics. At times, as in Gentile–Mormon tensions in Utah and Idaho or Catholic–Protestant antagonisms in the Southwest, religious affiliations have divided. But on other occasions—as in the role of Catholic schools in "Americanizing" Mexican and European immigrants or in the wide net cast by conservative Protestant evangelism—they have united. In truth, a shared faith perspective almost always *realigns* conventional social groupings. Membership in a particular denomination provides a common framework that transcends traditional divisions of gender, region, or ethnic grouping. Moreover, issues of faith have proven very democratic. Although not everyone shares strong views on politics, music, art, or architecture, virtually everyone has vigorous opinions on his or her own personal faith perspective or on the social value of this or that particular denomination.

Few would deny the role that religion has played in shaping the saga of early New Mexican history. From ancient times to the turn of the nineteenth century, religious themes have often held center stage: traditional Native ceremonies that ensured both social and individual harmony, plus abundant crops; the Franciscan missionaries who arrived with Coronado, Oñate, and Vargas; the Pueblo Revolt of 1680; the attempts by Jean Baptiste Lamy to "Europeanize" New Mexican Catholicism and the resulting opposition from Taos's Padre Martínez; the Italian Jesuits, the Sisters of Charity, and the Sisters of St. Joseph who built and staffed the turn-of-the-century schools and hospitals; the long-standing German Jewish mercantile community; the itinerant Protestant evangelists who handed out tracts in Spanish; the Presbyterian and Congregational missionary women who taught in a far-flung network of parochial schools; and Latter-day Saints who settled in the Farmington region. The list could easily be extended.

As these essays show, the oft-slighted religious history of twentieth-century New Mexico shares a similar significance. Indeed, by the 1990s New Mexico has evolved into a "spiritual magnet" for a wide variety of faiths, many of which extended far beyond the traditional nineteenth-century quartet of Native peoples, Protestants, Catholics, and Jews. From the 1960s forward, utopians of various stripes found homes in Taos, Sikhs settled in Española, Moslems in Abiquiu, Scientologists in Trementina, Pentecostals in the Llano Estacado and elsewhere, and a variety of "New Agers" in the region of Santa Fe. All these faiths jostled with one other and with the traditional groups, not always, it must be admitted, with the greatest of goodwill. New Mexico Archbishop Michael Sheehan's six 1994 public billboards in Albuquerque reflected both the hope and the reality of this unique situation. Said the archbishop: "Let us all live together as the sons and daughters of God."

In short, this collection of essays, the first attempt to assess the role of religion in modern New Mexico, makes important contributions to religious history and to western history. A pioneering effort in examining the varied religious cultures of the state, these articles also add much to our understanding of twentieth-century western cultural history, a field that many national or regional commentators have previously overlooked.

The editors are grateful to the volume's contributors who first presented their findings at a well-attended conference on "Religious Cultures in Modern New Mexico" at the University of New Mexico on September 11, 1993. The New Mexico Endowment for the Humanities, the University of New Mexico College of Arts and Sciences, and the Center for the American West in the UNM History Department generously supported that symposium. We also wish to thank Dan Carnett and John Griffin for preparing the annotated bibliography; Traci Hukill and Jill Howard for helping to plan and organize the conference; Jill Howard for preparing the index to this volume; and Florence Goulesque for aiding in the preparation of this manuscript.

FERENC M. SZASZ
RICHARD W. ETULAIN

1

Roman Catholicism in Modern New Mexico
A Commitment to Survive

Carol Jensen

PICTURE THE HIGH DESERT LANDSCAPE OF NEW MEXICO, its many miles of open space between population centers. Recall four centuries of political, economic, and social change. Consider the dynamics of diverse cultures striving for preservation of the past and development of a more prosperous future. New Mexico's Catholic culture has been shaped by these influences for over 450 years. Three consequent legacies characterize twentieth-century New Mexico Catholicism: an enduring missionary spirit, a troubled hierarchical structure, and a diverse grassroots creativity. Whether impacting each other or developing on their own, these three impulses illustrate a Catholic commitment to survive.

Interaction with Native Americans has accompanied a Catholic presence in the New World since 1521 and in New Mexico's Catholic culture since 1539. Consequently, this essay contains no special section highlighting Native American Catholics; Indian issues arise most appropriately in discussing the church's missionary efforts but appear throughout the essay. Likewise, Hispanic contributions and concerns are considered integral to the entire story of Catholicism in the state and are featured throughout the essay. Clearly, New Mexico Catholics' missionary spirit and grassroots creativity illustrate different forms of the pluralistic tendency in American religion, a tendency that can result in fragmentation. At the same time, the legacy of a struggling hierarchical structure, with traditional ties to the Roman pontiff, speaks to the counterbalancing tendency toward unity and order.

One might suppose that the Catholic missionary impulse in New Mexico faded away with the commencement of the twentieth century, but that is not the case. Political and ecclesiastical authority and leadership have consistently used a missionary approach toward Native Americans, and more Indians reside in northern Arizona and northwestern New Mexico than in "any other similar area in the United States."[1] Catholic policies for Christianizing those Indians, the stark geographic isolation of New Mexico, the long-term presence of Franciscan friars, and the establishment of the Diocese of Gallup all helped keep that missionary spirit alive. The inclusion of Native American rituals within Catholic worship, the appointment of an Indian bishop, increasing Native American self-determination, and a greater emphasis on social services reflect changes in missionary attitudes and practices.

Undoubtedly the instructions given to Juan de Oñate in 1595 represented Spain's intention to deal with the Pueblo Indians by Christianizing them, "always ordering everything for the glory of God and the increase of [the] holy Catholic faith."[2] That aggressive policy of church–state sponsored Christianization/colonization changed over the centuries to one of accommodation. For example, in 1987 Pope John Paul II addressed Native American Catholics in Phoenix, Arizona, encouraging them to preserve their cultures, languages, and customs.[3] Again, in 1993, Pope John Paul publicly admitted to a gathering of Indian Catholics in Izameal, Mexico, that Catholic colonizers failed to respect the basic rights of indigenous peoples in the Americas.[4] Such comments illustrate an official Catholic tolerance today for diverse cultural traditions within the church and a desire to keep those peoples within the church.

Just as missionary policies for Native Americans continued into the twentieth century, so too the geographic isolation that characterized New Mexico continued in many parts of the state to require a missionary approach. The distances were too great, the ministers too few. When the Franciscans returned to the Archdiocese of Santa Fe in 1897, after a seventy-year absence, 23 friars served 33,648 Catholics in eight parishes covering 56,000 square miles.[5] Recent harsh winters on the Navajo reservation remind us that rural communities can easily become federally declared disaster areas. Snow, sleet, and rain quickly turn open land and unpaved roads into impassable mud. National Guard helicopters still drop bales of hay for cattle and food for isolated families.[6] Missionaries of all religious cultures make extraordinary efforts to aid the people in this remote area, where only two towns have more than fifteen thousand people and "the majority of the population is widely scattered."[7]

Perhaps more important than either Catholic Indian policies or geographic isolation in continuing the missionary spirit is the long legacy of the Franciscan order of priests in the state. These friars currently serve in all three of New Mexico's Catholic dioceses and in 1985 were organized into a special province, the Custody of Our Lady of Guadalupe, formed specifically for serving and preserving Catholicism in the American Southwest.

Franciscan presence dates back to Fray Marcos de Niza, one of the earliest Spanish explorers in the Southwest, who visited the Zuni area in 1539. A series of friars, explorers, and colonizers followed, whose dual intention to colonize and Christianize the area resulted in the Pueblo Revolt of 1680. When the friars returned with de Vargas for the Reconquest in 1692 and found that "Zuni was the only pueblo to preserve any remnants of Christianity," they resumed their mission until a Mexican decree in 1826 exiled all Spanish-born residents of Mexico.[8]

It was the first bishop of Tucson, Peter Bourgade, who encouraged the Franciscans to return to Arizona and New Mexico. In 1897 they began their ministry at Mother Katharine Drexel's St. Michael's Mission; in 1900 they took over the parish at Peña Blanca; in 1902 they returned to Jemez Pueblo; and in 1903 they began their apostolate to the people of southeastern New Mexico. By 1918 twenty-three Franciscan priests remained in New Mexico.[9]

The value of the Franciscan labors to a missionary Catholic church in the early decades of the twentieth century was recognized in 1919 when Rev. Albert T. Daeger, OFM, was named archbishop of Santa Fe. It was even more widely recognized in 1939 when the Diocese of Gallup was established, with Rev. Bernard T. Espelage, OFM, as its first bishop. The purpose of establishing this new ecclesiastical jurisdiction was to coordinate Catholic ministry to the large numbers of Native Americans in northern Arizona and northwestern New Mexico: the Navajo, Laguna, Acoma, Zuni, White Mountain Apache, Hopi, and Jicarilla Apache. The new diocese served thirty thousand Catholics in seventeen parishes and fifty-six missionary churches covering ninety thousand square miles. Half of the thirty-two priests were Franciscans.[10] In 1940 the Diocese of Gallup was considered "almost exclusively a mission field"; even today it is considered "one of the last great mission territories in the United States."[11]

Clearly, Catholic missionary values have changed over the centuries in New Mexico as well as internationally. The policies of domination that once accompanied evangelization and colonization have been replaced by policies of service, accommodation to cultural traditions, self-determination, and social service.

Changes in missionary attitudes are evident in New Mexico's Catholic rituals. The Native Americans' ability to syncretistically combine elements from diverse traditions has, throughout the twentieth century, found support and opposition in the Catholic culture. Pueblo Catholics adopted those aspects of the yearly calendar of feasts that fit into preexisting cycles of tribal hunting and agricultural rituals. These celebrations often combine a Catholic Mass with traditional dances and processions, joining the two religious celebrations in one ceremony. For instance, Santo Domingo's August 4 corn dance, held on the universally celebrated feast day in honor of Saint Dominic, illustrates this syncretism. Another example of the missionary spirit's influence on church ritual is the creation of a Navajo Mass. Both clergy and laity contributed to the preparation of this Navajo liturgy, officially approved and celebrated for the first time in 1987.[12]

On other occasions, however, Catholic hierarchical leadership discouraged the Native elements in church worship. Ethnic conflict resulted. During the 1960s, German-born Frederick A. Stadtmueller was pastor of the Catholic community at Isleta Pueblo. His insistence on a style of Catholicism without elements of Native tradition angered the Isletas. When he poured a thirty-foot slab of concrete in the churchyard during the church's renovation and designated it the dance platform, the Isletas "charged him with gross disrespect for 'the Indian way of Life,' refused to use the dance platform, and circulated a petition for their pastor's removal."[13] The pueblo governor even threatened to evict Stadtmueller. In 1965 Archbishop Peter Davis had the church locked up; it was not until 1974, when Robert Sanchez became archbishop, that the church was reopened and the concrete slab removed.

Conversely, an example of increased sensitivity to Native traditions on the part of hierarchical leadership can be seen in the three-hundredth anniversary of the 1692 *reconquista* under de Vargas. One of the Catholic rituals included in the Santa Fe fiesta involves carrying a statue of Mary, the Mother of Jesus, in procession, under her title *La Conquistadora*. Originally brought to New Mexico in 1625 by the Franciscan superior of the missions, the little statue, symbolizing the part the church played in the Spanish conquest of New Mexico, was eventually enshrined in the Santa Fe cathedral. However, this title for Mary, "strongly detested by the Native American people," at last disturbed the consciences of the official church hierarchy as well.[14] Thus, in July 1992, Archbishop Robert Sanchez changed the statue's title from "La Conquistadora" to "Our Lady of Peace." This gesture was especially noted during the quincentennial of the Columbus discovery, an event that heightened ethnic sensitivities throughout the country.

One evidence of the Franciscan friars' reversal of earlier approaches to Native culture was their commitment to study and master the difficult Navajo language. Early on, Fathers Juvenal Schnorbus, Anselm Weber, Berard Haile, and Leopold Ostermann not only learned to speak and understand Navajo, they also began to write it. By 1912, after installing their own printing press at St. Michael's, the friars printed a *Navajo-English Catechism*, an *Ethnologic Dictionary*, and a *Vocabulary of the Navajo Language*, as well as articles for religious and scholarly publications. These Franciscans also set up an amateur radio station and in the late 1950s began broadcasting the *Padres' Hour* in the Navajo language.[15] Today, Father Cormac continues to compose Sunday sermons for this radio program. Cato Redhouse and Gilene Begay assist him in broadcasting an English sermon, a Navajo sermon summary, a hymn, and a bilingual news feature on Sunday mornings from 7:00 to 7:30 A.M. on KTNN-AM, the tribal-owned 50,000-watt station at Window Rock.

Another example of changing missionary attitudes and practices is the 1986 appointment of a Native American coadjutor bishop to assist Bishop Jermoe J. Hastrich in the Diocese of Gallup. Donald E. Pelotte, S.S.S.; of Abenaki Indian–French Canadian descent, has brought to the Catholic missionary mind in New Mexico firsthand experience with poverty, alcoholism, and Native American ways of worship.[16] The first Native American to be named a bishop, Pelotte became Bishop of Gallup in 1990.

Two twentieth-century secular enactments have further encouraged the new missionary values: the Native American Self-Determination Act, passed by President Gerald Ford in 1975, and the American Indian Religious Freedom Act, signed into law by President Jimmy Carter in 1978. The first act "clearly supported and encouraged Indian people to contract with the federal government for the operation and control of their institutions."[17] The Catholic response throughout the Intermountain West was immediate. At St. Stephen's Indian Mission in Wyoming, the control and operation of St. Joseph's School was turned over to the Arapaho and Shoshoni people in March 1976. In Phoenix, the Catholic missionary approach began to place greater emphasis on Native lay ministry and local decision making. In New Mexico, "Bishop Jerome Hastrich established a Personnel Planning Committee to study . . . the parishes and missions of the Diocese of Gallup."[18] One of the missionary needs identified at that time was "lay ministry presence and training," a Catholic form of self-determination.[19]

Two Catholic conferences for Indians also illustrate contemporary missionary values. In 1939 the Tekakwitha Conference was formed to provide advice and support for Catholic missionaries working with Native Americans; for forty years it had remained primarily a yearly gathering of priests from the northern plains states. However, by the mid-1970s, this conference of missionary priests decided that change was essential.[20] In 1976, Native American Catholics were invited to the conference, and its focus shifted to the interface between Native American religious traditions and Christianity. As a result, Indian participation in the Tekakwitha Conference has grown. The 1981 conference met in Albuquerque and drew more than a thousand participants, two-thirds of them Indians; the fiftieth anniversary conference, held in Fargo, North Dakota, in August 1989 drew more than two thousand.[21]

The growing self-confidence that comes with self-determination is apparent too in a yearly workshop sponsored by the Archdiocese of Santa Fe. The Sixth Native American Spirituality Workshop met in Santa Fe June 11–13, 1993, and drew participants from the Diocese of Tucson, as well as from the other two New Mexico dioceses, Gallup and Las Cruces.[22] Catholic missionaries in New Mexico are no longer partners of the conquistadors. Instead, they have become champions of the dispossessed.

One obvious example of this commitment is found in the increased effort to meet the social service needs of Indians, regardless of religious affiliation. The Diocese of Gallup identifies several areas of social crises, including alcoholism and substance abuse, child abuse and domestic violence, poverty, and mental illness among youth. Several regional agencies attempt to address such crises. Catholic Charities U.S.A. (also known as Catholic Social Services, CSS) is one of the nation's largest and most efficient church organizations, with many diocesan branches and many funding sources. In 1973 Catholic Charities started its work in the Diocese of Gallup as a social welfare department with a grant from the De Rance Foundation; in 1990, some 15,120 clients at six different sites in the diocese received a wide variety of services.[23] On another front, the Southwest Indian Foundation, established in 1968, "uses the labor of . . . Indians to provide roads, bridges, housing, and water wells in the remote areas and is supported by funds from all over the country."[24]

Despite or perhaps because of changes in policies and practices, the missionary spirit of New Mexico's Catholic culture endures. Its hierarchical structure endures as well, but, perhaps through its resistance to change, is far more troubled. Indeed, changes in hierarchical structure come very slowly, if at all. Some contemporary New Mexico Catholics wonder if change will come quickly enough to prevent collapse.

The hierarchical structure of New Mexico's Catholic culture can be seen in five levels of leadership: papal, episcopal, priestly, diaconal, and lay. All levels are today under challenge and/or vulnerable.

Papal exercise of authority in New Mexico is not often apparent to those outside the hierarchical structure. Whenever a new diocese is created, with a new bishop, most Catholics simply accept the Pope's jurisdictional change, adjust, and carry on. Perhaps the most noted exception to this tendency was the Hispanic Catholic community's resistance to Bishop Jean Baptiste Lamy in 1851. A more recent involvement of papal authority in New Mexican Catholic affairs occurred in 1993 with the resignation of Archbishop Robert Sanchez, due to a series of sexual scandals, and the appointment of Michael J. Sheehan as his replacement. Some analysts see this papal appointment as an unusual procedure in the U.S. church and suggest it clearly illustrates the Pope's concern for immediate authoritative action in this crisis.[25] Indeed, the episcopal level of New Mexico's hierarchy has experienced a long history of crisis.

From the seventeenth through the first half of the nineteenth centuries, ordained and lay envoys to Spain and Rome repeatedly attempted to obtain a bishop for New Mexico, all without success. Episcopal visits from the Diocese of Durango were rare. It was not until political authority changed in New Mexico that U.S. ecclesiastical leadership, convening at the seventh Provincial Council of Baltimore, petitioned the Pope for the establishment of a Vicariate Apostolic in the territory. However, this development brought with it ethnic conflict. Jean Baptiste Lamy, the New Mexicans' first bishop, was French, as were many of the imported clergy who served under him. On his arrival in 1851, the new bishop was critical of the Mexican clergymen who had been serving Hispanic Catholics in New Mexico. In turn, greatly influenced by the leadership of Padre Antonio José Martínez of Taos, they resented Lamy's imposition of the U.S. and European formal hierarchical authority. This ethnically based conflict of leadership resulted in what some call "Padre Martínez's schismatic church," and the split between New Mexico Catholics offered the Presbyterians in northern New Mexico and southern Colorado an opportunity to successfully evangelize many of his disaffected family members and followers. This moment of crisis in New Mexico's Catholic culture was indeed a challenge to its survival.

The eight archbishops of Santa Fe after Lamy were also "Anglos"; none were native sons. Thus, the 1974 elevation of Robert Fortune Sanchez from parish priest at San Felipe de Neri Church in Albuquerque to Archbishop of Santa Fe was cause for great elation and celebration among New Mexico Catholics. At age forty, Sanchez, a native of Socorro, New Mexico, was the youngest archbishop in the United States and the first Hispanic archbishop in the country. Also, as secretary of the National Conference of Catholic Bishops from 1990 to 1993, he was the group's first Hispanic officer. He likewise served fourteen years as chairman of the U.S. Bishops Committee for Hispanic Ministries and was extremely influential in the production of the U.S. bishops' pastoral, "The Hispanic Presence: Challenge and Commitment."[26] Obviously, he was a hero to the state's Hispanic Catholics.

Consequently, it was a tragic shock when, on March 9, 1993, Archbishop Sanchez was publicly accused of alleged sexual impropriety. At least three women said they had sexual relations with the archbishop during the 1970s and 1980s, when they were in their late teens and early twenties. These women appeared on CBS-TV's "60 Minutes" on March 21, 1993, to tell their stories.[27] As one newspaper reported, "The allegations came at a time when the archdiocese was wrestling with accusations of sexual misconduct by priests" and numerous civil suits filed against priests and the archdiocese for pedophilia.[28] Some archdiocesan officials suggested that Albuquerque attorney Bruce Pasternack, who was "representing more than 29 alleged victims of clergy abuse, tried to pressure the archdiocese into a settlement" by raising the issue of Sanchez's own sexual misconduct.[29] Many of the plaintiffs and their families believed that Sanchez was responsible for a cover-up by the church and called for his resignation.[30]

Although many religious scholars believed, at Sanchez's resignation, that New Mexico's next archbishop would also be Hispanic, others stated that "finding a strong leader for an archdiocese rocked with scandals . . . as well as dealing with the pain of victims and the low morale of priests and parishioners alike may be a stronger factor 'than the continuity of the faith of the people. . . . It may not be an Hispanic.'"[31]

There is no doubt that this crisis in episcopal leadership has devastated Hispanic Catholics in New Mexico. Sanchez made notable contributions to strengthen Hispanic Catholicism in the United States at a time when many of his people were being evangelized and converted by other Christian denominations. The archbishop extended his influence to Native American concerns as well, encouraging Indian leadership in the church and permitting the inclusion of more Native American traditions in Catholic worship. He also contributed to a certain atmosphere of optimism throughout his archdiocese by providing opportunities for individual parishes to pursue interests and experiments of their own. However, the linkage of this episode to the national scandal of pedophile priests and to the related issues of priestly celibacy and permanent deacons gives evidence of further trouble on the priestly level.

A recent study by Father Stephen J. Rosetti, program director at St. Luke's Institute in Suitland, Maryland, states that "revelations of priests having abused children are a major factor in the recent steep decline in American Catholics' confidence in their Church."[32] Nearly all observers agreed that disciplinary and diagnostic measures for offending clergymen, compassion and compensation for the victims, and perspective for the grieving Catholic community were in order. Much of this healing has been initiated at the episcopal level of hierarchical leadership. In the spring of 1993, the U.S. bishops presented their concerns regarding the issue to the Vatican Congregation for Clergy.[33] Progress was made in understanding the nature of pedophilia and the ineffectiveness of past disciplinary measures. By summer a national policy on clerical pedophilia had been created.[34]

In the Archdiocese of Santa Fe on April 29, 1993, the Independent Commission to the Archdiocese, established in October 1992 by former Archbishop Sanchez to study the problem of "clergy sexual misconduct," presented several recommendations to Bishop Sheehan.[35] In a July 1993 interview with the press, Bishop Sheehan reported that he had "acted on many of the recommendations" of that four member independent commission.[36] As apostolic administrator, he moved quickly to accomplish four goals: remove offending priests from the ministry, establish a counseling fund for victims, ask forgiveness in the name of the church, and "work to prevent such abuse from happening again."[37] Such decisive action was essential to uniting archdiocesan Catholics and encouraging their continued commitment.

These changes came too late for the twenty-nine victims of former priests treated and released to active ministry in the state of New Mexico, but they may have contributed to a successful suit against the Servants of the Paraclete, who treated many of these priests at a center in Jemez Springs, New Mexico, during the 1960s. This center, once the only treatment center in the world for pedophile priests, and the Paraclete priests who run it agreed in November 1993 to pay 125,000 dollars to the four New Mexico victims and another 400,000 dollars to the twenty-one Minnesota plaintiffs.[38]

The Archdiocese of Santa Fe, too, has faced extraordinary expenses in providing counseling to victims and in removing a number of priests from active ministry. An ongoing battle with insurance companies and some plaintiffs' attorneys has forced the archdiocese to sell some of its property to "pay for the settlement costs" and "to avoid bankruptcy."[39]

Although some commentators, including the famous American sociologist Father Andrew Greeley, reject "the argument . . . that the church's celibacy requirement is the cause of the problem," others strongly state that "the church needs to reexamine its policies requiring priests to be celibate and prohibiting them from marrying."[40] In fact, in a poll conducted by the *Albuquerque Journal* between June 3 and June 14, 1993, 68 percent of 403 practicing Catholics (289 of them Hispanic) said they thought the church should change its position and allow priests to marry.⁴¹ Such a change is possible since, the *New Catholic Encyclopedia* notes, the "law of celibacy is of ecclesiastical origin," not dogma, and "may, therefore, be abrogated by the Church."⁴² Clearly, the laity are more open to change on the priestly level than are those who have the power to make such changes. As in the nation at large, a decrease in the number of priests has reached crisis proportions in the state of New Mexico. Remaining clergy in the Archdiocese of Santa Fe are deeply concerned about declining numbers, high expectations, and changing roles.⁴³ Clearly the priesthood has survival problems of its own.

One means of alleviating the universal shortage of Catholic priests is the active renewal of the permanent diaconate. The papal authorization for the restoration of this ancient level in the hierarchical structure was given in 1967 in the document *Sacrum Diaconatus Ordinene*. Restoration of the order in the United States was approved one year later, and a committee, chaired by Archbishop Patricio Flores of San Antonio, Texas, was established to supervise the program.⁴⁴ Permanent deacons, like priests, may officiate at baptisms, weddings, and funerals. Unlike priests, however, they may not administer the sacraments of Reconciliation or Eucharist; like priests, and now lay ministers as well, they may preach and distribute Holy Communion.

The first group of deacons for the Archdiocese of Santa Fe were ordained in September 1972. In the summer of 1993, thirty-five men in the Archdiocese of Santa Fe were ordained to the permanent diaconate, bringing the total for that jurisdiction to 140.⁴⁵ For short periods of time a small number of these men have served as administrators of parishes without priests. Even though their congregations seem pleased to have them, the diocesan administration has, until very recently, been hesitant to place permanent deacons in regular administrative positions.⁴⁶

In keeping with its missionary approach, the Diaconate Formation Program in the Diocese of Gallup is separate from the Native American Diaconate Program, restructured in 1990 as the Diaconate and Lay Ministry Program. Whereas four men serve in the regular program at the present time, thirty work in the Native American program.⁴⁷ The noticeable difference in the numbers of men committed to these two programs gives evidence of papal, diocesan, and even federal policies regarding Native American leadership.⁴⁸

The Diocese of Las Cruces seems to be far less satisfied than those of Santa Fe or Gallup with the training and performance of their permanent deacons. In 1982, when the diocese was created, they inherited deacons from El Paso and Santa Fe. These men were judged by some to be unprepared for the special needs of the Las Cruces diocese and unable to work supportively and creatively with the pastors to whom they were assigned.[49] As pastors developed a negative attitude toward these inherited deacons, the diocese hesitated to develop a deacon training program of its own. Only now is it discussing the possibility and addressing the financial implications of such a commitment.

It may be that the permanent diaconate is a tempting, but not a sufficient, source of hierarchical leadership in a time of declining priestly vocations. Reluctance on the part of priestly and episcopal leadership to place deacons in administrative positions in the Archdiocese of Santa Fe, ineffective screening and training for some ministries, and the need for a separate Native American diaconate program in the Gallup diocese all indicate ongoing problems with this partly hierarchical, partly lay role.

In facing a shortage of priests, as well as other stresses in the hierarchical structure, dioceses have learned to use scientifically conducted self-studies and a consequent long-range plan. These sociological exercises, and the diocesan fund-raising campaigns created to support them, seem essential to a hierarchical structure struggling to survive.

During the 1980s, the Archdiocese of Santa Fe sponsored a series of discussion and planning sessions called "Growing in Faith Together." In 1988 an Archdiocesan Pastoral Plan resulting from that study listed several services, programs, and ministries as major goals.[50] Meanwhile a fund-raising program, called "Faith in Action," had been established in 1984 to support these expanded goals. During the past nine years, the program has averaged about 24 percent participation; currently, however, some contributors worry that their donations may be used for litigation expenses.[51] Although this is not the case, New Mexico Catholics see a clear distinction between having their contributions pay for legal costs and making donations that will be used for victims' counseling.[52]

During the last sixteen years, the Diocese of Gallup has gathered data from no less than four such studies. In 1977 Bishop Jerome Hastrich established a Personnel Planning Committee, which held consultations in fifty-six parishes and compiled a statistical report of needs.[53] In 1986–87, the Catholic Church Extension Society "conducted a study of ministry needs in home mission dioceses" and recommended "broadly based diocesan planning."[54] When the Southwest Catechetical Leadership Convocation held its regional meeting in Gallup in 1990 "to identify new issues and trends in religious education," twelve prioritized concerns were named.[55] Finally, in 1990 a Strategic Planning Committee was named to research both external and internal aspects of the Diocese of Gallup. The written description of the diocese, based on a parish self-evaluation survey, a diocesan survey, and a comparison with data from the Notre Dame Study of Catholic Parish Life, conducted during the 1980s, was then used to formulate "specific pastoral goals for the diocese."[56] In February 1993, the Diocesan Strategic Profile was presented to Bishop Pelotte and the people of the diocese.

In the eleven-year-old Las Cruces diocese, long-range planning has become the task of the Catholic Charities Office. It focuses on the socioeconomic needs of the people, which will be discussed later in this essay.[57]

It is conceivable that without these fund-raising programs, neither the traditional nor the contemporary programs of the hierarchical structure in New Mexico will survive. Add to that fiscal possibility the reality of litigation expenses for the Archdiocese of Santa Fe, and the economic picture is frightening, indeed. The changes in diocesan organization, creating new offices and consequent new expenses, may be in times of crisis a greater financial burden than the system can bear.

Perhaps as a result of self-studies and long-range plans, but certainly as a result of a serious shortage of priests, another technique has been adopted by the hierarchical structure in New Mexico's Catholic culture. It is called "collaboration in ministry" and is promoted by the Archdiocese of Santa Fe.[58] This emphasis on priests, sisters, deacons, and laity sharing more collegially in essential ministries of parish life is most evident in the newly established role of the Parish Life Coordinator, a sister or deacon who is officially assigned as administrator where there is no parish priest. In 1994 there were four Parish Life Coordinators in the archdiocese, one deacon and three sisters.[59] Since this new position was created with both papal and episcopal approval, its prospects for contributing to the solution of the current hierarchical crisis is good. Additionally, the reliance on Catholic sisters to fill the majority of these positions in the Archdiocese of Santa Fe raises the possibility of increased appreciation for the leadership of women in Catholic life. A public symbol of this new spirit of collaboration can be seen in the substitution of the term *Catholic community* for *parish*. The Archdiocese of Santa Fe's youngest parish, established on January 1, 1990, is called "Santa Maria de la Paz Catholic Community."[60]

The challenges and changes affecting New Mexico's Catholic hierarchical structure seem to indicate a movement away from an ancient, unquestioned bureaucracy toward a structure increasingly more open to the ethnic, social, and economic needs of the people. It is also more vulnerable to scandal and criticism. Today this structure is in crisis. Will it be able to retain necessary ingredients and let go of other elements of its ancient tradition in order to survive?

Finally, twentieth-century Catholic culture in New Mexico is characterized by a loyal but independent grassroots creativity. Much of this vitality and variety in lay leadership and ritual participation is conservative as well as innovative and has a long history. New Mexico's past cultural isolation was a breeding ground for grassroots Catholicism, a type of folk-religious tradition preserved today by non-Catholics as well. Other forms of lay leadership and liturgical life have been inspired by the changes of Vatican II and have national as well as regional impetus. Women's concerns are a case in point. As a result, new grassroots movements and social services (not always related to parish life or diocesan structures) counterbalance traditionally held beliefs and practices. If this diverse activity does not lead to factionalism, it may some day enliven and enrich the recent collaboration in ministry proposed and implemented by the hierarchy.

During New Mexico's colonial period, medieval Spanish Catholicism became in New Spain a religion of self-reliance. Many seventeenth-century Hispanic New Mexicans, often ignored by the friars, whose mission it was to convert the Indians, built several early churches "at their own expense," rather than at royal expense.[61] Santa Fe, Santa Cruz, and Albuquerque are sites of such early lay initiatives. Under later Mexican rule, and even under U.S. jurisdiction, grassroots Hispanic leadership produced the Penitentes and other *cofradías* or lay societies, which regularly gathered local parishioners when no priest was available.

The ancient Hispanic village celebration of *La Función*, the parish feast day in honor of the church's patron saint, continues to give full expression to earlier customs and continuing lay initiative, especially in the role of the *mayordomo*.[62] This lay person or couple, charged with care for the church building, its repair, maintenance, and seasonal decoration, has traditionally held a position of honor in Hispanic village life. Often mayordomos are publicly thanked at parish feast day or centennial celebrations for their valuable contributions to the parish community.[63]

Efforts to share restored folk celebrations with others include seasonal dramas like *Los Pastores* and *Las Posadas*, dancing *Las Matachines*, the use of *luminarias* or *farolitos* to commemorate the campfires of Christmas shepherds, and other public celebrations that contribute to the cultural richness of the state. These celebrations often include booths for *santeros*, whose traditional wooden renderings of Catholic saints have become prized art objects. Indeed, large Anglo collections of *santos* in villages like Arroyo Hondo and well-known collections of them, such as the one in the Taylor Museum of the Colorado Springs Fine Arts Center, evidence an interest in Catholic religious art beyond devotion. That contemporary santeros like

Charles Carrillo can make a living creating these pieces for church-affiliated and secular customers alike suggests that this aspect of the grassroots relationship with the larger society is growing.

Moises Sandoval, author of a history of the Hispanic church in the United States, speaks of the preservation of family-centered faith when he praises the accomplishments of Archbishop Sanchez: "He revived the many traditions of the Hispanic people.... To the people of the small towns, this was so important—the grassroots culture. Faith that had been gone for a long time came back. Pilgrimages that had gone out of use came back into being. He brought a renaissance of faith."[64] New Mexican Catholics have been more successful than other U.S. Hispanics in keeping ethnic religious traditions alive; they also gained an important boost to their grassroots faith when the official church, represented by one of their own, recognized and supported those ancient traditions.

Such ethnic pride is evident in a number of parishes who have worked together with the state to receive recognition as historic sites. For instance, at Santa Cruz de la Cañada, a restoration committee was appointed to research the history the church and to submit its findings to the State Cultural Properties Review Committee. As a result, the Santa Cruz church received a State Historical Site rating in 1972, and in July 1993, the church was named a National Historical Site.[65] Interestingly, these kinds of grassroots efforts have been so successful that the Archdiocese of Santa Fe has renamed its archives "The Office of Historic-Artistic Patrimony and Archives."[66]

Like this revived Hispanic tradition, the Second Vatican Council in our own time has inspired independence and responsibility on the part of lay Catholics. Some old attitudes regarding lay participation in hierarchical positions have changed.

On the diocesan level, lay coordination of many new ministries instituted at the parish level allows for initiative at the lower levels of the hierarchical structure. Within individual parishes, a lay person's employment as part of the official parish staff, membership on the parish council, or consistent commitment to a standing committee means that the opinions and energy of the laity are considered more essential to the Catholic culture than ever before. In New Mexico dialogue homilies, liturgical music, and even liturgical dance draw lay opinions, insights, and artistry into the communal act of worship. All of these inclusive gestures have encouraged lay commitment of a more participatory kind.

But the growing grassroots impulse of New Mexico's Catholic culture is nowhere more evident than in the diverse values that have been transformed into strong social movements and directed into a multiplicity of social services. These include women's concerns, the Charismatic Renewal, retreat houses, peace and justice issues, and social services offered to the society at large.

New Mexico's Catholic culture reflects the larger church in its concern for the place of women in church and society. Access to the priesthood is only one part of an international movement seeking "empowerment" for today's Catholic women. This grassroots movement also recognizes their past and present contributions to the survival and effective functioning of the church. A decrease in the number of religious women in the American church during the past thirty years has made the ministerial contributions of lay women during this period all the more vital. At the same time, new approaches to American Catholic history have resulted in more factual accounts of the many congregations of women religious who have served the educational, health, and welfare needs of the church here for centuries. Never considered more than lay women, these religious congregations and the hardworking individuals in them have served the needs of the church's hierarchy, the state, and the People of God selflessly, heroically, and creatively. Indeed, they may have been more influential in the survival of the modern Catholic culture than heretofore acknowledged. In an attempt to respond to the changing ministries and complex concerns of women in the American church, the U.S. bishops' process of composing a pastoral letter on women's concerns revealed the great diversity and deep divisions among U.S. Catholic women. These differences are apparent in New Mexico's Catholic culture as well.

"Extensive surveys have shown that the great majority of Roman Catholics are in favor of . . . women priests."[67] The idea of women priests in the United States became a serious campaign in 1975 with the creation of the Women's Ordination Conference. Despite a 1979 papal decree (reaffirmed in 1994) insisting on an all-male priesthood, the conference has continued to function. Today it boasts four thousand members.[68] Many U.S. Catholic women, including New Mexicans, have taken seminary courses and earned the necessary degrees in preparation for a changed Canon Law.

In the Archdiocese of Santa Fe, Catherine Stewart-Roache, a mother of five, prepared herself educationally for the priesthood, worked as a nursing-home chaplain, and in retirement, still hopes for a place in that ministry. However, her belief that women are just as fit as men for the priesthood is countered by others who say that "rules are rules."[69] Clearly, not all New Mexican Catholic women agree on this issue.

But the concerns of American Catholic women are more complex than disagreement over their access to the priesthood. They include recognition of a distinguished past and dedicated service and leadership in the present. According to the Notre Dame Study of Catholic Parish Life, "despite the lack of formal recognition or appropriate compensation, [women] do more than men to lead and minister in U.S. Catholic parishes."[70] No doubt Catholic lay women who are not members of religious congregations will need to assume more of these responsibilities, as the number of sisters, like the number of priests continues to decline. From a high of 181,421 in 1966, the number of U.S. sisters dropped to 99,337 in 1992.[71] New Mexico statistics parallel those on the national level. In 1960 the number of women religious in the Archdiocese of Santa Fe was 610; in 1994 it was 316.[72] Less than one-third of this loss was due to the creation of the Diocese of Las Cruces in 1982. Because the Diocese of Gallup resides in both New Mexico and Arizona, it is not clear just how many women religious reside in each state.

Like the loss of priests to Catholic ministry, the loss of sisters has been felt socially, spiritually, and financially. The story of their contributions to the church in New Mexico, as well as in other parts of America, bears this out. Although the earliest missionary activities in the state were conducted by priests, the establishment of official ecclesiastical jurisdiction under Bishop Lamy in 1850 brought several congregations of sisters to teach initially in academies, eventually in parochial schools, and temporarily in public schools. These services continued into the twentieth century. Sisters working in academies and parochial schools saved money for the church, while those engaged in public education saved money for the territory and later for the state.[73] Before 1891 three congregations of religious women maintained separate classrooms for public education; after 1891 the numbers increased due to a shortage of qualified public schoolteachers and a lack of public funds for building separate public schoolhouses.[74] Despite a law passed by the Albuquerque New Town school board in 1892 and the consequent withdrawal of the Sisters of Charity from four public schools in the city, the state continued to support the practice until 1947, when a civil suit was filed against the Archdiocese of Santa Fe by concerned citizens of Dixon, New Mexico.[75]

The educational work of sisters in New Mexico has included schools for Indians. Although their initial efforts to "Catholicize and civilize" Native Americans were characterized by resistance to the "influence of Indian culture on their lives," in more recent times, the sisters have demonstrated so deep an appreciation of Native American spirituality that they have included elements of it in their own communal worship and private prayer.[76] Despite diminishing numbers in their ranks, and diminishing finances to support their efforts, religious women continue their work in Indian education in

New Mexico. Sister Natalie Bussiere, S.N.D., serves as an elementary principal at Blessed Kateri Tekakwitha Academy, working "side by side with a nearly 50-member strong corps of dedicated lay missionaries."[77]

In addition to education and Indian mission work, New Mexico's religious women began their dedication to health care and social services with the establishment of St. Vincent's Hospital in Santa Fe in 1864; in the late nineteenth century and into the twentieth century, they contributed to New Mexico's sanitorium industry for victims of tuberculosis and, thus, to the population growth that would bring statehood in 1912.[78] The sisters' work with orphans as catechists and public health–social service ministers in rural areas of New Mexico earned them the respect of the citizens and new members for their orders.[79] Increased creativity in social service ministries will be described in the following paragraphs, particularly in reference to the dioceses of Gallup and Las Cruces.

It is likely that increased attention to social services by women religious in America and in New Mexico is directly related to their decreasing numbers and consequent decreasing presence in parochial schools, as well as to the decreasing number of parochial schools themselves.[80] But other factors may also have influenced this shift in ministry. During the 1950s and 1960s, the Sister Formation Movement provided women religious with even greater educational and leadership opportunities than they had previously received. Both those who left and those who remained in congregations and took advantage of these opportunities were well prepared for a wider range of professional positions.[81] These women were also among the most visible, committed, and enthusiastic proponents of greater attention to women's concerns in the church and society.

To address the issue of Catholic women's concerns, the U.S. bishops engaged in preparing an official pastoral letter on women. Between 1983 and 1992, many Catholic women on all levels contributed their insights and energies to its composition. The Archdiocese of Santa Fe was one of the one hundred U.S. dioceses that sponsored open hearings and communicated the results to the writers of and consultants on the letter. But the document in its multiple drafts proved to be so troubled that it was dropped, much to the relief of many who had earlier placed hope in it. One of the backlash grassroots groups that emerged and spoke out during this nine-year period was "Women for Faith and Family." These conservative Catholics were concerned about "feminist inroads in the church" and staunchly attempted to protect the hierarchical structure and magisterial authority of the past against what they perceived to be the subversion of the church.[82] They responded fearfully to the assertions of Catholic liberals "that the church is at the beginning of a massive disruption. . . . cultural change on the scale of the 1st century. . . . [the church's] most intense conflict in centuries."[83] Clearly, not all Catholic women were in accord on this issue.

In another area, the modern movement of the Charismatic Renewal has thrived, especially in the Hispanic communities.[84] Primarily lay inspired, this movement originated at Duquesne University in 1967 as a spiritual approach to God by means of ecstatic prayer. In this sense, it has much in common with Pentecostal churches. The Charismatic Renewal entered the Archdiocese of Santa Fe through independent clerical and lay initiatives. Abbot David Gereats introduced it at the Benedictine Monastery in Pecos, New Mexico.[85] Additionally, a young married couple began to hold prayer meetings in their home. These beginnings spawned parish-centered prayer groups as early as 1969, some of which still meet.[86] By 1975 this grassroots group was ready to sponsor the first Southwest Catholic Charismatic Conference; a year later it opened an office; and by 1978 it had a center of its own. Over the years, the "Center has added ministries of healing, intercession, and evangelization" to their original goals.[87] The yearly regional conference was replaced in 1993 by the National Catholic Charismatic Conference, held that year in Albuquerque. Many members of this movement place their hope for the survival of modern Catholic culture in devotion to the Holy Spirit's vibrant presence.

Yet another grassroots effort, retreat houses, provides a traditional Catholic opportunity for individuals to withdraw temporarily from the pace of daily responsibilities, expectations, and crises in order to become centered and to emerge a little more at peace with one's self and one's world. Often these prayerful centers are run by congregations of religious women. In the Archdiocese of Santa Fe, the Dominican Retreat House has, since 1957, invited people to a rural setting where either private or planned communal programs are available for less than the price of a hotel room. Unfortunately, the combination of a personnel shortage among the sisters and financial problems in the archdiocese (who owns the property) necessitated the retreat house's sale in 1994.[88] Some retreats are also offered at the Madonna Retreat Center, located on the Archdiocese Center campus, former site of Albuquerque's Catholic college. In the Diocese of Gallup, Sacred Heart Retreat, opened in 1977, is a center for spiritual renewal, days of recollection, conferences, or personal prayer.

Another concern for New Mexico Catholics is social action to achieve peace and justice. One of these actions is the Annual Prayer Pilgrimage for Peace, an interfaith event sponsored by the Archdiocese of Santa Fe, the brainchild of John and Joan Leahigh in 1983. A permanent element in the ceremony is the blessing of relay runners who travel, carrying the Flame of Peace and packets of healing soil, from Holy Family Church in Chimayo to Los Alamos, the birthplace of the atomic bomb.[89] Other elements of the event vary from year to year, but often include Native American healing traditions and the sharing of bread, a traditional Christian ritual. Other peace activists, drawing on a growing national and international community of peace pilgrims, stage demonstrations at Kirtland Air Force Base or join the parishioners of San Miguel Catholic Church in Socorro for a prayer vigil at Trinity site.[90]

An increasing environmental awareness, an offshoot of the peace movement among New Mexican Catholics, is another recent sign of grassroots awareness. One social activist and author, Joanna Macy, has conducted several workshops on this issue at the Center for Action and Contemplation in Albuquerque. She is particularly gifted in helping social activists to avoid burnout and despair.[91]

Meanwhile, in the Diocese of Las Cruces, where the population is predominantly Hispanic and of low income, social action focuses on poverty and racial discrimination. The diocese supports parish and community groups already responding to local concerns regarding immigration, economic development, civil rights, justice and peace. In so doing, the diocese aims to bolster and encourage further grassroots participation.[92]

Another grassroots program, the Center for Action and Contemplation (CAC) in Albuquerque, was founded during the 1980s by Father Richard Rohr. This center's goal is the training and spiritual formation of lay persons. Staffed by clerical and lay teachers, community organizers, and volunteers, CAC offers workshops, lectures, discussions, retreats, conferences, internship programs, advocacy actions, and a meditation chapel.

In the Gallup diocese, the Winslow branch of Madonna House, an international Catholic community of lay persons, was opened in 1957. Less focused on training than CAC, this community offers a variety of traditional social services as well as personal support for individuals.[93] It is the witness of this community, as much as the services offered, that illustrates the value of a life devoted to brotherly love.

Although these innovative movements and expressions of grassroots commitment to contemporary peace and justice issues are an important contribution to the pluralistic religious culture of New Mexico and to the survival of some important Catholic values in new forms, conservative values also characterize the state's lay mentality. The tension between U.S. Catholics and the Vatican caused by strong and vocal differences on such issues as abortion, birth control, married clergy, and the status of women find their parallels in New Mexico.[94] A recent poll in the *Albuquerque Journal* reveals that in regard to the last three issues, New Mexicans want change; however, in regard to abortion only 33 percent of New Mexico Catholics think a policy change is desirable.[95] And for the majority of New Mexicans participating in the poll, recent sexual scandals (both national and local) have not changed the way they feel about priests or their commitment to participation in church life.[96] Thus, despite many New Mexico Catholics questioning church policies on several key issues, they are, compared to U.S. Catholics in general, quite conservative.[97]

Finally, the establishment of lay-inspired social service agencies indicates a Catholic outreach to the entire society in New Mexico. As an example, Casa Angelica, a home for handicapped youngsters founded by the Daughters of Charity of Canossa, and staffed primarily by lay people, celebrated its twenty-fifth anniversary in 1992.[98] Presentation House, a "transitional living program for older homeless women with psychiatric disabilities," and Barrett House, a temporary shelter for battered women and their children, offer their services to people of all faiths.[99] These agencies benefit not only from private donations but from United Way and other community organizations.

In addition, through the Diocese of Gallup's independently funded Hispanic ministry, a Spanish-speaking individual or family may receive assistance with "employment, housing, medical care, interpretation, legal work, counseling, social services, adoptions, letters, etc. . . . Three Sisters are certified by the Immigration Authorization Service . . . to do immigration work."[100]

In the Archdiocese of Santa Fe, Catholic Social Services uses private as well as diocesan funding to offer an immigration program, a counseling program, a senior citizen meal site, senior home care and transportation services, a family life education program, and a "support line that offers information and referral to callers whose needs can't be met by CSS, but could be by another public or private agency."[101] All of these services are free or on a sliding scale for the society at large. The Diocese of Las Cruces also offers immigration services through official Catholic agencies and in cooperation with secular centers. All of these twentieth-century missionary outreach efforts resemble the Social Gospel ideas of nineteenth-century America. And while conservative Protestants may place more emphasis on personal salvation than social service, Roman Catholics have traditionally linked acts of charity with an eternal reward.

In short, twentieth-century Catholic culture in New Mexico is a mixture of healthy and troubled components. In this it is not unlike Catholic communities in other sections of the country at this time. Its uniqueness lies in the way that ethnicity, creativity, and crisis have shaped that mixture into a commitment to survive.

On the positive side, an enduring missionary spirit has adapted, through four centuries, to changing political and social circumstances while continuing to serve a large but widely dispersed Native American population. Although geographic isolation and the dedication of Franciscan priests are constants in this mission field, changing papal and episcopal policies have allowed for the establishment of the Diocese of Gallup, the appointment of a Native American bishop, the inclusion of indigenous traditions in Catholic ceremonies, increased self-determination, and an extension of social services offered by the church to all Native Americans in the region. The Diocese of Gallup's missionary commitment to Indians may be no different in quality than that of other dioceses, but it is more extensive than any other. Because of the episcopal and papal support it enjoys, this legacy will most likely continue to characterize New Mexico's Catholic culture.

Another positive contribution to U.S. Catholicism is New Mexico's long tradition of conservative grassroots Hispanic leadership, particularly in the rural villages. The Penitentes, La Función, the mayordomo, the support of former Archbishop Robert Sanchez, and historic preservation efforts all contribute to the richness of this cultural treasure. Although New Mexico may not have the largest Spanish-speaking population in the country, the vitality of its Hispanic Catholic culture is historically documented and socially visible.

A third strength found in New Mexico's Catholic culture is the creativity of its diverse grassroots movements and social services. Women's issues, the Charismatic Renewal, retreat houses, peace and justice centers and projects, and an increasing variety of social services extended to the society at large contribute to that vibrancy. If this legacy of independent action does not result in factionalism, it may well be the prophetic root of a renewed vision and commitment for a languishing liberal Catholicism.

However, an honest assessment of New Mexico's Catholic culture must include a presentation of the church's failures as well as its successes, discussion of its members' conflicts as well as their accord, and an evaluation of its limitations as well as its hopes. There is no denying that the hierarchical structure of Roman Catholicism is troubled in one way or another at this time. The severe shortage of priests, current limitations placed on existing roles of deacons, sisters, and laity, and recent scandals regarding sexual misconduct of clergy have created a crisis in leadership that challenges the fidelity of Catholics across the country as well as in New Mexico. The hierarchical tendency toward unity, often exercised at the price of uniformity, has been tempered by accommodation to tribal traditions and folk religious practices in New Mexico. But Native Americans and Hispanics have most often been conservative Catholics; they pose no major threat to the church's traditional structure. On the other hand, New Mexico Catholics who are neither Native American nor Hispanic often enter into tension with the hierarchical standard of unity, not only by the diversity of their grassroots issues and activities but by the spirit of independence and prophetic liberalism that motivates them. Perhaps the series of crises currently plaguing New Mexico's Catholic culture will force a closer encounter of these conservative and liberal interests. If this encounter is more than an appeal for money and/or service, if it is also a genuine extension of appreciation, support, and incorporation of grassroots efforts, there is hope that the Catholic church in New Mexico will not only survive but also find new life. Certainly its missionary spirit, its grassroots creativity, and some form of unifying structure are valuable legacies from which to draw strength for the ongoing struggle.

Notes

1. Elizabeth Kelley, *Diocese of Gallup Golden Jubilee, 1939–1989* (Albuquerque: Starline Printing, 1989), 9.

2. Luis de Velasco, "Oñate's Appointment as Governor of New Mexico," trans. George P. Hammond, *New Mexico Historical Review* 13 (July 1938): 246–48, repr. in *Foreigners in Their Native Land*, ed. David J. Weber (Albuquerque: University of New Mexico Press, 1973), 23–24.

3. James Cosgrove, "Caught Between Two Worlds," *Extension* 86 (March 1992): 11.

4. Victor Simpson, "Pope Admits Church Abuse of Indians," *Albuquerque Journal*, 12 August 1993, A1.

5. "The New Kingdom of St. Francis," in *The Franciscan Missions of the Southwest* (St. Michael's, Ariz.: n.p., 1913), 41.

6. Lorraine Keene, personal letter, 18 January 1993.

7. Strategic Planning Committee, "Diocesan Strategic Profile," Gallup, N.M: (Diocese of Gallup, 1993), Mimeographed, chap. 1:2.

8. Kelley, *Diocese of Gallup Golden Jubilee*, 7.

9. Provincial Archives of the Franciscan Province of Our Lady of Guadalupe, Albuquerque, N.M.

10. Kelley, *Diocese of Gallup Golden Jubilee*, 9.

11. Ibid., 10; Strategic Planning Committee, "Diocesan Strategic Profile," chap. 3:1.

12. Kelley, *Diocese of Gallup Golden Jubilee*, 15.

13. John L. Kessell, *The Missions of New Mexico since 1776* (Albuquerque: University of New Mexico Press, 1980), 220–21.

14. Joe and Peggy Savilla, "Native American Catholics Speak Out," *People of God* 11 (April 1993): 19.

15. Strategic Planning Committee, "Diocesan Strategic Profile," 3:4.

16. Kelley, *Diocese of Gallup Golden Jubilee*, 16.

17. Rev. Anthony Short, S.J., "1975—The Year of Self-Determination," *Wind River Rendezvous* 14 (January/February/March 1984): 1–2.

18. Strategic Planning Committee, "Diocesan Strategic Profile," chap. 13:1.

19. Ibid., chap. 13:2.

20. Rev. Carl Starkloff, S.J., "Arapahoe Service at the Tekakwitha Conference," *Wind River Rendezvous* 12 (July/August/September 1983): 12.

21. Ibid., 13; Catherine Walsh, "Walking the Sacred Circle with Christ," *Extension* 84 (February 1990): 8.

22. Joe Savilla, telephone interview, 2 July 1993.

23. Kelley, *Diocese of Gallup Golden Jubilee*, 75; Strategic Planning Committee, "Diocesan Strategic Profile," chap. 12:1.

24. Kelley, *Diocese of Gallup Golden Jubilee*, 74.

25. "Bishop Sheehan Takes Over Santa Fe Archdiocese," *Voice of the Southwest* 24 (May 1994): 2.

26. "Robert F. Sanchez," *Albuquerque Journal*, 20 March 1993, A4.

27. Bruce Daniels, "Sanchez Accusers Go Public," *Albuquerque Journal*, 22 March 1993, A1.

28. Bruce Daniels, "Sanchez Apologizes, Asks Forgiveness," *Albuquerque Journal*, 10 March 1993, A1.

29. Daniels, "Sanchez Accusers," A4; Bruce Daniels, "Pasternack Pressured Church Attorney," *Albuquerque Journal*, 13 March 1993, A1 and A5.

30. Eileen Welsome, "Archbishop Unfit Groups Say," *Albuquerque Tribune*, 10 March 1993, A1; Bruce Daniels and Art Geiselman, "Disbelief Turns to Division in Sanchez Controversy," *Albuquerque Journal*, 11 March 1993, A1.

31. Bruce Daniels, "New Archbishop Must Be Tough Yet Able to Heal," *Albuquerque Journal*, 25 March 1993, A10.

32. "Father Greeley Projects 2,000–4,000 Priests Have Sexually Abused Minors during the Last Quarter Century," *Voice of the Southwest* 24 (May 1993): 24; Paul Wilkes, "Unholy Acts," *The New Yorker*, 7 June 1993, 72.

33. Cindy Wooden, "U.S. Bishops Say Curia Heard Their Concerns about Sexual Abuse," *People of God* 11 (April 1993): 18.

34. Garry Wills, "The Real Problem with the Priesthood," *Las Vegas Review Journal*, 23 June 1993, 9B.

35. "Independent Commission Presents Report and Recommendations," *People of God* 11 (June/July 1993): 1.

36. Bruce Daniels, "Bishop: Church Recovering," *Albuquerque Journal*, 2 July 1993, A6.

37. Daniels, "Bishop," A6.

38. Bruce Daniels, "Paraclete Settles 25 Sex Cases," *Albuquerque Journal*, 11 November 1993, A18.

39. Archbishop Michael J. Sheehan, "The First Twelve Months," *People of God*, 12 (October 1994): 2.

40. "Father Greeley," 24; Thom Cole, "Legislature Shows Its Respect For Archbishop," *Albuquerque Journal*, 20 March 1993, A4.

41. "The Journal Poll: N.M. Catholics Want Some Change," *Albuquerque Journal*, 1 August 1993, special section 17.

42. *New Catholic Encyclopedia*, 1969 ed., s.v. "Celibacy, History of."

43. Phil Casaus, "Father Luna: Pastor on a Tightrope," *Albuquerque Journal*, 1 August 1993, special section 16.

44. *Catholic Almanac*, 1993 ed., s.v. "Permanent Diaconate."

45. Deacon Richard Prentiss, KAFB, "Ordinations to the Permanent Deaconate," *People of God* 11 (June/July 1993): 5; Berna Facio, telephone interview, 26 July 1993.

46. Berna Facio, telephone interview, 26 July 1993.

47. Strategic Planning Committee, "Diocesan Strategic Profile," chap. 11:5.

48. Ibid., chap. 11:6.

49. Father Denis Tejada, personal letter, 24 June 1993.

50. Linda J. Garcia, "Faith in Action '93," *People of God* 11 (June/July 1993): 4.

51. Garcia, "Faith in Action '93," *People of God* 11 (April 1993): 3; Garcia, "Faith in Action '93" (June/July 1993): 4.

52. "*Journal* Poll: Impact of the Scandals," *Albuquerque Journal*, 1 August 1993, special section 2.

53. Strategic Planning Committee, "Diocesan Strategic Profile," chap. 13:1.

54. Ibid., chap. 13:2.

55. Ibid., chap. 13:4.

56. Ibid., chap. 1:1.

57. "Forward," *A Study on Social Concern* (Las Cruces, N.M.: Diocese of Las Cruces, 1985), Mimeographed.

58. Archbishop Michael J. Sheehan, "In the Risen Lord: Collaboration in the Archdiocese of Santa Fe," *People of God* 12 (November 1994): 2.

59. Ibid.

60. Robert D. Habigee, "Santa Maria de la Paz Catholic Community, Santa Fe," *People of God* 11 (February 1993): 8.

61. Kessell, *Missions of New Mexico*, 82.

62. Thomas J. Steele, "Funciones of a Village," in *Funciones: Communal Ceremonies of Hispanic Life* (n.p., 1983), 5.

63. *Our Lady of Guadalupe, Taos, New Mexico* (White Plains, N.Y.: Monarch Publishing, 1976), 32.

64. Phil Casaus, "Sanchez: When a Hero Stumbles," *Albuquerque Journal*, 14 March 1993, A10.

65. 250th Anniversary Book Committee, *La Iglesia de Santa Cruz de la Cañada, 1733–1983* (Santa Cruz, N.M.: n.p., 1983), 37.

66. Marina Ochoa, "New Mexico's Historic Churches," *People of God* 11 (February 1993): 6.

67. Patrick J. Roache, "Denial of Sexuality Is Real Problem," *Albuquerque Journal*, 23 March 1993, A7; Andrew M. Greeley, *American Catholics since the Council: An Unauthorized Report* (Chicago: Thomas More Press, 1985), 182.

68. Richard N. Ostling, "Cut from the Wrong Cloth," *Time*, 22 June 1992, 64.

69. Leslie Linthicum, "Excluded Women Hope to Redefine 'Priest,'" *Albuquerque Journal*, 1 August 1993, special section, 13.

70. "Women and Parish Life," *People of God* 3 (June 1985): 7; Jay P. Dolan, *The American Catholic Experience: History from Colonial Times to the Present* (Garden City, N.Y.: Doubleday, 1985), 439.

71. Ostling, "Cut from the Wrong Cloth," 64; Dolan, *American Catholic Experience*, 438.

72. Carol Jensen, "Deserts, Diversity, and Self-Determination," in *The American Catholic Parish*, ed. Jay P. Dolan, 2 vols (Mahwah, N.J.: Paulist Press, 1987), 2: 273; and *The Official Catholic Directory* (New Providence, N.J.: P. J. Kennedy and Sons in association with R. R. Bowker, 1994), 972.

73. Phyllis Rapagnani, "A Tradition of Service: Roman Catholic Sisters in New Mexico, 1852–1927" (master's thesis, University of New Mexico, 1988), 57.

74. Ibid., 65.

75. Ibid., 72 and 81; Jensen, "Deserts, Diversity, and Self-Determination," 190.

76. Rapagnani, "Tradition of Service," 93, 96.

77. "Sister Pleads for Struggling Indian Mission School," *People of*

God 12 (October 1994): 19.

78. Rapagnani, "Tradition of Service," 113, 116–117, 122.

79. Ibid., 145.

80. *The Official Catholic Directory*, 1994 Supplement (New Providence, N.J.: P. J. Kennedy and Sons in association with R. R. Bowker, 1994), xxiii, xxi, and xxii.

81. Helen Rose Fuchs Erbaugh, *Women in the Vanishing Cloister* (New Brunswick, N.J.: Rutgers University Press, 1993), 92, 135, 174.

82. Ostling, "Cut from the Wrong Cloth," 65.

83. Ibid., 65.

84. Stephen J. Shaw, "The Cities and the Plains, A Home for God's People: A History of the Catholic Parish in the Midwest," in Dolan, *American Catholic Parish*, 2: 373.

85. Catholic Charismatic Center, Albuquerque, N.M.

86. Catholic Charismatic Center Staff, telephone interview, 26 July 1993.

87. Catholic Charismatic Center, Albuquerque, N.M.

88. Sister Nancy Kazik, OSF, ed., "Around the Archdiocese: Dominican Retreat House," *People of God* 12 (October 1994): 7.

89. John Leahigh, "Priest and Navajo Spiritual Leader to Preside at Peace Pilgrimage," *People of God* 11 (April 1993): 12; "11th Annual Peace Pilgrimage," *People of God* 11 (May 1993): 18.

90. "Prayer Vigil Set for July," *People of God* 11 (May 1993): 6.

91. Joanna Macy, "Working for the Earth without Going Crazy," *Radical Grace* 6 (February-March 1993): 1.

92. "Organization History," *A Study on Social Concerns* (Las Cruces, N.M. Diocese of Las Cruces, 1985), Mimeographed.

93. Kelley, *Diocese of Gallup Golden Jubilee*, 74.

94. Victor L. Simpson, "Pope Takes the Hard Line," *Las Vegas Review Journal*, 15 August 1993, 1A.

95. "The *Journal* Poll: N.M Catholics Want Some Change," *Albuquerque Journal*, 1 August 1993, special section 17.

96. "The *Journal* Poll: The Scandal's Legacy," *Albuquerque Journal*, 1 August 1993, special section 2.

97. John Fleck, "Despite Deep Loyal Core, New Mexicans Have Doubts," *Albuquerque Journal*, 1 August 1993, special section 13.

98. Geraldine Esquivel, "1992: Casa Angelica's 25th Anniversary Year," *People of God* 11 (February 1993): 10.

99. "Spotlight on Barrett House," *People of God* 11 (May 1993): 8.

100. Strategic Planning Committee, chap. 12:3.

101. "Catholic Social Services Fills Gap," *Albuquerque Journal*, 21 March 1993, C1.

2

Protestantism in Modern New Mexico

Randi Jones Walker

DURING THE TWENTIETH CENTURY, PROTESTANTISM BECAME AN increasingly influential part of the religious culture of New Mexico. The censuses and surveys of church membership in this century continually showed New Mexico to be one of the most religious areas of the country. Protestants account for an increasing percentage of church members, and Baptists for an increasing percentage of Protestants. A map of religion in New Mexico would show Protestant, primarily Baptist, strength in the counties near Texas and in other largely Anglo counties.[1] Even in the largely Hispanic and Roman Catholic counties in the north-central part of the state, there are sizable numbers of Protestant church members. These Protestants are mostly Anglos with increasing numbers of African Americans and Asians. There are old Protestant mainline churches in Hispanic communities, as well as newer Pentecostal and evangelical congregations. Protestantism has also appealed to a small number of Native Americans.

All of these Protestants have had to come to terms with the twentieth century. The issues they have faced have ranged from temperance to public schools, from war to the economy. All have had to cope with distance from national denominational centers of power, the large indigenous Roman Catholic presence, and the increasing secularization of the modern world. This essay will address this story. How the Protestants in New Mexico were shaped by the twentieth century and how they influenced life in New Mexico is not a question that allows attention isolated from trends in Protestantism in the wider world, nor does it allow us to pass over the unique aspects of the New Mexican context.

Protestantism is a complex phenomenon. What differentiates Protestant from Roman Catholic or Orthodox Christianity is not as pronounced as might first appear. Perhaps the most characteristic Protestant traits include an emphasis on the word, both Bible and sermon, and a sense of discontinuity with the majority of Christian history. The discontinuity entails both a break with the old authority structure and a sense of recovery of the earliest forms of Christian life.

There are several kinds of Protestantism in the United States, and all of them are represented in New Mexico in the twentieth century. The mainline, liberal, more modernist denominations tend to have longer histories and deeper European roots. They share common ecumenical ideals, social-justice agendas, and historical critical analyses of biblical texts, and they tend to accept a variety of theological points of view and tolerate a wide variety of lifestyles. The mainline churches were the first Protestants to move into New Mexico, and though they are not the largest group, they are well established and influential.

Evangelical, conservative, or fundamentalist denominations emphasize a more literal interpretation of the Bible than is found among the mainline churches. Salvation of individual souls is their primary focus. They are more inclined to be exclusive, to have more rigorous standards of belief and personal morality. Another group of Protestants, the Pentecostal denominations, emphasize religious experience, and may or may not be particularly conservative or literal in their approach to the Bible. Often mutual suspicions exist among the mainline, evangelical, and Pentecostal denominations.

Newer independent or nondenominational churches have a wide range of theologies and are difficult to categorize. Sometimes they originate as a reform of mainline or evangelical Protestantism. Often they are formed by a strong leader who becomes the center of the life of the church. Usually they address what they consider to be contemporary religious concerns that others are neglecting. Finally, there is the Church of Jesus Christ of the Latter-day Saints, a reform of mainline Protestantism that includes a new scripture. This essay will touch in some manner upon all of these groups and tie all of them to the larger trends in religion in this century.

Martin Marty, in his introduction to *Altered Landscapes: Christianity in America, 1935–1985*, makes several observations about the changes affecting the churches in the twentieth century. Some of these changes he characterizes as glacial (deep and very slow moving) while others are swift, arriving with the force of a hurricane.[2] The civil-rights movement, the changes in women's roles in society, and the effects of electronic media such as television have pushed on the churches as inexorably as a glacier. The world wars and the Second Vatican Council swept onto the scene with the force of a mighty wind. The increasing splits between the sacred and secular, the rich and poor, the fundamentalist and modernist, the ecumenical and denominational continue to rend American Christianity.

Leonard Sweet's essay in the same volume focuses on the modernization of religion in America. Sweet names 1935 as the end of the "Protestant era in American Religion." Shifting values and family structures, demands for cultural equality, great population migrations, new technology, including automobiles and television, all combined to undermine the previous hegemony of the mainline Protestants (Methodist, Presbyterians, Congregationalists, Episcopalians, many Baptists, Disciples of Christ, and Lutherans). Sweet suggests that Protestantism at first embraced modernism, only later becoming more critical of modern trends.

In his essay Sweet outlines the process by which American mainline Protestantism came to terms with the modern age. The first step, beginning in the nineteenth century, was to develop a modernist Protestantism, enthusiastically embracing the technological developments and many of the social changes that accompanied modernization, for instance the acceptance of divorce. World War I shook the belief in the ever-growing progress of human good and spurred the turn to pacifism and socialism—especially among the mainline Protestant clergy, though this turn was not shared by the laity. World War II dealt the final blow to liberalism's illusion of progress and innocence. Neoorthodox theology restored a healthy notion of human sin and the witness of Christian tradition over against modernist ideals. But again the developments were confined to the seminaries and the clergy, never becoming widely discussed among the laity. The mainline Protestant critique was too little, too late, and contributed to its decline.[3]

Sweet defines the values characteristic of modernism as "rationality, objectivity, relativity, novelty, science and technology, social action, organizations, differentiations, and distributive justice."[4] Bruce Lawrence, a student of Islam, gives an even more complex definition:

> Modernism is the search for individual autonomy driven by a set of socially encoded values emphasizing change over continuity; quantity over quality; efficient production, power, and profit over sympathy for traditional values or vocations, in both the public and private spheres. At its utopian extreme, it enthrones one economic strategy, consumer-oriented capitalism, as the surest means to technological progress that will also eliminate social unrest and physical discomfort.[5]

Modernism is an ideology of uncritical acceptance of life shaped by the bureaucratization, rationalization, and technological developments of the last two centuries. One might say, following Lawrence, that the strength of fundamentalism lies also in a critique of modernism.[6] Fundamentalist Christianity is also clearly uncomfortable with and resistant to the modernist set of values. The opposition, whether to the secularization of public schooling, the theory of evolution, or the availability of abortion, is focused on some aspect of the use of empirical or scientific method to discover the truth. Ironically, however, the same rationalist thought process is used to "prove" the case of creation science or to argue the validity of moral law rationally derived from Scripture.[7] Also, worldwide, fundamentalism as an ideology sustains its influence by means of the quintessential modernist electronic media.[8]

None of the essays in Lotz's volume dwell on what is perhaps the most influential factor of twentieth-century life—its violence. This has been humankind's most destructive century. The two world wars were the most destructive events, in terms of loss of human life, since the Great Plague in the fourteenth century. It can also be argued that these were simply two flare-ups of an otherwise constant global war that raged throughout the century. The issues of rage, grief, and guilt that have faced humanity in this century have touched every soul, and all religions have struggled to come to terms with them.

Sweet characterizes the post–World War II era with two statistics. At the same time that church membership reached an all-time high in the United States (69 percent), biblical literacy reached an all-time low. Membership became equated with "going to church" rather than "being the church." Religion became something to be packaged and consumed. Little wonder the clergy became silent about controversial issues facing society. National church bodies engaged in making social and political pronouncements "which one old parson termed the most harmless form of amusement ever designed by the human mind."[9] Such pronouncements rarely resulted in significant change. The constant violence is one of many effects of modernism. Because it is a pervasive element of twentieth-century life, it is almost impossible for any segment of society alone to oppose its influence successfully.

The need to unite religious bodies for common activity created another characteristic of Protestantism in the twentieth century, ecumenism. Beginning with the Edinburgh International Missionary Conference in 1910, the churches began to engage in conversation about their theological similarities and differences, and they began to look for ways to cooperate. By midcentury, the formation of the Federal Council of Churches (later the National Council of Churches) and the founding of the World Council of Churches and the Evangelical Alliance had given institutional form to this desire to work together. Over the course of the century, substantial agreement has been achieved on matters of doctrine, several major denominational families have accomplished reunions, and cooperation among denominations on social service and evangelism projects has greatly increased the effectiveness of those programs.

Ecumenical activity has influenced the liturgies of the mainline Protestants. As hymnals and books of worship have been revised, the forms of worship are growing more and more alike. The Presbyterian scholar Jane Dempsey Douglass, president of World Alliance of Reformed Churches, pointed out that this was a result of renewed interest in the history on the part of each denomination.[10] When each group separately did its homework it found itself on common ground with the others. A comparison of the new worship books of the United Methodists, the Presbyterians, the Episcopalians, and the United Church of Christ shows substantially more similarity than one would have found fifty years ago.

Denominational identity is now based more on polity than unique theology. Indeed, the business of church unions focuses almost exclusively on polity concerns, where the maintenance of personal power and influence of individuals become factors in the discussion. Here again, many lay people and clergy tend not to participate in ecumenical conversations in the same way as national denominational representatives. In the union negotiations between the Congregational Christian Churches and the Evangelical and Reformed Church to form the United Church of Christ, for example, the plans were made at a high level. Communication of the arrangement to the grassroots level precipitated an unexpected level of controversy. The greatest concerns were polity concerns, and theological issues were passed over lightly.

Ecumenical bodies, still modernist in Sweet's sense, are more able to do things together than simply believe together. It is easier to form committees and measure Christian faith by acts of social work, though by those acts of social work the ecumenical activity is often subversive of the modernist agenda (registering with dismay in *Reader's Digest* and *60 Minutes*).

In additional to these trends in American Protestantism of the twentieth century, developments in the economic and cultural and political atmosphere in the Southwest, particularly in New Mexico, require attention. Whereas in the East and Midwest, Roman Catholics are recent immigrants, in New Mexico Protestants are the newcomers. Although there is a sense of Anglo-Protestant hegemony in the larger cities, in Albuquerque, where the majority of the population is Anglo, almost half the people are Roman Catholic, and 60 percent of all church members are Roman Catholic.[11] Culturally the area north of Albuquerque is Roman Catholic, and even in the southeastern part of the state, where there has been a long-standing Baptist presence in the shape of immigrants from Texas and the south, Mexican immigration fuels a sizable Roman Catholic community.

Not only is there an old Roman Catholic religious tradition in New Mexico, the cultural tradition is largely Hispanic, with twelve of thirty-three counties retaining a Hispanic majority population, especially in the southwestern and northeastern sectors of the state. In addition there are sizable Native American communities (McKinley County is 61 percent Native American),[12] which, by their inescapable and ancient presence, have modified Hispanic and Anglo life.

Like other parts of the West, New Mexico is dependent economically on extractive industries (mining and logging controlled by companies centered elsewhere), on ranching and farming, and increasingly on government-funded projects. Its cities have experienced rapid growth since World War II, with great dependency on the federal government as an employer. The prevalence of single-industry areas, plus the low-paying nature of extractive labor, creates an economy unable to support Protestantism's expansive dreams.[13]

A small, widely scattered population and the relative poverty of the state create difficulties for the churches. Reliance on financial assistance from large denominational structures looking for large numbers to justify their expenditures create frustrations compounded by the distances that must be traveled to supervise and encourage the work of the various churches. It is also difficult to attract ministers to all but the largest cities and towns. Low salaries, lack of employment opportunities for spouses, and isolation discourage many qualified pastors.

The automobile, airplane, the telephone, and television have had an impact on life in New Mexico. All these inventions serve, on the one hand, to overcome the isolation of both individual and communities in the West, and on the other, to further isolate people from one another. One cannot stop to chat with neighbors one meets driving a car down the street, though one can see friends several miles away more easily. The Protestant churches likewise benefited and suffered from the development of these technologies. The very car that made it easier to get to church also made it less difficult to get out of town for the weekend. Although the mainline Protestants made good use of radio, the fundamentalists have made better use of television. It remains to be seen what effects the computer will have.

New Mexico also became one of the centers of the Cold War defense economy. Many of the military personnel and others who came to the state because of such work belonged to Protestant churches. In all of these churches, painful dilemmas were faced concerning the wish to be patriotic, the need to feel secure, and the imperative to make Christian witness against the mass destruction of life that this industry made possible. Into the neighborhoods of some of the most ancient communities in North America came high technology, seeing itself as the wave of the future, making the past irrelevant.

In the last century New Mexico has attracted people seeking economic opportunity, health, better weather for retirement, and even holy ground. Who among them were Protestants, where did they settle, how did they cope with life, and what part did they play in the shaping of society? And how have the churches they built fared, and what part do these institutions play in shaping people's lives?

Protestant Demographics[14]

From the beginning of the twentieth century, church membership has been high in New Mexico. In 1906 the territory of New Mexico led the nation in the percentage of the population reported to be members of religious organizations.[15] Sixty-three percent of the people of New Mexico were religious enough to be claimed as church or synagogue members, compared with a nationwide figure of 39 percent. Of these 137,009 members, almost 90 percent were Roman Catholic. The three largest Protestant bodies—Methodists, Presbyterians, and Baptists—accounted for about 90 percent of the remaining church members: the Methodists with 6,560 members, the Presbyterians with 2,935, and the Baptists with 2,403.

Throughout the twentieth century, Roman Catholics maintained their majority among church-going New Mexicans. Although the level of church membership of all adherents in New Mexico declined during the course of the century, it did so less dramatically than in the rest of the trans-Mississippi West. Although Southern Baptists and Methodists remained among the largest Protestant bodies throughout the century, the Presbyterians, fourth largest through most of the century, have dropped to eighth in the last twenty years. Not only did the percentage of Presbyterian membership decline; a rapid increase among such bodies as the Churches of Christ, Assemblies of God, and independent noncharismatic churches also became apparent in the years after 1956. The Latter-day Saints have remained among the top ten largest religious bodies throughout the century, moving solidly into fourth place.

The most dramatic increase in Protestant numbers came in the more than 500 percent growth of the Southern Baptists between 1936 and 1956. In 1941 the Baptists began setting goals for their home mission and evangelism projects. In his *History of New Mexico Baptists*, Lewis Myers lists the

Table I: New Mexico Church Membership

Churches	1906	1916	1926	1936	1956	1971	1980	1990
Percentage of Total Population	63.3	64.1	50.9	45.7	64.9	63.3	59.1	58.7
Catholics	121,000	177,727	174,287	196,759	293,683	363,518	435,241	467,356
Baptists	2,403	6,721						
Southern			9,570	8,687	61,759	116,869	131,575	158,873
Black			408	542				7,046
American						2,092	1,298	1,885
Methodist	6,560				34,898	58,700	53,185	54,664
Methodist Episcopal Church South		7,120	3,914	2,363				
Methodist Episcopal Church		4,385	8,848	10,225				
African Methodist Episcopal		79	238	310				
Christian Methodist Episcopal		69	64	181				
Presbyterians	2,935	4,208	5,227	5,623	12,370	19,813	16,652	14,730
Congregational	270	366	709	802	1,003	2,564	2,273	2,556
						[ucc]	[ucc]	[ucc]
Disciples	1,092	2,284	2,662	2,249	4,165	4,123	4,147	4,224
Episcopal	869	1,718	2,258	3,479	9,233	14,731	13,692	10,691
Latter-day Saints	738	1,484	1,497	2,296		21,843	28,804	39,429
Church of God		1,333	17[1]	224				
Cleveland, TN					501	1,802	1,710	2,240
Anderson, IN					210	904	1,137	536
Church of Christ		1,333	2,032	3,077		6,238	17,414	19,780

Churches	1906	1916	1926	1936	1956	1971	1980	1990
Seventh-day Adventists		323	221	484	1,051	2,945	3,555	4,523
Assemblies of God			135	989	5,725	5,838	15,345	20,841
Nazarene			450	832	1,510		6,663	6,571
Jewish			367	553	1,245		1,137	6,075
Lutherans	100	509	397	595				
Missouri Synod					2,377	5,788	5,543	6,604
Lutheran Church in America					2,215	6,652	7,139	
American Lutheran Church								
Evangelical Lutheran Church in America						11,378		2,098
Reformed Church in America	70		206			296	487	575
Christian Reformed				899	164	712	1,561	
Friends					57	153	204	396
Unitarians					99	1,273	1,189	1,301
Independent / Non Denominational								
Charismatic								5,075
Non-Charismatic								23,078

Figures are from:

U.S. Bureau of the Census, *Religious Bodies: 1906, 1916, 1926 and 1936* (Washington, D.C.: Government Printing Office).

National Council of Churches of Christ, *Churches and Church Membership in the United States* (New York: National Council of Churches, 1956-58).

Douglas Johnson et al. *Churches and Church Membership in the United States, 1971* (Washington, D.C.: Glenmary Research Center, 1974).

Bernard Quinn et al. *Churches and Church Membership in the United States, 1980* (Atlanta: Glenmary Research Center, 1982).

Martin Bradley et al. *Churches and Church Membership in the United States, 1990* (Atlanta: Glenmary Research Center, 1992).

[1] A split occurred in the Church of God in this decade, and only one group reported membership. The group was not identified.

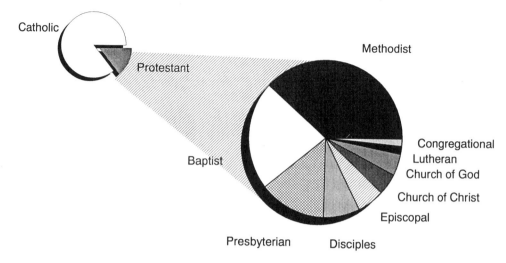

Chart 1. New Mexico Church Membership in 1916.
Information for this chart and those following is found in Table I, pages 34–35.

following goals, as found in the annual reports of the Baptist Convention of New Mexico: "every church open every Sunday . . . , at least one revival, . . . a paper in every home and the Lord's Supper at least once per quarter. . . . agreeing to attempt the goals of "Every Two Win One" on the New Mexico Front.[16] The year 1949 was the year of a great Baptist revival in New Mexico celebrating the centennial of the first Protestant sermon delivered in the Southwest, and part of a national upsurge in Southern Baptist activity, which eventually made them the largest Protestant denomination in the United States. In addition, the African-American Baptist churches together presently rank as the eleventh largest religious body in New Mexico. Some are growing fast. One of these is the New Hope Missionary Baptist Church in Albuquerque, one of the largest African-American churches in town.

Between 1936 and 1956 the Latter-day Saints increased tenfold, the Methodists tripled, and the Presbyterians more than doubled their numbers, while the Roman Catholics increased by only one-third. It is more difficult to trace the growth of independent churches because their membership figures are not so readily available. They are included for the first time in the 1990 statistics from the Glenmary Research Center. In 1990, the number of independent, noncharismatic church adherents stood at 23,078, making them collectively the fifth largest religious body in New Mexico. By 1995, Calvary Chapel in Albuquerque claimed nine to ten thousand members, although they do not keep an official membership list.[17]

In the course of the century several denominational unions and splits affected the size of certain groups. For example, in 1939 the Methodist Episcopal Churches South and North reunited to form the Methodist Church, and by 1956 Methodist increase proved the union to be a success. The Methodists continued to grow after their union with the Evangelical United Brethren in 1968. The Lutherans were also strengthened after the union that formed the Evangelical Lutheran Church in America in the eighties. Although the Congregational churches initially lost members at the time of the formation of the United Church of Christ in 1957, they have recovered their 1956 membership level. In contrast, the Disciples of Christ divided in 1927 with the formation of the North American Christian Convention, the "Independents," in a controversy over the Disciples' move into mainstream liberal Protestantism.[18]

Most religious bodies have shown steady growth throughout the twentieth century, largely following trends of immigration from other places. For instance, though the Congregationalists are one of the oldest Protestant denominations in New Mexico, not many New Englanders moved to New Mexico to augment their ranks in the way that southerners brought increasing numbers to the Baptist and Methodist churches.

Table II: Percentage of New Mexico Church Members in Each Group

Churches	1906	1919	1926	1936	1956	1971	1980	1990
Catholic	88.7	84.7	80.8	80.8	66.4	56.4	56.7	52.6
Protestant	10.7	11.7	18.0	18.1	33.4	40.3	39.4	39.4
Mormon	.5			.6		3.3	3.8	3.8
Jewish				.2	.2		.1	.1
Other	.1	.3	.6					

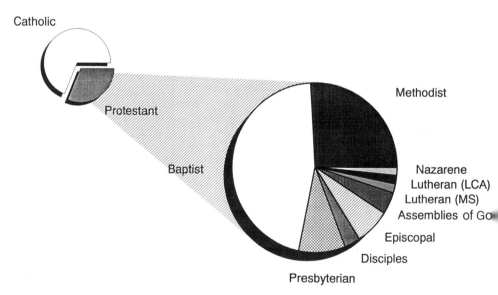

Chart 2. New Mexico Church Membership 1956.

On the other hand, the percentage of New Mexicans claiming membership in religious bodies has gradually diminished over the century, following a nationwide trend; the numbers reached a low point in the thirties, when confidence in traditional institutions was also low. If it were not for the large Catholic population and growing number of Latter-day Saints, the percentage of church adherents in the population would look more like that of the West Coast.[19] The growth rate of all groups, except apparently that of the independent noncharismatic churches, has slowed in the last twenty years.

The demographic geography of church membership in New Mexico deserves brief comment. The counties with a majority of Protestants—Chaves, Curry, Eddy, Lea, Quay, and Roosevelt counties—tend to be located in the southern and eastern areas of the state. In 1971 five counties, including San Juan and McKinley, had fewer church members than nonchurch members. One should note that San Juan and McKinley counties have a large Native American population whose own religions are not included in the surveys of membership. The rest of the counties in New Mexico remain largely Roman Catholic.[20]

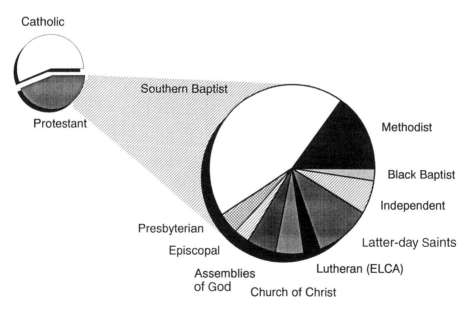

Chart 3. New Mexico Church Membership 1990.

Table III: Ten Largest Churches in New Mexico for Each Year

Date Rank	1890	1906	1916	1926	1936	1956	1971	1980	1990
1	Catholic	Catholic	Catholic	Catholic	Catholic	Catholic	Catholic	Catholic	Catholic
2	Methodist	Methodist	Methodist	Methodist	Methodist	Baptist	Baptist	Southern Baptist	Southern Baptist
3	Presbyterian	Presbyterian	Baptist	Baptist	Baptist	Methodist	Methodist	Methodist	Methodist
4	Episcopal	Baptist	Presbyterian	Presbyterian	Presbyterian	Presbyterian	Presbyterian	Latter-day Saints	Latter-day Saints
5	Baptist	Disciples	Disciples	Disciples	Episcopal	Episcopal	Latter-day Saints	Church of Christ	Independent Non-Charismatic
6	Congregational	Episcopal	Episcopal	Epicopal	Church of Christ	Assemblies of God	Episcopal	Presbyterian	Assemblies of God
7	Disciples	Latter-day Saints	Church of Christ	Church of Christ	Latter-day Saints	Disciples	Lutheran Church in America	Assemblies of God	Church of Christ
8	Lutheran	Congregational	Church of God	Latter-day Saints	Disciples	Lutheran Missouri Synod	Church of Christ	Episcopal	Presbyterian
9	Other	Lutheran	Lutheran	Congregational	Assemblies of God	Lutheran Church	Nazarene	Church of Christ / Christian Church	Evangelical Lutheran Church in America
10		Reformed	Congregational	Nazarene	Christian Reformed	Nazarene	Lutheran Missouri Synod	Lutheran Church in America	Episcopal

Latter-day Saints information not available for 1916 and 1956.

How Have Protestant Churches in New Mexico Come to Terms with the Twentieth Century?

The twentieth century has presented churches, and indeed the world, with uniquely complex challenges. The social changes wrought by industrial development and urbanization have puzzled governments, schools, and businesses as much as they have churches. Ironically, at the same time that society has increasingly found itself in need of moral guidance, the credibility of the churches has been eroded. Yet the churches have continued as viable institutions, able, upon occasion, to trouble society with claims that go beyond economic survival.

On the great issues of the century—war, technology, race relations, economic disparity, and women's rights—churches, like most institutions, have usually reacted to these developments rather than anticipating or shaping them. This is not to say that any institutions in society could have wrested the twentieth century from one course onto another; however, the multinational corporations and the military forces of the various nations have shaped the world in which we live far more effectively than churches. Instead, the power of churches lies in the multitudes of people who gather regularly to attend to the life of the spirit and remind themselves of ideals and values that shape their behavior. Rather than gaining world dominion, a kind of moral imagination, fed by biblical and nonbiblical sources, has shaped the churches' struggles with the ethical dilemmas of our times.

In addition to these secular forces, other factors related to the life of the churches have influenced their development. The ecumenical movement, the continuing development of historical and literary analyses of biblical texts, the increasing secularization of society, and family issues related to the liberation of women, divorce, and homosexuality have created new divisions in already splintered churches. These are issues that, along with war, technology, and economic disparity, are forcing churches to redefine themselves, to clarify again their theological premises, and to influence the rest of society. It is time to take a look at the ways in which Protestants in New Mexico have come to terms with these issues.

At the turn of the century, saloons, gambling, the lack of Sabbath observance, and graft in government were among the top issues facing the major Protestant groups. In addition, they were concerned about the non-Anglo society around them. The Presbyterian synod stated its concern for "tens of thousands of Indians and Mexicans . . . living without the Gospel of Jesus Christ, which alone can mould and fashion and fit for true citizenship here and happiness hereafter."[21] Concern about both Mormons and Native Americans influenced the Synod to endorse a petition to Congress to amend the constitution prohibiting polygamy.[22] The Methodists, Congregationalists, and Baptists all had similar concerns.

Some of these concerns had long histories before they attracted the attention of New Mexico's Protestants. With the rise of an industrial economy came the distillation of more potent alcoholic beverages and an increase in drinking, noticeable by the early nineteenth century. Churches began to speak out about the harm alcohol caused to individuals and to the community. Protestants organized temperance societies. The movement became a well-organized political crusade after the Civil War; the Prohibitionist party was formed in 1869, and churches strongly supported its candidates. The Anti-Saloon League, organized in 1895, also drew its members primarily from the Protestant churches. But temperance as such was not as large a concern in New Mexico as it was, for instance, in Kansas. Perhaps the concern among New Mexico Protestants lay in the association of Roman Catholics and Indians with drinking and gambling.

Concern about polygamy among the Mormons in Utah was an important issue for Anglo Protestants in New Mexico because it also affected the territory's application for statehood. Thomas Harwood, the superintendent of the New Mexico Methodist Spanish Mission Conference, in his report to the conference in 1906, reflected on the statehood issue with these words:

> Statehood is now upon us. While our people hate to lose the long cherished, historic, romantic name, "New Mexico," yet, almost to a man they favor statehood even at the loss of the name, as it adds so many advantages to the new state, all of which lies in the line of progress; yet, as our good Bishop has said, "One would naturally suppose that the necessity of making good citizens out of the Mexican people, who have become an integral part of our nation, would be sufficient even without the higher gospel motives to cause benefaction to that end to flow in deep and constant streams."[23]

"Are you ready for statehood? Is the Mexican a safe and intelligent citizen? Will the political bosses control or will you have a popular government by the people?" These questions from friends outside New Mexico were sent to John R. Glass, Presbyterian synodical missionary, and reported in the synod meeting in 1910. He continued:

> The eyes of the nation are upon us and our successes and defeats in our missionary enterprise are more eagerly watched by intelligent people in the east than any of the plans of the would-be political bosses. After all, the shaping of the destiny of these new states is not

primarily in the hands of the political leaders but with the moral and religious teachers of the states. As is the Church, so is the State.[24]

Protestants distinguished themselves from the largely Hispanic Roman Catholics as well as from their secularized Anglo neighbors by their manner of keeping the Sabbath—attending church, closing their stores, and foregoing entertainments on Sunday. Still, even in their own ranks, people did not attend church as regularly as they had. The Sabbatarian movement among Protestants in the early years of the twentieth century was born out of the marked decrease in Reformed-style Protestant Sabbath keeping in the face of industrialization and the immigration of large numbers of people who did not customarily keep the Sabbath. Evidence of Sabbatarian success lies in the "blue laws" regulating public activity on Sunday in many places. In New Mexico there was additional Protestant effort to instill a more puritan Sabbath observance in communities accustomed to a more festive Hispanic Catholic Sunday.

In 1899 the Methodist annual conference recommended that its churches not announce their services or advertise in any newspaper that published a Sunday edition.[25] The Presbyterian synod recommended that each presbytery organize a Social Service Committee that would work against Sunday labor and "great corporations that employ Sunday labor."[26] The church folk of the early twentieth century tended to see social ills as matters of individual responsibility. When Protestant convictions led to political action, it was generally an attempt to regulate personal behavior, as in the temperance crusade.

Early in the twentieth century, the woman suffrage movement made more progress in the West than in the rest of the country. Although New Mexico lagged behind other western states in granting women the vote, Lewis Myers points out that in the 1870 New Mexican Southern Baptist Convention, women and men had worked on an equal basis in the territory. A decade later, women's equal participation was open to debate.[27] Methodist activity in New Mexico at the turn of the century depended upon funds raised by women and on women teachers. Emily Harwood wrote, translated, and edited much of the Methodist paper *Abogado Cristiano*, and taught at the Harwood girls' school in Albuquerque.[28] The Methodist conference women's organization owned and operated a hospital in Albuquerque through much of this century, and the Women's Missionary Society supported and supervised teachers in Methodist schools. Women controlled missionary funds and served as teachers in the Presbyterian schools, and the wives of Hispanic Presbyterian ministers, such as Petrita Rendón and Margarita Cruz, preached in their husbands' absence and performed other ministerial tasks.[29]

As in other parts of the West, women preachers began to appear, especially in places where men were reluctant to serve. An ordained Congregational woman, Mrs. M. J. Border, was president of the New Mexico W.C.T.U. in the early 1890s and was preaching in Cabezon at the turn of the century.[30] The United Brethren licensed women to preach, and Mellie Perkins held regular worship services in Santa Cruz in connection with her work at the Evangelical United Brethren's McCurdy School.[31] Tabytha Watson, an African-American evangelist, founded the Mount Olive Baptist Church in Albuquerque at the turn of the century, and in 1918 a Mrs. Wilson of Indianapolis held services at the African Methodist Episcopal Church in Gallup.[32]

As early as 1900, the Presbyterians also gave indication of increasing their understanding of the Native Americans. In one incident, the missionary Charles Cook requested the New Mexico synod to consider "a water supply for . . . [the] Pimas, a water supply of which they have been robbed by the whites."[33]

The Social Gospel was developed in the Progressive era as an attempt by thoughtful church leaders and theologians to persuade churches that moral reform and charity were not enough to remedy the injustices of society. Many activists, like Frances Willard of the W.C.T.U., embraced socialism and spoke on behalf of labor. As we shall see, by the end of the twentieth century such reformist thought informed many denominational and ecumenical projects and caused dissension in church ranks. However, the majority of Protestant church members early in the twentieth century believed that personal conversion and reform were the keys to bringing the Kingdom of God into reality.

The illusion that personal morality was enough to repair the ills of the world was shattered for the Protestants in 1917 with the entry of the United States into World War I. Until then, New Mexico Protestants had been largely silent about the war. It was not our war after all, they said; it was Europe's war. Until the United States entered the fray, the loss of some eight million lives in the course of four years was passed over lightly in the religion pages of New Mexico's newspapers. A few exceptions can be found. The *Albuquerque Evening Herald* noted in May 1918 that the Episcopal chaplains were addressing their district convention on the subject of Christianity and patriotism, announcing that the church bells of both Catholics and Protestants would be rung at noon every day in May, "calling people to prayer for the country in war times."[34] In December 1917, Reverend Pratt, rector of Grace Episcopal Church in Carlsbad, published one of his sermons on the front page of the *Carlsbad Argus*. In it, he likened the trials of the war, especially having one's children killed for the cause of civilization, to Abraham's trial when God required the sacrifice of his son, Isaac. Pratt not only asked readers to face this test with faith, but also requested that they enter into the active service of God and humanity.[35]

This war was seen as the last gasp of a corrupt old order, with the aftermath providing a clean plain upon which to build a new world. Presbyterians made a similar call in their September 1917 synod meeting:

> War's fierce ravages are wasting the world with a devastating power which destroys in a day what it took years, even centuries, to build up. With the ending of the war or even before, the slow, patient work of rebuilding must begin. The sort of world which will be built upon the wreck of the old will depend largely upon the spiritual leaders who shape the destiny of the new era.... We would recommend that there be ... a definite campaign to enlist young men and young women in some definite Christian service to meet the vast need which is presented to the church at this time.[36]

But the new world was not built. War broke out again in the thirties and forties. Between the wars, Protestant churches generally took a more clearly pacifist position. An editorial in the *Artesia Enterprise*, on December 20, 1940, expressed the prevalent position:

> The spirit of Christ is perhaps the only influence in the world today which can bring order out of chaos, peace out war, salvation out of sin; life out of death. It is the only influence in all the world that can bring hope to the human soul.... And Christ, whose birthday Christmas commemorates ... was not a fighting man.... The only fight he was interested in was a fight against the devil, not waged with a sword. There is small justification here for the waging of war. ... Today many people hurl slurs and epithets at "pacifists." But when they do this, they are striking at ... Christ.... Christmas has nothing to do with war.... Its chief beauty is the fact that it claims the things that war abhors.[37]

But a year later, the editor of the *Alamagordo News*, C. W. Morgan, wondered why Protestant churches seemed so ineffective in bringing peace to the world. People have not abided by their religion, the editor suggested, because the religions are divided by "a bewilderment of creeds and denominational bickerings.... We can only conjecture what the result would be if even all of the Protestant religious groups would unite on the simple fundamentals and seek a world-wide betterment of human relations."[38] The United States had just entered the war, and the article concluded by identifying the United States with God's will for human liberty.

Echoing these sentiments was an article in the *Farmington Times Hustler*, by the local Methodist pastor, Rev. D. W. Brashear, who called for Protestant unity in the face of the war: "The need for a more pronounced spirit of unity is not only necessary but essential to our success," he wrote. "Some minds are muddled with partisan politics and religious bias.... This, I insist, is the first line of defense. The Churches should be full of worshipers."[39]

The identification of the liberty of the human race with the cause of the United States in World War II was not seriously challenged in the churches, at least not in public pronouncements. True, there were a few conscientious objectors, but these were rarely mentioned in either newspapers or in denominational records. Neither was much attention paid to the plight of European Jews. In March 1942, however, New Mexicans were called upon to think about the Japanese. Both the Taos and Farmington newspapers reported community reactions to the request of forty thousand Japanese Americans to relocate from California to New Mexico. There was widespread opposition to a plan for Japanese to buy irrigable land and settle on it. Still, the communities reluctantly agreed to cooperate with the U.S. Army in establishing concentration camps in their neighborhoods.

Some editorials warned that the creation of the camps jeopardized American ideals. Ruth Taylor's editorial in the *Taoseaño* was biblical. She wrote, "We must not echo the actions of our enemies by persecution of the enemies in our midst.... It is a direct denial of the American Way of Life."[40] Orval Ricketts of the *Farmington Times Hustler* was more careful about defining the enemy: "The Japanese problem in America is indeed a hard one to approach with the usual fair-mindedness and leniency that marks our country's attitude toward other nationalities.... To place loyal Japanese who are American born citizens in the same camp and class with the aliens is certainly an injustice."[41] Ricketts acknowledged that it was impossible to separate the two groups but concluded that "the Japs brought some of the trouble on themselves when well to do persons of that nationality sought to move inland from the coast and purchase land for colonization."[42] Ricketts's editorial, although citing an American ideal of justice, did not have the moral force of Taylor's, but probably gave a better expression of popular opinion. Two things can be noted in the discussion of the internment issues in the New Mexico secular press. The Protestant churches had little or no identifiable voice in the editorial discussion, and the arguments were framed without overt reference to Protestant theological ideals. Most often, interested Protestant church members heard the discussion within their denominational press. But even journals such as the *United States Baptist* or *The*

Methodist Woman focused attention after December 1941 on support of those who were involved in the war effort or were facing the pain of loss. The *United States Baptist* before 1942 gave specific advice about conscientious objection, but after 1942 did not.

Though they seldom spoke clearly and publicly against any part of the war effort, the mainline Protestant churches concentrated their efforts on the pastoral care of those involved in, or touched by, the war. This included chaplaincy, assistance to churches located near military bases, home church contact with young men and women serving far away, and community comfort for those who lost loved ones.[43] It would be hard to find a congregation in those years that had not lost at least one young member to the war.

Since World War II, mainline liberal Protestants have been ambivalent about war. They supported the formation of the United Nations and the World Council of Churches. Other, more theologically conservative Protestants were concerned that cooperation with nations and churches whose creeds differed significantly from theirs would dilute their Christian witness. Some of them identified their ideals with those of the secular United States (as Billy Graham often did). Others lived in visible opposition to the secular society, especially in matters of personal moral behavior.

Liberal mainline Protestants also took note of the profound change signaled by the American use of the atomic bomb in Japan. Appropriately, this view was expressed most strongly in an editorial appearing in the *Los Alamos Skyliner* of December 17, 1948:

> Our moral position in the world has been sacrificed. Our government and the scientists led us blindfolded to the abyss and say, "Now be careful." . . . The American people woke up to find themselves irrevocably committed to merciless destruction by surprise agencies. Gone was our moral position. We gave no mercy and we cannot expect mercy for ourselves in the future.[44]

Again, although this editorial was rooted in the moral code that Protestants shared, the view was not identified as "religious."

From the fifties until the eighties, the voice of the churches in the newspapers, aside from their ads, is difficult to discern. It is ironic that a bank in Carlsbad becomes the vehicle for encouraging people to look to the churches for help with the issue of war. "All you hear about is war. Where is God?" the headline on the quarter-page Commerce Bank ad asked. "You may find some surprising approaches developing in your church or synagogue. And with your help, your place of worship can, after all, become an important voice in establishing our country's moral position in matters that profoundly affect every one of us."⁴⁵ The only indication on that day's religion page that any of the local churches planned to be of help was the announcement of the sermon topic at Immanuel Lutheran Church. "Christ expects us to be obedient to God," the Reverend Nickel said, "and, if there is no conflict, also [to] the government in whose country we live. Civil disobedience is possible only when the government commands us to sin against God." One hopes that this pastor was of help to the troubled young man (perhaps facing the draft) pictured in the Commerce Bank ad.

In addition to conflicts on these matters, a crisis in theological thinking gripped mainline Protestants and contributed heavily to their loss of membership and influence. In the sixties a number of disturbing and widely read books were published. Gabriel Vahanian's *The Death of God: The Culture of Our Post-Christian Era* (1961), and Harvey Cox's *The Secular City* (1965) were among the most popular. These books called into question the basic assumptions that people had about the Bible, the church, and Christian morality. Moreover, these questions were asked thoughtfully out of a post-- World War II consciousness that realized that things could never be the same again. The postwar generation admitted that the possibility of human goodness and God's reality could not be assumed and certainly were difficult to demonstrate in the face of the holocaust, the Cold War, and racial injustices. Mainline liberal Protestants took these criticisms to heart, but they were not able to answer them easily. They became paralyzed in a way that more conservative churches who simply rejected the critique did not.

The liberal churches' engagement with the issues of the twentieth century is illustrated in the windows of the First Congregational Church, United Church of Christ, in Albuquerque. Pictured in the windows are an open Bible, a balanced scale "representing concerns about justice, racial justice, justice among people with different sexual preferences to issues of who gets the food in this world," a dove, sword, and plowshare "representing concerns for peace," stalks of wheat, a loaf of bread, a cross, a circle, "one symbolizing the birth of Christ and the other his resurrection," and finally, a nucleus with electrons orbiting around it "to represent church members' concerns for the proper use of nuclear energy."⁴⁶ In 1993, the *Albuquerque Tribune* published an interview with the pastor, Francis Rath, who explained that the windows mirrored the open-minded attitudes of members, some of whom were involved with Sandia Laboratories, where research on the application of nuclear energy for both war and peacetime was pursued.⁴⁷

Discussion about the issues of racial and economic injustice, women's rights, and the environment have followed similar patterns. Through most of the century, Anglo Protestant churches exhibited the racial prejudices of the general culture. Even proponents of the Social Gospel, and those concerned with the education and medical care of Native American and Hispanic peoples of New Mexico, did their work in a paternalistic way, feeling good about fulfilling a need but reluctant to trust those in need with responsibility. After World War II, the issue of prejudice became more pressing. In 1950 the Presbyterian synod passed the following resolution:

> In view of the General Assembly's assertion that policies of racial discrimination and segregation are undemocratic and unChristian, we recommend that you authorize your chairman to write a letter to the Board of Christian Education of the Presbyterian Church, U.S.A., urging the removal of all Jim Crow barriers from the doors of our Presbyterian schools of higher learning.[48]

In the late seventies, the United Methodists likewise began to emphasize the development of the ethnic-minority local church, resulting in the development of new but often financially poor congregations. By the eighties many Anglo Protestant congregations hosted congregations of non-Anglo Christians who rented worship space from the Anglo church. Denominational literature and programs increasingly included non-Anglo images and voices. In New Mexico, as in most of the United States, however, Sunday morning worship was still largely segregated by race. Anglos remained in control of all the mainline denominations. Even the statistics compiled by the Glenmary Research Center do not give an accurate picture of the non-Anglo churches. Clearly, there is much work to be done in this area.

Although total membership can never be deduced from such a source, the variety of Protestant groups in present-day New Mexico can be shown by looking at the telephone books in the largest communities in New Mexico: Santa Fe, Los Alamos, Española, Gallup, Grants, Silver City, Deming, Las Cruces, Roswell, Artesia, Belen, Los Lunas, Las Vegas, Raton, Farmington, Hobbs, Lovington, Carlsbad, Clovis, Portales, Tucumcari, Alamogordo, and Albuquerque. This source is limited to those churches that can afford to advertise, and that choose to do so, but the telephone books provide a more extensive list than the Glenmary Research Center figures. In counting the churches advertising in the yellow pages, one finds this rough distribution by non-Anglo ethnic group and denomination.

Hispanic Congregations

7 Methodist
5 Seventh-day Adventist
2 Church of God

2 Jehovah's Witness
2 Nondenominational
2 Mennonite
2 United Church of Christ
1 Disciples of Christ
1 Nazarene

NATIVE AMERICAN CONGREGATIONS
(mostly Navajo)

5 Southern Baptist
1 Assemblies of God
1 Bible Missionary
1 Church of God
1 Evangelical Church of North America
1 Free Methodist
1 Independent Fundamentalist
1 Nazarene

AFRICAN-AMERICAN CONGREGATIONS

1 Pentecostal
4 National Baptist
4 Christian Methodist Episcopal
4 African Methodist Episcopal
1 Presbyterian

In addition, one finds five Korean congregations: two Southern Baptist, two United Methodist, and one Assemblies of God; one Laotian and one Chinese Southern Baptist Church, and a Filipino Bible Missionary congregation.

The *Albuquerque Tribune* features some of these non-Anglo Protestant churches in its "Albuquerque Congregations" column. One article highlights Grant Chapel African Methodist Episcopal Church, which celebrated its 110-year anniversary in December 1992. It was started as the Colored Methodist Mission by Rev. Spotwood Rice, and in 1883 it was one of five churches to receive a plot of land in the city's Newtown. Another congregation, the New Hope Missionary Baptist Church, where the pastor's goal is to create a multiracial fellowship, was featured recently as the fastest growing African-American church in Albuquerque. Also featured were the Mount Olive Baptist Church, nearly one hundred years old, and the Mount Zion

Baptist Church, both African-American congregations. An article about Cristo del Valle Presbyterian Church focused on the Hispanic congregation's Methodist woman pastor.

The Hispanic Methodist Churches of the Rio Grande Conference have always dealt with issues of racial and cultural relations. Interesting in this regard is the use of the term *Mexican*, common in Texas but not used in New Mexico as a reflection of the cultural differences between the old, settled population in the northern Rio Grande valley and the new immigrants in the South. As one scholar has noted, "The main argument [made in 1947] for eliminating the word, 'Mexican,' was that the conference had nothing to do with the work in Mexico and there was no such thing as a 'Mexican race.'"[49] Another cultural problem the conference faces is that many of the pastors come from Latin America, rather than from the Rio Grande Conference.[50] In 1973 priorities for the conference included what Alfredo Náñez called working for better relations between *hispanics* and *méxico-americanos*, the problem of paternalism, and *conscientización de anglos*.[51] In common with other mainline Protestants, evangelism and church growth are the highest priorities for the Rio Grande Conference, in addition to the challenge of living on its own resources and depending less on the agencies of the general church.[52]

Because of its relatively large population of Native American and Hispanic people, whose cultures remain intact after a century and a half of Anglo immigration, northern New Mexico was chosen as the site for a cross-cultural ministry with families that the Garrett-Evangelical Theological Seminary, a Methodist school in Chicago, sponsored. The plan was to see if families from three different cultures can gain strength from each other and learn from each others' experience without giving up loyalty to their own heritage. One experience in this project was related in the progress report:

> In the summer of 1982, three churches in Albuquerque, one Spanish and two Anglo, set up a day-long cross-cultural workshop, Hispanic and Anglo. We called it "Tres Familias de Tres Iglesias" and each church recruited three families willing to spend the day in exploring similarities and differences. As the day started, it was almost totally adults.... But the C. family from El Buen Samaritano church did not leave it at that. They were a couple in their late forties, and as their teenage and young adult children finished chores and got off work from their many jobs, they came one-by-one to the meeting. Characteristically, each would whisper a bit to find out what was going on, and then would unabashedly move into the discussion and activity. By the time we broke up, there had been nine members of the family taking part. Now the parents knew that since it was

mostly Anglos who had set the day up, we expected them to come and to talk *about* their family. But, in what proved to be the most lasting impression of the day, they remained true to their heritage and called the family in to speak for themselves.[53]

In another area the post–World War II era marked the culmination of years of ecumenical hopes among Protestant churches worldwide. In 1948, the same year as the organization of the World Council of Churches, a New Mexico Council of Churches was discussed: "Elder Dale Bullock reported" to the Presbyterian synod meeting "a communication pertaining to the organization of the New Mexico Council of Churches, for which a meeting has been scheduled to be held in Albuquerque on November 1 & 2, 1948. Synod voted to encourage and support such an organization."[54] But the council was not founded until 1964. Soon after the Second Vatican Council, the Archdiocese of Santa Fe joined some ten Protestant and Orthodox denominations, the first Roman Catholic diocese in the United States to join an ecumenical council. The focus of the council's work was then primarily to foster cooperation in human service ministries. In the seventies, it was renamed the "New Mexico Inter-Church Agency" to reflect this emphasis.[55]

In the eighties, after the publication of the World Council of Churches' consensus document *Baptism, Eucharist and Ministry*,[56] there was a renewed international interest in Faith and Order concerns in ecumenical councils. Taking this into account, the New Mexico Inter-Church Agency restructured itself again in 1983, calling itself the "New Mexico Conference of Churches."

One significant Conference of Churches discussion focused on the particularly difficult matter of proselytizing, always a point of contention between Protestants and Roman Catholics in New Mexico. Since evangelism and church growth have become priorities for each group, they inevitably compete with one another, and they often are tempted to exploit people's dissatisfactions. A protocol was developed that affirmed the essential mandate of the churches to evangelize but provided a process by which one church could complain of proselytizing by another.[57]

Another protocol established by the New Mexico Conference of Churches related to differences over ethical issues. The executive director wrote:

> A biblical model became our keystone: the Jerusalem Council as reported in Acts 15. From this event the task force discovered four key elements: 1) there is clear evidence that the Jerusalem Council affirmed the integrity of all those in fellowship with the church; the Council did not impugn the motivation or "quality" of faith among those who were disagreeing over the application of the Mosaic

regulations; 2) the Council wanted both to resolve the differences and at the same time maintain the unity of the churches; 3) the Council wanted ethical requirements to be guides for believers and not burdens; 4) and the Council was able to separate out what were "essential" matters and what were of secondary concern.[58]

Ecumenical activity in New Mexico continues its focus on social justice. In 1987 a Prayer Pilgrimage for Peace united Anglos, Hispanics, and Native Americans, Protestants and Catholics, in a journey from El Santuario de Chimayo to Los Alamos, in a prayer for peace. Today the Conference of Churches sponsors many social services: the New Mexico Alliance for the Mentally Ill; the Southwest Organizing Project, which draws attention to issues of toxic waste in minority communities; the New Mexico Community Development Loan Fund, which promotes self-help projects and socially responsible investment; as well as services to people with AIDS, advocacy for humane public policies, care for the aging, and many other projects.[59]

Congregational Life in Twentieth-Century New Mexico

Attention to family life is probably closer to the heart of church life for the average member of a Protestant church than all of the foregoing concerns about the twentieth century. Another look at the telephone books reveals the following descriptive phrases used countless times in Protestant church advertising: "a friendly church," "a place for you," "the church that cares," "recognizing the worth and dignity of every person," "a great church for you and your family," "where the family can grow," "experience a warm family feeling," "where friendliness is a way of life and the Bible is our guide," "a friendly New Testament congregation," "spirit-filled and Friendly," "a place to belong," "a family of believers," "a family for all ages," "a Fellowship of Friendly Christians," "a loving fellowship sharing the excitement of Jesus," "ordinary people experiencing God," "a small friendly church." Second in number to these phrases are those identifying the church as Christ-centered, Spirit-centered, Bible-centered or Fundamentalist, and specifically denominational descriptions such as "The Church of the Lutheran Hour." In a time when family life is rapidly changing and traditional family patterns are weakening, Protestant churches seek to strengthen family life and to serve as family for those facing life alone.

Yet a commitment encouraging youth to be active in the church is not new. Early in the century it was taken for granted that young people would become adult members of the church, and special programs were devised to encourage them to commit themselves to full-time Christian service as ministers or missionaries. Organizations such as the YMCA, YWCA, and Christian Endeavor were thriving. By the end of the century the effort has shifted. The goal now is to get the youth in the door, youth who may never have been to church before. As early as 1948 the Presbyterian synod recognized the need to interest young people in the church. The report noted: youth want to discover God's will in their lives and do it and that gives them work to do in the church, in the presbytery, and in the synod.[60]

The Albuquerque newspapers recently noted an increase in young families attending mainline Protestant churches, as well as Roman Catholic parishes and the newer, nondenominational, more conservative Protestant congregations. Part of the change is demographic, of course. Not since the postwar population boom in Albuquerque in the fifties have so many children resided in the city. For example, Immanuel Presbyterian Church, featured in the "Albuquerque Congregations" column of the *Tribune*, benefited from this change. "Young families are beginning to move back into the Nob Hill area, so we're building programs, like our Logos and our music programs for children, to become attractions to those young families," said the pastor James Rucker.[61] Part of the change, however, is not simply demographic. In April 1993 the *Albuquerque Journal* explored one change in Albuquerque church-going. Many people who dropped out of organized religion earlier in their lives were returning when they had children. What they wanted for their children varied. Some wanted their children to have faith in God; others hoped for a sense of community; still others sought values of kindness and sharing. Some wished their children to know "the truth" and to find salvation. Some simply wanted them to be familiar with their family traditions and maintain a sense of spirituality. It is too early to tell what effect this trend may have on the life of Protestant churches, but it has increased attendance across the denominational spectrum in the city.[62]

In another area during the last quarter of the century, churches have faced challenges to an idyllic picture of churches filled with happy, two-parent families. The women's rights movement has profoundly challenged the notion of family and women's place and role in the church, and the issue of homosexuality also has raised deep questions about the meaning of family, marriage, and sexual morality.

In mainline Protestant churches it is no longer unusual to find a woman pastor. The New Mexico Conference of the United Methodist Church now has a woman district superintendent; this in a conference where this writer was told in 1978 that there was no future for clergywomen. The women's movement has changed lay women's roles in the churches as well. Obviously, women who work both outside the home and within it have little time for volunteer work in the church. Although churches can count on more financial contributions from women with earned incomes, they have fewer Sunday school teachers, fewer fund raisers, and fewer volunteers available for service to the community. Even though retired men take up some of this work, all churches find their cherished programs threatened. Moreover, in the mainline Protestant churches, women are raising theological questions that reach to the very heart of the traditional concepts of God. At the Women-Church conference in Albuquerque in April 1993, an ecumenical group of women borrowed forms of worship from a variety of world religions and spoke of the divine as goddess.[63] In the more conservative Protestant churches, women who contemplate such questions often simply leave, perhaps never to return to church. Reverend Kay Huggins, a Presbyterian pastor in Rio Rancho, illustrates what many women feel: "The Presbyterian church has ceased to nurture its spiritual power. That to me is the biggest reason the church does not have a strong future."[64]

Other Protestants besides women are concerned that the church is losing its spiritual power. Hillside Community Church, Del Norte Baptist Church, and West Mesa Christian Church—all in Albuquerque—are experimenting with the presentation of traditional Christian spiritual principles in nontraditional ways. Hillside, using jazz and Native American stories, advertises in the phone book as combining "the best of eastern and western spiritual traditions." Del Norte Baptist Church has Saturday services (something Roman Catholics have done for years), and West Mesa Christian Church cooperates with other neighboring churches to celebrate such festivals as Easter.[65] In another change, the New Life Presbyterian Church seats its congregation at round tables.[66] Nationwide, mainline Protestantism seems to be "reinventing itself." The emphasis is on community, spiritual life, and, in some cases, multicultural/multiethnic experience, where creed or doctrine takes a back seat.

Church buildings have also changed over the course of the century. First United Methodist Church in Albuquerque preserves its nineteenth-century stone church building with its tall steeple surmounted by a cross. Its mid-twentieth-century sanctuary is still recognizable as such, with its tall arched doorway and long nave windows. But churches built in Albuquerque in the last few years could easily be mistaken for shopping centers or movie theaters.[67] Hoffmantown Baptist Church worships in a building identifiable unmistakably as a church by large crosses at the entrances, but otherwise it resembles a small southern California shopping center. Perhaps it is a building that would attract the generation of young families familiar with shopping plazas but made uneasy by gothic-style church architecture. In addition, such buildings cost a fraction of the amount it would take to build a traditional stone church, like that of First Methodist. Sierra Vista Bible Church in Albuquerque is similar. Its sanctuary looks like a modern auditorium or theater and its office/education building could be any modern business. It looks very little like a traditional church or school.

Two other churches on the growing western edge of Albuquerque, West Mesa Christian Church and Mesa View United Methodist Church, are actually located, for the time being, in buildings that house commercial businesses. The most common type of Protestant church building in New Mexico is more modest than Hoffmantown Baptist, but more recognizable as a church than is West Mesa Christian. It features a plain building with a pitched roof, a white steeple, and windows of tinted colored glass. If there is a building for classrooms or a fellowship hall, it is an attached wing of the main building. The church may or may not have an exterior cross, but it does not need one to be identified as a church. Generally these buildings reflect the generally modest financial means of New Mexico churches. Many are built, at least in part, by labor donated by the congregation.

Often New Mexico Protestant church buildings employ the unique New Mexican architectural styles. First United Methodist in Albuquerque has red Spanish tiles on the roof. Immanuel Presbyterian Church in Albuquerque is built in the territorial style, with brick topping the walls. Further north, in Santa Fe or Taos, it is difficult to distinguish Protestant and Catholic churches. Both use the common adobe style of the seventeenth-century mission churches.

Conclusion

The influences shaping Protestantism in New Mexico are of three kinds. The environment of vast space and the isolation from centers of ecclesiastical power affected all the churches. Isolation resulted in lack of money and the reluctance of highly skilled people to serve as ministers, but it also allowed, for example, for the independent development of the Presbyterian school system of the nineteenth century and the Union Church in Los Alamos that embraces all the liberal Protestants in the area except the Methodists. The largely extractive economy of New Mexico, with its boom-and-bust cycles and one-company towns, its reliance on defense-industry employment, and an underlying cycle of poverty and dependence, has limited the life of the churches. Clergy were not well paid, and the most talented could get better work elsewhere; resources for buildings and service ministries also have been limited. And because growth was slow, denominational bodies were reluctant to support work in New Mexico. Finally, the troubles of the twentieth century and its technological advances have challenged the theology and shaped the congregational life in the Protestant churches of New Mexico.

Clearly, the distinctive cultural makeup of New Mexico, with its relatively large Native American and Hispanic populations and the Roman Catholic majority, has challenged Protestant assumptions and practices. In the nineteenth century, Protestant missionaries found themselves unable to make inroads into the Catholic communities, but at the end of the twentieth century mainline liberal Protestants are cooperating with the Catholics while fundamentalist Protestants are proselytizing from both communions. Protestants of all kinds in New Mexico have never been able to forget they are not the majority, as are their sisters and brothers in other parts of the United States.

Anglos have, by and large, held on to positions of control in the Protestant churches. The African-American Methodist and Baptist churches have been traditionally independent from the white churches. Hispanic Protestants have strong congregations in many denominations, but there are few Native American Protestants. The First Indian Church of the Nazarene in Albuquerque has only fifty-six members.[68] These congregations have a voice in the larger body but cannot of themselves sway the whole. The Church of the Nazarene has a Native American Indian district. There is only one group of non-Anglo-controlled Hispanic Protestant churches in New Mexico, the United Methodist Rio Grande Conference. In the Rio Grande Conference the Hispanic members control their own affairs in a larger arena than the local church, although, according to historian Alfredo Náñez, the conference's early dependence on the leadership of Thomas Harwood hampered the development of a strong indigenous organization.[69] There is pressure to end this separation of the church by language and culture, as the African-American United Methodists have been integrated into the denomination, but the Rio Grande Conference has so far resisted such a move. It continues to provide a unique cultural expression of mainline Protestantism. Its hymns are even beginning to appear in the main denominational hymnal. Hymn No. 180 in the 1989 *United Methodist Hymnal*, "Jesus Es Mi Rey Soberano," is from the Hispanic Protestant tradition, as is the Spanish translation of "Jesus Loves Me" from the 1968 *Himnario Metodista*.

Another contribution of the mainline Protestants to New Mexico has been the shaping of its public school system, and, indirectly, as a spur to the development of the Roman Catholic parochial schools. Most of the early public schoolteachers in the rural Hispanic communities, whether they were Protestant or Catholic, were graduates of Protestant mission schools.[70] In fact, the public school has been largely a secular Protestant school, inculcating in young citizens a basic Protestant set of values, hard work, individualism, and conventional morality. Even the demonstrations at the public universities in the sixties were rooted in values fundamental to the mainline Protestant tradition, such as freedom of individual conscience.

Values of community, family, personal morality, and social justice, born of a sense of God's care for every person, have been characteristic of the mainline Protestants throughout the century. Their fundamentalist brothers and sisters root the same values more thoroughly in a sense of the primacy of concern for individual salvation, coupled with a literal understanding of biblical promises and commands. These values have shaped the Protestant churches in New Mexico, and they continue to shape the concerns of Protestant citizens as they struggle with the public issues of the day.

Notes

1. Paul E. McAllister, "Major Religious Denominations," in *New Mexico in Maps*, ed. Jerry L. Williams and Paul E. McAllister (Albuquerque: Technology Application Center, University of New Mexico, 1979), 88.

2. Martin Marty, "Introduction: Religion in America, 1935–1985," in *Altered Landscapes: Christianity in America, 1935-1985*, ed. David Lotz (Grand Rapids: William B. Eerdmans Publishing Company, 1989), 1–16.

3. Leonard I. Sweet, "The Modernization of Protestant Religion in America," in Lotz, *Altered Landscapes*, 19–41.

4. Sweet, "Modernization of Protestant Religion," 20–21.

5. Bruce Lawrence, *Defenders of God: The Fundamentalist Revolt against the Modern Age* (San Francisco: Harper and Row, Publishers, 1989), 27.

6. Ibid., 2.

7. James Turner, *Without God, Without Creed: The Origins of Unbelief in America* (Baltimore: Johns Hopkins University Press, 1985), 266–67.

8. Lawrence, *Defenders of God*, 232.

9. Sweet, "Modernization of Protestant Religion," 22.

10. Personal conversation with Professor Douglass.

11. Williams and McAllister, *New Mexico in Maps*, 67, 80.

12. Ibid., 66.

13. Wallace Ford, executive secretary of the New Mexico Conference of Churches, comments further on this problem in "The View from Atop the Sandias," *Christian Social Action* 2 (December 1989): 6–9.

14. Statistical figures for individual states are available in several places. The Bureau of the Census issued reports on religious bodies in the years 1906, 1916, 1926, and 1936. After that the National Council of Churches of Christ in the United States and the Glenmary Research Center published church membership statistics for 1956, 1971, 1980, and 1990. In addition to these listings, some denominations provide yearly figures. All of these materials must be used carefully for purposes of comparison because denominations have different criteria for counting members. For example, Roman Catholics count every baptized Catholic in the parish, but Episcopalians count only confirmed members. Other denominations have changed their criteria for membership over the years. The Congregational churches at the beginning of the century admitted only some of the congregation to full membership, based on the outward quality of their moral lives, and, in some cases, evidence of conversion. Later in the century, many of the same congregations admitted to membership anyone who asked, sometimes without even requiring baptism. This study uses the largest reported number, which, in most cases, includes all those who would be likely to attend a church of that denomination regularly. Because not every denomination reported its numbers in every

study, some denominations are easier to study in this way than others. Table 1 shows the number of members reported in New Mexico by most of the religious organizations present in the state. Noticeably absent are the traditional religions of the Native American communities and most other non-Christian faiths. Table 2 compares the percentage of members of religious organizations who are Catholic, Protestant, Latter-day Saints, and Jewish. Table 3 shows the top ten religious organizations for each year in terms of numbers of adherents. I am grateful for the technical assistance of Audrey Englert, Barbara Anderson, and Mark Parsons in the preparation of the tables and charts in this essay.

15. U.S. Bureau of the Census, *Religious Bodies: 1906*, Part 1 (Washington, D.C.: U.S. Government Printing Office, 1910), 52, 601.

16. Lewis Myers, *A History of New Mexico Baptists* (n.p.: Baptist Convention of New Mexico, 1965), 479.

17. Telephone conversation with Calvary Church official, 20 October 1995.

18. Edwin Gaustad, *Historical Atlas of Religion in America*, rev. ed. (San Francisco: Harper and Row, 1976), 66.

19. The Glenmary Research Center, a Roman Catholic center for the study of statistical information about American religion, publishes statistics and maps periodically based on survey research. Their figures show that the percentage of church members in the population declines noticeably as one moves west.

20. Williams and McAllister, *New Mexico in Maps*, 88–89.

21. Presbyterian Church in the U.S.A., *Minutes of Synod of New Mexico* (1900): 32–33.

22. *Minutes of Synod of New Mexico* (1900): 35.

23. Thomas Harwood, "A Few Reflections," *Minutes of the New Mexico Spanish Mission Conference, Methodist Episcopal Church* (1906): 25–26.

24. *Minutes of the Synod of New Mexico* (1910): 13.

25. Methodist Episcopal Church, South, *Minutes of New Mexico Annual Conference* (1899): 190.

26. United Presbyterian Church, *Minutes of the Synod of New Mexico* (1910): 27.

27. Myers, *History of New Mexico Baptists*, 114–15.

28. Harriet Kellogg, *Life of Mrs. Emily Jane Harwood* (Albuquerque: El Abogado Press, 1903).

29. Randi Jones Walker, *Protestantism in the Sangre de Cristos* (Albuquerque: University of New Mexico Press, 1991), 59; and Mark T. Banker, *Presbyterian Missions and Cultural Interaction in the Far Southwest: 1850–1950* (Urbana: University of Illinois Press, 1993), chap. 4.

30. Mrs. M. J. Borden, letter to Rev. A. B. Cristy, 20 April 1893, and letter to Rev. Dr. Kincaid, 26 April 1893, New Mexico File, Archives of the American Home Missionary Society, Amistad Research Center, New Orleans, La.

31. Richard Campbell, *Los Conquistadors: The Story of the Santa*

Cruz Evangelical United Brethren Church (Santa Cruz, N.M.: n.p., 1968).

32. *Gallup Independent*, 6 June 1918, 2.

33. *Minutes of the Synod of New Mexico* (1990): 37–38.

34. *Albuquerque Evening Herald*, 1 May 1918, 3.

35. *Carlsbad Argus*, 28 December 1917, 1.

36. *Minutes of the Synod of New Mexico* (September 1917): 8–9.

37. *Artesia Enterprise*, 20 December 1940, 22.

38. *Alamogordo News*, 25 December 1941, 2.

39. *Farmington Times Hustler*, 27 February 1942, 12.

40. *The Taoseaño*, 12 March 1942, 2.

41. *Farmington Times Hustler*, 27 March 1942, 6.

42. Ibid.

43. *Minutes of the Synod of New Mexico* (October 1942): 17.

44. *Los Alamos Skyliner*, 17 December 1948, A4.

45. *Carlsbad Current-Argus*, 3 November 1967, 6.

46. Jim Wagner, "Albuquerque Congregations," *Albuquerque Tribune*, 1 April 1993.

47. Ibid.

48. *Minutes of the Synod of New Mexico* (1950): 26.

49. Alfredo Náñez, *Historia de la Conferencia Rio Grande de La Iglesia Metodista Unida* (Dallas: Southern Methodist University Bridwell Library, 1981), 104; translation mine.

50. Ibid., 166.

51. Ibid., 142–43.

52. Ibid., 150.

53. Taylor McConnell, "Cross-Cultural Ministries with Families," *Religious Education* 79, no. 3 (Summer 1984): 360–61.

54. *Minutes of the Synod of New Mexico* (1948): 21.

55. Wallace Ford, "The New Mexico Conference of Churches: A Profile of Regional Ecumenism," *Ecumenical Trends* 17 (December 1988): 169.

56. *Baptism, Eucharist and Ministry*, Faith and Order Paper, no. 11 (Geneva: World Council of Churches, 1982).

57. Ford, "New Mexico Conference of Churches," 170.

58. Ibid., 171.

59. Ford, "View from Atop the Sandias," 8.

60. Report of the Committee on Education, *Minutes of the Synod of New Mexico* (1948): 20.

61. *Albuquerque Tribune*, 14 January 1993, C3.

62. *Albuquerque Journal*, 11 April 1993, C1, C3.

63. Kate Nelson, "Church Women Broaden Their Rituals," *Albuquerque Tribune*, 17 April 1993.

64. Ibid.

65. *Albuquerque Journal*, 11 April 1993, A1, A5.

66. Jim Wagner, "Albuquerque Congregations." *Albuquerque Tribune,* 4 February 1993.

67. This became clear to me in a conversation with Doug Adams, Professor of Worship and the Arts at Pacific School of Religion, and John Dillenberger, Professor Emeritus of

the Graduate Theological Union, as we looked at slides of dozens of New Mexico church buildings.

68. Jim Wagner, "Old Benches Spark Vision," *Albuquerque Tribune*, 20 November 1993.

69. Náñez, *Historia de la Conferencia Rio Grande*, 30–31.

70. Sarah Deutsch, *No Separate Refuge: Culture, Class, and Gender on an Anglo-Hispanic Frontier in the American Southwest, 1880–1940* (New York: Oxford University Press, 1987), 67.

3

The Religious Culture of the Jews in Modern New Mexico

Henry J. Tobias

FOR THE PURPOSES OF THIS ESSAY, THE JEWS OF NEW MEXICO are defined as those immigrants from central and eastern Europe and the American East who arrived from the 1840s on, and who continue to arrive to this day, or the local descendants of those earlier generations of immigrants. Excluded from the discussion are the crypto-Jews, the descendants of Spanish Jewry, who still claim a relationship to Judaism and practice their faith as it has come down to them. The two cohorts have remained essentially separate.

To speak of the religious culture of these immigrants raises certain questions, such as the following: who were these Jews, how did they define themselves, and how did they intend to live among the non-Jews who were their neighbors? Each issue involves questions about how they felt and behaved as Jews. In addition, one must ask about the effects of their behavior on the internal development of the Jewish community. Conversely, one must consider how the non-Jewish population viewed Jews and how the latter were affected by such views.

The specific environment of New Mexico into which Jews moved provides some important conditions of development. Those who came to New Mexico from the 1840s to 1880, the era of the Anglo pioneer, did so predominantly along the Santa Fe trail.[1] The traits that characterized that route limited the population using it. The journey was difficult, the area isolated from other parts of the country, and the rewards relatively modest, as compared to those of the California gold rush, or even the Colorado mineral fever. The Santa Fe Trail was not essentially an immigration route for the purposes of agricultural settlement, but a trade route. Moreover, New Mexico had many aspects of a foreign land rather than an American farm frontier where one broke virgin sod. Such conditions assured relatively slow settlement from the East and produced conditions of selectivity unique to the area, not only for Jews but for all those who came.

From the 1830s through the early 1880s, Jewish immigration to the United States came heavily from the Germanic states of Europe—from Germany after 1870. That wave of immigration was distinguishable from an earlier seventeenth-century influx of Sephardic or Spanish-Portuguese Jews from the Caribbean and Brazil who settled in a number of cities along the East Coast of colonial America. The conditions under which these Ashkenazic or Germanic Jews left their old homeland affected the early social and religious character of the Jews of New Mexico. Afflicted by special laws in some of the German states that limited their place of residence and their occupations, as well as obligations toward military service, these Jews, along with millions of non-Jewish Germans, who had their own reasons for emigrating, came to the United States.

The plight of these Jews was not as extreme as that of the East European Jews who formed a wave of immigration after 1880 or the Jews of Hitler's Germany in the twentieth century. The impulse to leave was certainly more economic in character than religious. Many who came to the United States did so as young, single men rather than as whole families. The older generations tended to stay behind to continue their lives of middle- or lower middle-class existence. The newcomers, at least those who came to New Mexico, were not penniless, but neither were they wealthy. They left a homeland in which their religious community was defined by law and came to a society in which the responsibility for the practice of their religion rested solely on themselves.

Until the late 1870s, all the adult Jewish inhabitants of New Mexico were of Germanic birth. It was characteristic of the Jewish migration to New Mexico that many were related to each other—brothers or cousins—while others knew of each other in the old country or were family friends. The earliest Jewish community thus resembled an extended family of related males engaged almost exclusively in merchant enterprises and of those serving as clerks for the proprietors. Most came to New Mexico with the intent of joining an already existing enterprise. From an economic standpoint they appeared as a caste rather more than a full-bodied community.

To a great extent, those young German Jewish males who moved to New Mexico were, from a religious perspective, products of changes that had occurred as a result of the emancipation that followed the French Revolution and the Napoleonic era. Whereas before the French Revolution Jews had considered themselves, and were considered by others, a separate nation, afterward they were regarded, at least in part, as Frenchmen, Germans, and others of the Jewish persuasion. Partially as a result of these political and cultural changes, which broke down the isolation between Jews and non-Jews, German Jews, in particular, altered or discarded many of their traditional religious practices to be more in accord with the larger, more modern society in which they lived. That phenomenon took on the general appellation of Reform Judaism.

The experience of outward assimilation in Europe prepared the new immigrants for life in New Mexico. Not only did they adapt to American—that is, Anglo—culture, but also to the special conditions of the Southwest. Learning Spanish was as much a part of the expected experience of adaptation as learning English. They could not communicate with the surrounding population without it. Moreover, they were ambitious, willing to go out into the hinterland to trade. Such flexibility in attitudes and behavior played no small role in allowing them to fit in and survive well in their new surroundings.

The first two generations of Jewish residence in New Mexico provide little evidence of open religion. These immigrants created no congregations before the 1880s, and one hears little of religious practice. Their small numbers, about one-fourth of 1 percent, may have contributed to such lack of organization. The isolated condition of New Mexico probably forced them, out of necessity, to ignore or forego many traditional practices of their heritage. They did not, for instance, normally close their places of business on Saturday, the day of the Jewish Sabbath. The known nature of their destination, however, may have preselected those whose adherence to traditional religious custom was already weak. Furthermore, because they were mostly unmarried until the 1870s, there was little need for them to seek religious training for young children, an important consideration for a community wishing to continue its historic religious existence.

Yet bits of information indicate an internal desire to remain Jews. In 1881 an article published anonymously in *The American Israelite*, a paper published by the German Reform Jews in Cincinnati, gave a touching account of the first commemoration of Yom Kippur in Santa Fe in 1860. Levi Spiegelberg, a brother of the putative first Jewish settler in Santa Fe, had recently married a German Jewish lady and brought her to the city. The Jews of the city, perhaps sixteen in all, observed this most solemn occasion, which, the writer noted, evoked for them sweet memories of their old home.[2]

On another occasion, the charge of wrongdoing against a Jewish trader appeared to draw Jews together. In 1859 a Jew was accused of swindling

James J. Webb, a prominent Santa Fe merchant, by one of his employees, John Kingsbury. The latter, in reporting to Webb, noted, "We have had considerable excitement in our little Jerusalem of Santa Fe." He continued, "The whole Jew outfit are more or less interested in this nest," and concluded, "the excitement is really laughable."[3]

It appears that the misdeed of one Jew affected the attitude of all. They possibly assumed that all would feel the stigma of the charge of dishonesty rather than the guilty party alone, and one may infer a communal sense of fear that drew them together in the face of accusation of wrongdoing by an individual. Kingsbury's stereotypical observations uphold as rational their common reaction of fear to the charge of dishonesty.

In the last analysis, however, it was probably the family bond, beyond any other factor, that enabled these Jews to maintain their existence as Jews. The fewest cases of intermarriage occurred where brothers and cousins lived and worked together; the largest number, where Jews lived alone. When a solitary Jew in the West, as well as New Mexico, intermarried, he almost invariably disappeared within a generation as children were reared in the faith and culture of the non-Jewish mother. It is also clear that the most successful and long-lasting businesses in New Mexico were those composed of brothers.

Caution in religious expression by New Mexico's early Jews carried over into public affairs in these first decades of their settlement. Although asked at times to participate in political life, they refused. Charles P. Clever, a possible German Jew who converted to Catholicism and ran for office after the Civil War, found himself attacked in the press for his action on the basis of this supposed opportunism.[4] Involved in a contested election for territorial delegate to Congress, Clever had his Jewish supporters. They found themselves attacked as Jews, who were described in a published letter as "a party of men which is causing the inhabitants of this unfortunate Territory great injuries to free ourselves from which it is necessary to cut them up root and branch."[5] The caution of the Jews toward too public an appearance did seem to appear warranted when their presence aroused in some elements of the population an ire expressed in the hostile language of anti-Jewish sentiment.

Unlike their early experience in politics, however, Jews participated heavily in the social and economic activities of the places in which they lived. Much of Hispano life, centered in Catholic activity, by its nature excluded Protestant and Jewish populations. Still, economic activity fostered its own forms of cooperation, ranging from helpful favors among competing merchants to partnerships between Christian and Jewish merchants. In addition, the creation of Masonic and other fraternal lodges served as meeting places, provided burial grounds, and drew together persons who sought to escape the pain of social isolation and have an alternative to the environment of the gaming saloon.

In the 1870s, the first stirrings toward the creation of public institutions occurred among New Mexico's Jews. By then their numbers had grown, and the effects of marriage became evident in the slow establishment of the nuclear family as the basic social unit of the community. Children born in New Mexico became numerous and the felt need to educate them in the ways of their parents became a gnawing concern. Late in the seventies, criticism of the older generation of Jews for not doing more to reaffirm their religion emerged from within the Jewish population.[6] Circumcision of male children, a basic rite of Jewish practice, became known through traveling practitioners of the art, who came from Denver periodically to perform their services.

The few public comments on Jews up to the early eighties seem indicative of a general openness often attributed to the frontier. Their economic success up to that time certainly belies any widespread animus against them. In the late 1870s, important Jewish holidays were celebrated openly in Santa Fe (the Spiegelberg family obtained the Germania Hall for such events), and one hears of no negative repercussions. Tolerance and a generally benign attitude characterizes non-Jewish Anglo views toward their Jewish neighbors on religious grounds. Indeed, as Germany moved into a period of intolerance toward Jews, the *Santa Fe Weekly Democrat* found that country's attitude incomprehensible. The paper depicted Jews as good, law-abiding citizens, charitable and public spirited, and the Germans' attitude toward them as barbaric.[7]

The Jews in New Mexico thus spent nearly two generations as a private community that gave almost no public evidence of itself in matters of religion. Small numbers and the need to fit in, dictated by economic circumstances, contributed to the caution they displayed. That caution itself was probably the result of their experience with a Christian Europe that had often regarded them with hostility. American Christian culture inherited elements of that hostility, but conditions in New Mexico permitted economic opportunity and individual freedom to a degree hitherto unknown to the Jewish immigrants. Having come west primarily to make their way economically, adaptation to the existing cultures superseded any urge to achieve public religious expression that might prove divisive. In any case, those young men, ready to move into the remote West, did not, like the Mormons, come there to establish a Zion. Despite their caution, however, they did not abandon their religious identity, and by their continuing existence and development as a social community they left a presence upon which later generations built.

The first public Jewish institutions appeared in the 1880s. The impetus for such development appears directly linked to changes brought about by the coming of the railroad to New Mexico, the beginning of the modern period. In Las Vegas and Albuquerque, where the main line of the Santa Fe ran, new towns grew up along the rails. These communities not only contained growing numbers of Jews, they also reflected a more American rather than a Hispano presence. Protestant churches flourished in the new environment. Whether that rupture of the near monopoly of the Catholic church strengthened concrete expression of urges already present in Jewish family life cannot be documented, but within four years of the railroad's appearance, the Jews of Las Vegas formed a congregation and those in Albuquerque a chapter of B'nai B'rith, a Jewish men's organization dedicated to fraternity and mutual aid. Santa Fe, which did not receive the main line of the railroad and developed no new town, did not develop any Jewish institutions, even though it had a sufficient Jewish population. In 1897 Albuquerque added a congregation, Congregation Albert, which exists to the present day.

Similarly, changes in political form, longevity of residence, and economic success brought Jews into local political arenas around 1880. The creation of the county commission system in 1876 opened new levels of government to the elective process. From that time on Jews began to run for offices, and successful candidacy for the legislature did not lag far behind. The late seventies and early eighties proved to be a watershed after which full Jewish participation in public life came into existence. It continues to this day.

The early modern period of New Mexico's history, from the coming of the railroad to the eve of World War II, coincided with a period of sharp changes in American Jewish history. During that period, immigration from Germany began to decline and a new, far larger influx arrived from eastern Europe. These Jews clung to the northeastern United States, particularly New York and vicinity. From a religio-cultural standpoint, this migration had not undergone the reforming experiences of German Jewry, and most of those who sought modernization were influenced by movements for change in the Russian empire. There, the presence of a late medieval tsarism and culture, unaffected by the emancipatory tendencies of the French Revolution and the Enlightenment, produced radical solutions to economic and political problems. Many Jews adhered to older, premodern forms of Orthodox religious practice or adopted extreme forms of national or universalist doctrines, such as a revitalized Zionism or the new secular religion of socialism. The newcomers, far more impoverished than their German brethren and often without a modern educational background or an environment that allowed them immediate access to the world of commerce, provided a large laboring class of craftsmen, workers for a growing clothing industry, and a cultural life based on Yiddish, the language of millions of East European Jews. New Mexican Jewry, isolated and without need of factory workers, received few persons of this background.

Instead, the diminishing wave of newcomers from Germany left a Jewish population in New Mexico that slowly leveled off in its growth. It also assimilated to local cultural life, gradually becoming native in its origins and sustaining, to a large extent, that commercial background that it had established in the nineteenth century. Unlike the Jews of the Northeast, who arrived with a full range of Jewish cultural heritage, New Mexican Jewry retained the version of Reform Judaism that it had brought from Germany, which had developed its own lines of thought in America. One might say that the Jews of New Mexico were far less like the majority of American Jews on the eve of World War I than they had been in 1880.

The earliest Jewish religious institutions showed clearly the powerful influence of Germanic origins and reformist thought. The constitution of Congregation Montefiore in Las Vegas of 1886 (the congregation was formed in 1884) justified its existence on the grounds of the faith taught them in their youth, which recalled to them the heroic deeds of their ancestors. Their own deeds, they hoped, would be worthy examples to the children of Israel who would perpetuate the teachings and practices of Faith, Hope, and Charity. They adopted the newly formulated views of the Reform movement as their own and still offered to teach German to the children as part of the curriculum of their religious school.[8]

An amended version of that constitution adopted in 1898 displayed their Reform character even more strongly. It showed a sharp preference for the religious and moral principles of the Prophets as the truest guide for the ordering of lives and the organization of society on the basis of justice and righteousness. The constitution expressed the belief that the spread of that knowledge would draw closer the Messianic age "of a humanity united in love and sanctified by duty."[9]

The thrust of the documents demonstrated that New Mexican Jews who adhered to religion did so in a modern social context. The universalism of prophetic belief, rather than emphasis on the legalist tradition that separated Jews from others by custom or reference to Jewish ethnicity, appeared among the strongest characteristics of their religious practice. The service of man, which, as taught by Judaism, was the service God demanded, became the dedication of the new constitution.[10]

Reform Judaism left the Las Vegas Jewish community in a position of openness toward the surrounding population. The larger population of Las Vegas recognized this and wished their Jewish townsmen well. The day after the founding of the congregation in 1884, the *Daily Optic* of Las Vegas noted: "The Israelites have cause to be proud of yesterday's work. It is not often that so small a community exerts itself for the promotion of Judaism to such an extent."[11] And again in 1886, when efforts to build a temple began, half of the contributors on the subscription list to raise funds came from nonmembers, many of whom were prominent non-Jewish citizens, Hispano and Anglo alike.[12]

The attitude of goodwill and support reflected a spirit that could be found in many instances among the religious communities in the larger towns of New Mexico. Bishop Jean Baptiste Lamy in Santa Fe had also found that he could rely on support from Santa Fe's Jews for the building of his cathedral during times of financial stress. Perhaps this spirit of cooperation in the still relatively isolated West, where communities had to rely on themselves to get things done, allowed all to benefit. Churches and temples both permitted the use of their facilities by other religious groups while their own buildings were being constructed. One may also consider that the absence of competition from Jews, who sought no converts, made cooperation easy. But one would also have to point out the experience of two generations of tolerance and trust and a willingness on the part of the Jews to fit in and engage in good works, as defined by the population as a whole, as part of the process that led from the mere presence of Jews in New Mexico to a Jewish presence in the form of religious institutions.

The achievement of formalized status for the expression of Jewish religion marked a distinct step in communal development and, for the first time in New Mexico, placed on record Jewish reactions toward public social issues. The appearance of rabbis as congregation leaders meant that their behavior could reflect upon the congregation or even upon the whole Jewish community. Still fearful of encouraging displeasure, congregational leaders demanded caution from their clergymen when they voiced their views on moral or social issues.

In the early twentieth century, for example, Rabbi J. H. Kaplan of Temple Albert incurred displeasure from parts of the medical establishment when he sought, with others, the creation of a nonsectarian charity hospital in Albuquerque.[13] And again, working with a Christian clergyman, the Rev. E.

E. Crawford of the Christian Church, Rabbi Kaplan published a small magazine, *The Barbarian*, which attacked a lynching in the city in 1907. Hostile public reaction to this stand led congregation leaders to demand his resignation. Although the offending rabbi had to leave, the congregation voted him generous severance pay, possibly indicative of sympathy for his position.[14]

Even in the 1930s the congregational leaders felt it necessary to rein in their spiritual leaders. One popular rabbi, A. L. Krohn, who taught in the University's Sociology Department and was judged "the only faculty member who could fill [Rodey Hall, the largest classroom on campus] with students," incurred displeasure with his advocacy for small, mostly Hispanic farmers, who were in conflict with the Middle Rio Grande Conservancy District. Arrayed against them were such persons as Clinton P. Anderson, the future secretary of agriculture under President Harry Truman and senator from New Mexico. On the other side stood Dennis Chavez, another senator from New Mexico, who regarded Krohn as a man of justice. In 1937, Krohn, although withstanding a vote to relieve him, nevertheless felt compelled to resign his pulpit because the small Jewish community still feared controversy and the loss of general goodwill.[15]

Thus, the Jewish population of Albuquerque up to World War II still reflected its traditional cautiousness. Many congregational leaders were persons who had come to Albuquerque in the later decades of the nineteenth century or were their descendants. Despite the town's growth from twenty-three hundred in 1880 to thirty-five thousand in 1940 and a commensurate growth of its Jewish population, the latter retained the feelings of a small, isolated community. Only about 18 Jews lived in Albuquerque in 1880, while in 1900 there were about 120. By 1940, there were about 450. In 1900 they represented about 1.9 percent of the total population of the city and in 1940, about 1.2 percent.[16] In 1900 Albuquerque's Jews counted about 25 percent of all New Mexico's Jews and in 1940, about 39 percent.

Even in this quiet period between 1900 and 1940, when cultural assimilation worked its way and Jewish growth barely kept pace with general growth in New Mexico, the ground began to change under the feet of the Jews. The late nineteenth and early decades of the twentieth century were extraordinary years for world Jewry. Pogroms in eastern Europe, monumental disruptions caused by World War I, and the rise of Nazism in Germany in the thirties forced even the isolated Jews of New Mexico into active concern where the lives of their coreligionists were involved. New Mexican Jewry showed little evidence before 1921 of the Orthodox or Conservative wings of Jewish religious practice. But in that year a new congregation, B'nai Israel, was formed in Albuquerque. It indicated a growing diversity, however small, among New Mexico's Jews that had as its basis a more traditional practice of religion than offered by Reform Judaism. Only in 1941 did the new congregation acquire its own synagogue. By then, however, it had moved to a Conservative rather than Orthodox position, some indication of how difficult it was even in the twenties and thirties to maintain in New Mexico such customs as dietary laws and separate seating for men and women in New Mexico.[17]

It was from among the leaders of this congregation that Zionism, which was just entering its modern stage of organization at the end of World War I after the Balfour Declaration promised the Jews a homeland in Palestine, had its first adherents and organizers in New Mexico. Participation in the philanthropic efforts to relieve the sufferings of their brethren long predated those events. The rise of Nazism in Germany of the 1930s also led to a renewal of immigration and a sharpened demand for philanthropy to ease the suffering of their fellow Jews elsewhere.

Those efforts revealed continuing good relations with the general community, which joined the Jews in relief efforts at times. One such campaign in 1938 evoked an editorial from the *Albuquerque Tribune* that praised Albuquerqueans for their support of justice and noted, by way of historical recognition, that the city's inhabitants understood the debt they owed to Jews who had helped build the city and state, had proven themselves a mainstay of civic life, and had contributed generously to common causes.[18] In this early modern period, then, one may speak of the creation of an institutionalized Jewry based on religion in New Mexico. The larger numbers who adhered to organized religious practice still did so in forms most adapted to American life. They found common cause with non-Jews in the name of justice or against discrimination on the grounds of religion or even, on occasion, on the basis of wealth. But Jews were also increasingly driven by the needs of their own broader community. Easy relations between Jew and non-Jew remained present in New Mexico and did not demand exceptional effort on their part in local matters. They participated strongly in political and social life, even as their own community slowly defined itself.

If the fate of world Jewry before World War II slowly closed in on New Mexico's Jews, what occurred during and after the war proved a firestorm that occupied their attention in major ways. New Mexico as a whole felt the effects of the war to a degree that defined it as a new historical period. As a result, little-known, quaint New Mexico became the site for military bases, hospitals, and, certainly not least, the most advanced technological innovations of the twentieth century. These developments, heavily funded by the federal government, drew highly educated newcomers in large numbers to its remote mesas and mountains in numbers heretofore not even imagined.

Population growth itself indicates the scale of the change. Between 1940 and 1980, the state grew from over a half-million to nearly one and one-third million souls; the Jewish population from under 1,200 to over 7,000. Albuquerque burgeoned from 35,000 to 330,000, nearly a tenfold increase in forty years. The town's Jewish population expanded from 450 to 6,500, a fourteenfold increase. The new massive immigration nearly inundated what had been a fairly stable, slowly changing community.

The postwar period also produced sharp changes within the Jewish population. Although commerce remained an important component of the economic life of the Jews, in Albuquerque, where by 1980 close to 90 percent of the state's Jews lived, a new economic mix had grown up. By then those Jews engaged as professionals and technicians were double the number of proprietors.[19] And even though New Mexico's Jews were fairly well educated in 1940, by 1980 the level of educational attainment among them had reached astonishing heights. Over half of Albuquerque's Jews under the age of forty had attended or completed graduate schools; over 90 percent had attended college-level institutions.[20] It becomes difficult to see how those figures could go any higher.

Social change accompanied economic change. The middle-class Jewish family of the prewar period had witnessed a slow rise of women as proprietors, teachers, and office workers. In the postwar period, however, a veritable revolution took place. In the early 1980s, of Jewish women over sixty, half had ended their formal education with high school and nearly half with some undergraduate or graduate college education. Of those under forty, only 5 percent had ended their education with high school, while 85 percent had at least some exposure to college-level study.[21]

The heavy trend toward educational attainment reflected more than the need to achieve a respectable literacy. It revealed a desire for career goals and, perhaps, independence. Indeed, well over half of Jewish women under the age of fifty engaged in full-time employment, many of them professionals. Their grandmothers, who had not often worked outside the home, would have been astonished.

At major touch points the changes in the Jewish community matched the broader changes resulting from this mass influx. If Los Alamos represented the most radical innovation within New Mexico, then a Jewish congregation was already formed there during the most secretive years of the atomic city's history. As the new professional population of engineers and scientists gave Albuquerque one of the highest ratios of Ph.D.s per capita in the United

States, the new Jewish population formed a significant portion of this contingent. And if New Mexican Jewry reflected New Mexico's relatively settled ways prior to World War II, then the new wave of Jews, far less commercial and more professional in their economic makeup and more cosmopolitan in tone, unsettled them.

But the war alone did not end the changes. The rapid influx of people altered the relationships between all parts of the American continent, and New Mexico found itself drawn into every issue that affected Americans. The movement for civil rights, and every form of minority and feminist challenge, entered the concerns of New Mexicans, as it did all other Americans. International problems and conflicts took on an unaccustomed immediacy, with New Mexicans responding to them at times as issues of direct relevance. In short, New Mexico lost most of those facets of isolation that had characterized its earlier history.

The Jewish community, possibly as much as any other single group within New Mexico, reflected the changes that were taking place. The postwar issues themselves forced a heightened level of concern that had only begun to impinge upon New Mexico's Jews before the war. The creation of Israel, for example, and the dangers it faced in the early decades of its existence, produced an activism from those Jews to whom its fate was important, and in the face of all this a great deal of the accustomed caution of the Jewish community faded. Since Americans often held differing views on such matters, the Jews at times took positions that were controversial. Yet they had to do so out of their sense of relationship to their own broader cultural heritage. And in civil rights, they could not silently ignore racial discrimination when agents of that discrimination often had Jews in mind one step behind their primary targets. Group interests and values collided and re-aligned, and both cooperation and tension became more marked in a society that had often sought to downplay differences, or that had been isolated from the broader American scene.

Even symbols became an issue. In the early eighties, for example, a Jewish student called for an end to the use of the swastika, the major symbol of the Nazis, as a logo for the yearbook at New Mexico State University at Las Cruces. Students and faculty rallied to both sides of the issue. The swastika was, after all, an old Indian symbol and had been in common use before the Nazis adopted it. It had also been dropped during the war and reinstituted afterward. Regardless of the arguments for and against, the controversy drew considerable antagonism from students who regarded denial of its use as a denial of their rights and from others who, in letters to editors, attacked the Israeli treatment of Palestinian Arabs and denounced Jews for feeling sorry for themselves; still others defaced a sculpture by Sol Lewitt on campus. In the end, Governor Toney Anaya's insistence that use of the symbol cease carried the day.[22] One can hardly imagine such a discussion before World War II.

To meet the effects of the Holocaust and the creation of Israel, the American Jewish community assumed burdens that not only taxed its resources, but also demanded a degree of organization never before achieved. New Mexico's Jews responded to that challenge as did the entire American Jewish community. Even though the process of engagement in national organizations of congregations preceded the war, the new communal efforts superseded congregational structures and sought the participation of all Jews. In Albuquerque, which included an ever-larger proportion of the state's Jews, a Jewish Welfare Fund established in 1948 grew to a Jewish Community Council in 1972 and to a Jewish Federation in 1984. Annual fund-raising drives became a way of life for American Jews and New Mexico was no exception.

The increased concern with the fate of Jews and the religious needs of newcomers also brought changes to New Mexico. New congregations grew up in many towns, with Las Cruces and finally even Santa Fe among them. Albuquerque's Jews joined the Conservative synagogue as never before, approaching equality with the older Reform temple. New groups of Jews joined in *chavurot*, groups of families who sought their own Jewish ways together. Santa Fe even witnessed the creation of an Orthodox group. A survey undertaken in the mid-eighties found that about 55 percent of Albuquerque's Jews considered themselves very or fairly religious, one-third not very religious, and 12 percent not religious.[23] All this attested to a new sense of awareness and a continuing commitment to Jewishness.

Yet the sense of openness in the growing Jewish population did not cease. Intermarriage, always present in the country, continued and increased with time. It occurred at a higher rate where the density of Jewish population was low, a condition that described New Mexico. The survey taken in the mid-eighties found about a 35 percent rate in Albuquerque, higher than that of New York or Chicago.[24] Unlike the older experiences of the "disappearing Jew" of the nineteenth century, however, the children of these mixed marriages often were raised as Jews.

A major shift had occurred in the stance of Jewish expression. Always open, but long cautious, it now took ever more varied and forthright forms. However small the Jewish population, its spectrum of action was wide. On one end, there was greater adherence to traditional religious practice, even among Reform Jews. On the other end, there existed the closest interaction with the general population as evident in the phenomenon of intermarriage. Moreover, Jews were no longer a community driven by foreign immigration; however they expressed themselves as Jews, they were Americans and at least as New Mexican as other Anglos.

The trends of Jewish history in New Mexico for one and a half centuries moved toward greater numbers, more diverse religious organization, greater confidence in allowing institutional visibility of themselves, and, ultimately, greater social mixture with the population at large. Jews fared well in general. They came and went in numbers that matched the growth and decline of New Mexican communities. Their occupational trends matched the growth of the needs of the territory and state: they were merchants when the territory was opening to Anglo commerce, and professionals when New Mexico developed its educational, medical, and scientific characteristics.

The keys to Jewish well-being in this process rested on a combination of adaptation and preparation. Jews in New Mexico sought to fit in as Americans and as New Mexicans. They brought with them their preparation for life as reflected in their own traditions and attitudes with respect to education, work, and a sense of the meaning of their small numbers. In work and education, especially as the experience of immigration faded, they tended to match the performance of Anglo-Saxon Protestant groups.[25] The open, individual character of the American economic order and political system contained the criteria by which they judged themselves and were judged, even though some always begrudged them their success.

It should be noted that their behavior reflected the general modernization of New Mexico and America. Jews adjusted in a major way to the demands of New Mexico's environment when it was isolated and highly distinct. The skills they brought with them, however, reflected the power of American commerce on the local scene. When New Mexico itself changed sharply after World War II, they adjusted in a minor way to changes occurring on the American scene. One could, after all, be a nuclear physicist, still learn some Spanish, and appreciate Indian and Spanish colonial arts and crafts.

Religion did not rule their lives. In any case, Reform Judaism had already presented a modern form to Jews, and western Jews in particular had used that as a yardstick for fitting in. Few in numbers, they adapted their religious or ethnic identity to coexist with the larger groups that defined the religious map of New Mexico—that is, they sought not to be conspicuous and yet perform the obligations of their religious traditions. As they grew in number and diversity, they organized to meet the problems of their own larger community and their differing versions of religious practice. In so doing, the consequence of organization was to strengthen group feeling and to ease the path of newcomers to associate as they moved into New Mexico. In their voluntary association, a large segment of the community was, in effect, redefining and asserting its identity. If the range of their organizations was still limited, as compared with areas where large numbers of Jews lived, it nevertheless displayed a vigor that boded well for their future.

In terms of political and social behavior, American Jews generally, and more than likely those in New Mexico, heavily aligned themselves with forces that sought to alleviate social injustice.[26] Whether that viewpoint stemmed from a passion for justice derived from the Prophets or a background of historic experience with European injustice is, Nathan Glazer tells us, difficult to say.[27] One may argue that the Jews' awareness of their own insecurity led them to positions seeking general justice, which promised well-being for them in well-being for others who felt the pain of discrimination.[28] Jews, more than many other immigrant groups, had long experience as a minority and of the uncertainties such status carried.

New Mexico's Jews were mainstream, cautious, middle class. They differed to some extent from many American Jews in the Northeast before World War II, who were often advocates of liberal and even radical positions. After World War II—indeed, even before—those positions modified. Much more native in their origins and middle class in their economics, American Jews tended to become liberal rather than radical. New Mexico's Jews, as a result of the great immigration since World War II, probably also reflect such views. To the best of our knowledge—and a body of data does not exist to characterize the politics of New Mexican Jews—they still hold to liberal positions on social justice, as noted in such congregational stands as support for pro-choice positions in the abortion debate. On the other hand, there is no unanimity on any issue among Jews except survival.

New Mexico's Jewish community reflects characteristics of Jews in middle-size rather than large communities, especially in Albuquerque. Conditions in New Mexico invoked for them a somewhat higher level of professionalization, education, and intermarriage and a narrower range of Orthodox and traditional practice, leaving an impression of assimilation with the non-Jewish community greater than that in larger cities.

However much the world impinged on New Mexico, however, no local sense of a beleagured community exists. Jews and Christians remain good neighbors in accord with their individual nature and a common moral ground, called Judeo-Christian ethics, which allows each to practice religion without infringement on the other. In any case, it is difficult to say that religious issues are so powerful in New Mexico that they incline New Mexicans to behave in an openly hostile manner toward each other on a sustained basis. Whether it is the oft-proclaimed openness of the West or a learned balance between Anglos and Hispanos that allows cooperation or space between the differing groups, the result is a general tolerance that forms the dominant expression of relations between the groups. Jews participate in the general affairs of the community and are elected to high office, even in the face of more marked identity with their own community and special stances on issues of particular importance to them.

Insofar as Jews are treated as participants in the state's Anglo chapter of history, they are comfortable and at home. In any case, the major ethnic fault line of New Mexico's history is between Anglos and Hispanos. The Jews appear mostly as a part of the Anglo experience rather than as an important entity in their own right.

Flexibility and versatility characterize the growth and development of Jewish history in New Mexico. Those traits have enabled them to survive and prosper. Continued survival as a religious and ethnic community in New Mexico would seem to rest on the same features. The variety of religious organization and expression achieved over time offers more options by which Jews can identify themselves. In few instances are these choices of such an extreme order as to cut Jews off from the larger New Mexican world in which they live. There is a well-roundedness to this experience that bespeaks a high degree of health for a community that has experienced vast movement in immigration, survival over attempts at genocide, and high levels of discrimination throughout the world. For New Mexico's Jews, comparisons of their lot with the fate of their brethren elsewhere over the last century and a half are highly positive, and they have every reason to be pleased with the results while remembering that conditions change and that little is permanent under the sun.

Notes

1. The conclusions for this essay are drawn mainly from Henry J. Tobias, *A History of the Jews in New Mexico* (Albuquerque: University of New Mexico Press, 1990).
2. Cited in Ibid., 42-43.
3. Ibid., 45.
4. Ibid., 86; see also Floyd S. Fierman, *Guts and Ruts: The Jewish Pioneer on the Trail in the American Southwest* (New York: Ktav Publishing House), 69–70.
5. Cited in Tobias, *History*, 87.
6. Ibid., 59–60.
7. 13 January 1881, 2.
8. *Constitution and Bylaws of Congregation Montefiore* (Las Vegas, N.M., 1886), 3–5. *Jewish Families and Congregations in New Mexico and Southern Colorado* (Cincinnati: American Jewish Archives, 1982–1986), reel 12.
9. Montefiore Congregation, *Constitution*, adopted 1 January 1898 (Las Vegas, N.M.), 2.
10. Ibid.
11. Cited in Tobias, *History*, 111.
12. Ibid.
13. Gunther Rothenberg, author; Israel C. Carmel, research, *Congregation Albert* (Albuquerque, 1972), 22.
14. Ibid.
15. Tobias, *History*, 142–43.
16. Ibid., 139.
17. Ibid., 145-46.
18. *Albuquerque Tribune*, 7 December 1938, 10.
19. Tobias, *History*, 176.
20. Ibid., 175.
21. Ibid., 177.
22. Ibid., 189–91.
23. Brigitte K. Goldstein, "Jewish Identification among the Jews of Albuquerque, New Mexico: The Maintenance of Jewishness and Judaism in the Integrated Setting of a Sunbelt City" (Ph.D. diss., University of New Mexico, 1988), 186.
24. Ibid., 172.
25. David L. Featherman, "The Socioeconomic Achievement of White Religio-Ethnic Subgroups: Social and Psychological Explanations," *American Sociological Review* 36 (April 1971): 207, 217.
26. R. Laurence Moore, *Religious Outsiders and the Making of Americans* (New York: Oxford University Press, 1986), 101; Nathan Glazer, *American Judaism*, 2d ed. (Chicago: University of Chicago Press, 1972), 136.
27. Glazer, *American Judaism*, 141.
28. Moore, *Religious Outsiders*, 101.

4

Competition for the Native American Soul

*The Search for Religious Freedom
in Twentieth-Century New Mexico*

Kathleen Egan Chamberlain

TRUE OR FALSE: THE FIRST AMENDMENT OF THE CONSTITUTION guarantees freedom of religion to all U.S. citizens? Most Americans, who take religious freedom more or less for granted, would probably reply "true." Some Native Americans, however, would counter with a resounding "false," a reply that might astonish a sizable portion of the non-Indian population. After all, the Constitution has been stretched to safeguard religious faiths that fall outside the Judeo-Christian tradition, such as Buddhism or Islam. New Age adherents, even cults, enjoy a degree of protection under the Constitution. Why then do some American Indians feel that they often fall outside the scope of the Bill of Rights?

The problems are complex, and the answers defy easy solutions. Simply stated, the issue is this: although Native Americans do not possess a single, monolithic theology, their traditional beliefs regarding sacred space often challenge Judeo-Christian ideology and even some secular precepts upon which the United States was established. Their need for privacy arouses the curiosity and animosity of some Anglo-Americans who seek to share their own beliefs and cannot understand exclusion. Historically, these rival views have coexisted primarily by remaining separate and have produced a cultural gulf that has, in many respects, grown deeper throughout the twentieth century.

The Native American demand for First Amendment protection of traditional religions has complicated the often-heated ideological standoff. To make things more confusing, missionaries of various Christian denominations have, over the years, converted thousands of Pueblos, Navajos, and Apaches in New Mexico, many of whom no longer value traditional beliefs or support their protection under the Constitution. Although the state of New Mexico represents only one area where Native and non-Native views clash—sometimes quite bitterly—it provides an excellent case study for this complex struggle; after all, in New Mexico, the encounter between Indian and European religions began four hundred years ago. However, rapid population growth in this Sunbelt state has made some solution imperative, particularly as continual development crowds Indian land. Even though solutions lie beyond the scope of this study, perhaps the major problems can be explained.

The Battle over Indian "Salvation"

Clearly, neither the Spaniards who settled Nuevo México nor the men who framed the Constitution of the United States anticipated the perseverance of traditional Indian religions. By the eighteenth century, Franciscan friars had introduced the Roman Catholic faith to most of the Pueblo people living along the Rio Grande, plus those in Acoma, Laguna, and Zuni, which lay to the west. The majority appeared to accept the faith, although as anthropologist Alfonso Ortiz, himself a Tewa Pueblo, points out, the Indians preserved much more of their traditional religion than either the friars or later historians had previously suspected.[1] Conversions to Christianity often lacked conviction. Some of the Pueblo people participated in Catholic rituals without internalizing their meaning. Others integrated Christian catechism and symbols with their old religion—a response called "syncretism"—hoping that the fusion of old and new might successfully ward off disease, assure a good harvest, or even—as many surely prayed—make the European invaders disappear.

Today, some Pueblos still syncretize Christianity with their Native beliefs. Others "compartmentalize" the two belief structures. They practice Catholicism through the intermediary of a Roman Catholic priest, but also participate in Native ceremonies with Native priests.[2] The early Franciscan friars, however, made few inroads among the Apaches or Navajos. Not until the nineteenth century did Christian missionaries focus their efforts on these tribes, both of whom were located in remote regions.

Attempts to Assimilate the American Indian

New Mexico came under U.S. jurisdiction in 1846. The Treaty of Guadelupe Hidalgo, which ended the war between the United States and Mexico, contained a provision granting American citizenship to Mexican nationals, including the Pueblos. In 1876, the Supreme Court upheld Pueblo status because they were largely Christian and farmed in settled communities. In 1913, the Court reversed the earlier decision and declared the Pueblos to be Indians and wards of the federal government, a decision that profoundly impacted them legally, but also explains why they were not subjected to federal Indian policy prior to 1913. The nomadic Navajos and Apaches, however, were confined to reservations and placed under the jurisdiction of the federal Indian office.

Many nineteenth-century Americans believed that once Indians were converted to Christianity, learned English, and adopted Anglo-American agricultural methods, they would easily and eagerly shed their "heathen ways" and assimilate into mainstream culture. Indeed, from the early days of the republic, the federal government worked closely with Protestant missionaries to accomplish these tasks. To speed the process along, reformers in 1869 initiated what became known as President Grant's "peace policy." This plan established a board of commissioners to advise the federal Indian office on how best to implement Indian policy. One of the board's primary goals was to turn over the administration of reservation agencies, religious instruction, and education to religious denominations, which obtained exclusive rights to specific reservations. For example, the Presbyterians took over the Navajo mission, and the Quakers were offered one among the Mescalero Apaches.[3] Other Apache groups were not assigned specific denominations because there remained no official agreement or treaty with them until later.[4]

The board largely bypassed the Roman Catholic church, which as we have seen, had long since established itself among the Pueblos. Instead, Presbyterian missionaries James Roberts and William Truax tried to convince those living in San Felipe and Santo Domingo pueblos to accept the Protestant faith, but failed miserably. The board shunned the Latter-day Saints (Mormons) whose theology was also deemed unacceptable, but who already had begun outreach programs among the Navajos. Similarly, it overlooked the Moravians, whose missionaries had worked with Native Americans in the East and South since before the American Revolution, as well as the southern branches of those denominations that divided during the Civil War: the Southern Baptists, Southern Methodists, and Southern Presbyterians.[5] Because of these omissions and the controversial selection process, Grant's peace policy generated tremendous discontent on the reservations and caused bickering among the denominations.

This policy lasted about ten years, after which time—as so often happens—the government changed its mind and mode of dealing with Indians. Assimilation continued to be the major goal, however, and New Mexico churches remained interested in assisting the process. As the twentieth century dawned, some denominations maintained a long-standing interest in "their" reservations. The Roman Catholic presence continued unabated among the Pueblos. The Presbyterians and Dutch Reformed remained active among the Navajos and Apaches. Northern Presbyterians did some work at Laguna Pueblo.

Other denominations arrived as well. On the Navajo reservation, for example, the Methodists obtained 400 acres in 1890 for a mission. That same year, 160 acres at Two Grey Hills, New Mexico, were donated to the Women's National Indian Association for an interdenominational mission, which was taken over by the Baptists in 1901. In 1894, Episcopalian missionaries organized a hospital, and in 1900 the Christian Reformed Church, under the Reverend James DeGroot, established an outstation at Tohatchi. Early in the twentieth century, the Christian Reformed, Mennonites, the Faith Mission, Mormons, and the Roman Catholic churches all sent missionaries to the Navajos.[6] Although these efforts led to the conversion of some New Mexico Indians, most remained faithful to traditional ways. As anthropologists Clyde Kluckhohn and Dorothea Leighton explained, "Christianity speaks of far-off lands and places," whereas Native stories "tell of the four sacred mountains, at least one of which is visible almost everywhere in the Navajo country."[7]

It became increasingly difficult during the twentieth century to safeguard traditional Native faiths because Native Americans sometimes found the federal government actively lined up against them. For example, in 1920, the Reverend E. M. Sweet, inspector for the U.S. Department of the Interior, submitted a report designed to discredit the Roman Catholic missionary effort in the Southwest, weaken tribal governments, and expand Bureau of Indian Affairs (BIA) control over the lives of Native people, particularly the Pueblo Indians whose disputed land was about to be settled. Government officials generally assumed that to assimilate individual tribal members into the American mainstream, traditional religions first had to be dismantled, priests and spiritual leaders removed, and tribal governments, which in most cases were inseparable from the religious structure, severely weakened. The Sweet report labeled traditional worship "obscene" and argued that it interfered with agricultural development and the establishment of a work ethic. The report portrayed spiritual leaders as particularly harmful to school-age children because they periodically removed the children from school for traditional religious instruction.

On April 26, 1921, Commissioner of Indian Affairs Charles Burke issued his infamous Circular 1665. This directive ordered Indian agents to suppress tribal dances and ceremonies, the very core of Pueblo religious observances. It made participation in ceremonies punishable by fines and imprisonment. On February 14, 1923, Burke issued a supplement to Circular 1665 that limited tribal dances to one day per month and banned them entirely between March and August, when planting and harvesting dominated their time. Ten days later, on the twenty-fourth of February, he sent a letter to the New Mexico Pueblos and the Hopis of Arizona giving them one year to abandon their religions or "some other course will have to be taken." Later, Burke visited the Taos Pueblo Council and during his stay referred to them as "half animals" because of their "pagan" religion. The Pueblos countered. Indian children, they argued, were compelled to learn Christianity in their schools regardless of parental or clan wishes and without a choice of denomination.[8] Their protests fell largely on deaf ears, although they were allowed to keep their sons out of school for some religious instruction in the kivas. Commissioner Burke's actions served only to push traditional practices deeper underground.

In 1933, John Collier was appointed commissioner of Indian affairs by the Franklin Roosevelt administration. Collier, who had vehemently protested Burke's actions throughout the 1920s, argued that although Native people possessed cultures different from those of Anglo-Americans, they were not inferior, and they deserved respect.[9] As one of his first acts, Collier rescinded Circular 1665. Still, First Amendment protection did not automatically extend to American Indians under tribal jurisdiction. It was virtually nonexistent until Congress passed the Indian Civil Rights Act of 1968. Even then, that legislation prohibited tribal governments, but not necessarily federal or local governments, from interfering with the free exercise of religion.[10] The American Indian Religious Freedom Act of 1978 (AIRFA) formally extended protection to traditional religions, but lacked enforcement provisions. In addition, federal courts have ruled in ten consecutive cases during the 1980s and early 1990s "denying any practical content to indigenous spiritual rights."[11]

Different Traditions, Different Views

Over the past century, non-Indian Americans have seldom understood the distinctiveness of native religions.[12] In 1890, for instance, an unnamed Indian agent to the Navajos wrote that the people in his charge were "entirely devoid of any religious instruction." He added that "from what I can learn [the Navajo] has never had any."[13] For this agent, views different from his own apparently lacked validity.

It should be noted that although early Europeans often assumed that all Native people were alike, nothing was further from the truth. Even in a relatively small area like New Mexico, Native Americans possessed very different social and political structures and often spoke mutually unintelligible languages. Similarly, the Pueblos, Navajos, and Apaches held no single world view or tradition. Each had unique origin myths, stories, and deities. Generally, however, each believed in a universal spirit that infused all matter with divine energy and ordered the cycles of birth and death. In fact, traditional Pueblos have no separate word in their vocabulary for "religion" since it is not viewed as a separate concept.[14] The spiritual world unfolds, and everything exists as part of an eternal whole with no predestined role. The past is present in each moment. The earth is not theirs to subdue, but to protect. Their ceremonies revolve around relationships between the individual, the community, and the cosmos.

By contrast, the Judeo-Christian tradition values a personal God, stresses individual salvation, and usually places an emphasis on proselytizing. During the Renaissance, Christians positioned mankind, animals, and nature on what became known as the "Great Chain of Being," a hierarchy whereby humans took priority over animals and nature, and wealthy men were generally deemed superior to poor ones.[15] This philosophy survived in America, especially in the Puritan tradition. Since this Christian ideology was diametrically opposed to Native American beliefs, differences led to misunderstanding and animosity from the beginning. In New Mexico, culture clashes have continued into the twentieth century. A primary battleground has been over the use of land.

The Issue of Sacred Land

The Spanish who first ventured into the arid, sun-baked Southwest saw little aesthetic appeal in the "unbridled wilderness" that stretched endlessly about them. Neither the Roman Catholic faith nor personal histories tied them spiritually to the land. Instead, Spanish explorers and colonists sought wealth in the mythical seven cities of Cíbola. They searched for silver mines like those that made men rich in Zacatecas, Mexico, whereas Catholic friars sought Native souls.

Nor did Protestant denominations equate religious beliefs with the land. Rather, they often associated prosperity with salvation, thereby encouraging capitalism, and by the mid-nineteenth century when Anglo-Americans arrived in New Mexico, the pattern of unbridled land use and exploitation was well established. Wed to a rags-to-riches myth, the Protestant tradition depended upon "unlimited" land and abundant natural resources to be maximized rather than saved and protected. Whereas Native Americans preserved their ancestral land, non-Indian Americans used land and then moved on. Thus, land was a commodity for private gain, a view at the very core of Manifest Destiny.

New Mexico's Pueblos, Navajos, and Apaches all attributed religious significance to the land. Mountains, lakes, and rivers were sacred. Prominent natural features marked the borders of traditional land or indicated where the people originated. Mountains revealed locations where deity, mortal, and spirit intersected or where communication with ancestors might occur.[16] Spiritual leaders gathered plants, rocks, or other sacred material for ceremonial purposes at specific places and designated times of the year. Unfortunately, non-Indians who failed to understand this concept of "sacred land" tended to trivialize it, an attitude clearly illustrated by events in twentieth-century New Mexico.

Confiscation and Return of Blue Lake

The competing concepts of "sacred land" versus "land as commodity" intersected in 1906, when President Theodore Roosevelt established the Carson National Forest in northern New Mexico and, in so doing, arbitrarily assumed jurisdiction over some fifty thousand acres of Taos Pueblo land, including their sacred Blue Lake. Taos Pueblo immediately requested return of their land. Preservation of Blue Lake in pristine condition was a sacred obligation, they claimed. Their ceremonies and prayers paid homage to the land, and in turn, the land nourished them. These rituals, they cautioned, had to be performed in solitude, not contaminated by the presence of curious onlookers. Although anxious to regain Blue Lake, the Pueblos hesitated to discuss the area with officials or reveal their beliefs to the public.

Their request ran into a brick wall named Gifford Pinchot, chief forester of the U.S. Forest Service, who had personally approved the reserve in 1906 and insisted that the inclusion of Blue Lake in Carson National Forest best served everyone. Pinchot believed wholeheartedly that the national forests existed for multiple land use, which included lumbering, grazing, mining, and recreation. By 1916, Elliott Barker, the supervisor of the Carson preserve and a particularly bitter foe of the Taos Pueblo, cut trails into the area, stocked Blue Lake with trout to encourage fishing, and permitted non-Indian livestock to graze on land of the sacred watershed.

In desperation, the Pueblos agreed in 1926 to surrender some contested land within their village in exchange for Blue Lake. Commissioner Burke supported the exchange, not out of sympathy for the tribe, but because he believed that once Blue Lake fell under Pueblo control, it would come under direct BIA supervision. His field agents could more closely monitor those ceremonies forbidden by Circular 1665. The Pueblos appealed to the Department of the Interior and Department of Agriculture: "This region is like a church to us, and if you look at it this way you will understand how deeply we feel."[17] No action was taken in 1926, however, and the Pueblos lost both claims.

The Forest Service constructed a cabin, outhouse, corral, and garbage pit on the shore of Blue Lake and allowed its personnel to live there during summer months. This proved a devastating blow to the Taos Pueblo. Spiritual leaders found their land strewn with garbage and their privacy threatened. The Department of Agriculture offered a fifty-year permit to the tribe allowing them to graze their stock, cut timber, and use water, further proof that federal officials failed to comprehend the religious significance of Blue Lake. At no time had the Pueblos requested their land based on monetary value. The Pueblo plea continued to be for the right to conduct religious ceremonies without interference by federal authorities or Park Service personnel.

In 1946, the federal government established the Indian Claims Commission (ICC) to examine Indian land claims across the country and make monetary compensation where appropriate. It could not, however, authorize the return of land. As a first step in a legal struggle, Taos Pueblo filed a claim in August 1951 over BIA objections. The ICC finally reached its decision in 1965 that Blue Lake had been taken unjustly by the federal government. The government offered compensation, but Pueblo leaders refused the money. Despite opposition by Senator Clinton P. Anderson (D-N.M.), the Department of Agriculture, and U.S. Forest Service, the Pueblo launched a campaign to acquire trust title to all fifty thousand acres of their sacred area. At the same time, they began a media crusade directed at the general public, which explained the religious significance of Blue Lake and the lack of religious protection granted Native people in the United States.

Alarmed by the apparent disregard for religious beliefs, a number of Christian organizations offered assistance to the Indians. The Reverend Dean M. Kelley, director of the Commission on Religious Liberties of the National Council of Churches, visited Taos Pueblo and wrote: "The tribe and the valley have grown old together." Furthermore, "anything which mutilates the valley hurts the tribe. If the trees are cut, the tribe bleeds. If the springs or lakes or streams are polluted, the lifestream [sic] of the tribe is infected." The tribe's spiritual relationship, he said, clearly extended to the entire region.[18] The New Mexico Council of Churches wrote to Senator Henry Jackson (D-Wash.), chairman of the Senate Committee on Interior and Insular Affairs, which heard testimony regarding Blue Lake: "the heart of the issue is the simple right of the Taos Indians to the same principles of religious freedom as are guaranteed to all Americans."[19] The Roman Catholic Archdiocese of Santa Fe also affirmed the right of the Taos people to religious protection. Vice-Chancellor Luis D. Jaramillo declared: "As a Christian and American citizen, I strongly hold that the federal government has no alternative but to return ownership of the Blue Lake area to the Taos Pueblo. Whatever arguments may be proposed in opposition are in violation of a people's religion."[20]

Opponents depicted Native people as "anti-progressive" and accused them of trying to expand their economic land base in the name of religious freedom. Return of the lake would only preserve an "Indian ghetto." Senator Lee Metcalf of Montana said that legislation would encourage other Indian religions to spring up. "It will set a precedent allowing every other tribe to come in and ask for like treatment."[21] A Pueblo delegation testified before the Interior and Insular Affairs Committee. They said: "We have had to contend with the irreverent curiosity and even mockery," including a 1968 threat by "a stranger who declared that he would force his way with a gun into our ceremonies." Furthermore, they argued, "we assert the profound belief . . . that the trees and all life and the earth itself . . . must be protected."[22]

Fortunately, Arizona Republican Senator Barry Goldwater, an authority on Indian affairs, and the Richard Nixon administration provided support. On December 2, 1970, the Senate passed the Blue Lake bill by a margin of six-to-one. It was signed into law on December 15 by President Nixon. Thus, a sixty-four-year battle that held Pueblo beliefs up to ridicule and forced them to reveal far more about their spiritual realm than they deemed safe ended happily. The lengthy battle also helped passage of AIRFA, but the controversy over sacred places in New Mexico has not ended. The most recent debate has pitted Albuquerque urban developments against several pueblos nearest the city. Because the Supreme Court has punched holes in AIRFA, Native Americans have lacked legal leverage. Historian R. C. Gordon-McCutchan, who has researched the Blue Lake controversy, points out that most recent attempts to protect American Indian sacred sites have fared poorly.[23] Walter Echo-Hawk of the Boulder, Colorado-based Native American Rights Fund, wrote amendments to AIRFA in an attempt to strengthen the law.[24] Congress held hearings across the country, and legislation passed on October 6, 1994.

Albuquerque's Petroglyphs

A proposed highway to connect the new western developments of Albuquerque with the east side of the city has threatened to slice through Petroglyph National Monument, a thousand-year-old site containing over fifteen thousand Indian rock art carvings. The petroglyphs were designated part of the National Park system in 1990. Even more important, the monument lies on land sacred to the Pueblos near Albuquerque.[25] They use the site for prayers and other religious ceremonies. As one observer pointed out, "We've already dug up just about every site in New Mexico."[26]

Pueblos describe the site as a "church," but it is far more than a simple structure that can be added to, moved, or rebuilt as a congregation grows or changes. A church, of course, can be destroyed and replaced, but according to Pueblo spokesmen, "the Great Spirit is here." The deities are "in the sand, the bushes, the pictures on the rocks."[27] As before, these Native people feel bound by secrecy, prohibited from talking about their sacred beliefs to outsiders. "Fear still persists," claims Jemez Pueblo historian Joe Sando.[28] Secrecy and fear make things doubly difficult, however, when non-Indians line up behind wealthy developers and politicians such as Mayor of Albuquerque Martin Chavez, who promised during his election campaign in 1994 to pursue construction of this highway.

Commenting on the tendency to downplay the importance of Indian sacred sites, former Navajo president Peterson Zah observed that "in the Gulf war, Gen. Norman Schwarzkopf told pilots to avoid bombing Iraq's sacred areas. . . . Wouldn't it be nice to have this guy as a BIA director?"[29] Unlike Pueblo land, much of which lies adjacent to growing cities in New Mexico, Navajo and Apache territory has, thus far, remained largely free of urban interference. Nevertheless, it has been threatened by economic development such as mining, timbering, and recreation, and by archaeologists and collectors. Proposals to drill for oil peaked in the 1970s, often in areas within the eastern checkerboard of Dinetah—traditional Navajo land—on terrain that falls under U.S. Forest Service, Bureau of Land Management (BLM), or Park Service jurisdiction. San Francisco Peak, one of the four sacred Navajo mountains, has seen continued enlargement of the Snow Bowl Ski Resort by the Forest Service. The Ramah Navajo, who live on land southeast of the main reservation, along with the Acoma Pueblo, have opposed BLM plans to expand tourism into El Malpais, a sacred landscape to them and other

New Mexico tribes. In addition, some of the more remote reservation sites have frequently been ransacked by archaeologists. Native Americans are often forced to back up their claims to sacred sites by revealing information that they prefer to keep private. Revelation, however, provides no guarantee that sites will be protected. Moreover, neither AIRFA, as it was written in 1978, nor other legislation has offered safeguards against the commercialization of other aspects of native religions. Exploitation of sacred artifacts can be as devastating to Native Americans as the destruction of their sacred land.

The Native American Religious Market

The Land of Enchantment in the twentieth century attracts tourists from all over the world. It is, in fact, one of the most popular vacation spots in the nation, and many visitors come specifically to enjoy American Indian culture and purchase Native arts and crafts. Tourism assists the tribes economically, even though many still remain cautious; some fear exposing their beliefs too readily. They are "afraid of losing the same thing they have lost for 200 to 300 years: their land, their life [sic], their religion."[30]

This dilemma may be seen in the commercial sale of Indian spiritual objects. For example, the kachina holds a sacred place among Hopi religious beliefs. Kachinas are also widely prized by collectors of Indian art. They were once carved by Hopi artisans during only two months out of the year. Even those made to be sold were crafted with utmost respect. They might cost hundreds, even thousands, of dollars. Today factories in northern New Mexico, staffed almost exclusively by non-Hopi, mass-produce kachinas in about two and one-half hours, an affront to those who hold them sacred. Recently, Marvel published a comic book about a "kachina gang" that terrorized people, and in the end the kachinas were unmasked. Horrified Hopi religious leaders claimed that not only did the comic book trivialize their religion; it also interfered with the religious training of their children, who are not allowed to see kachinas unmasked until they are about nine years old. The publisher, they argued, had no right to appropriate the Hopi religion in that manner.[31]

In another incident, the Hopis threatened to sue Hollywood producer Robert Redford for filming the motion picture *Dark Wind*, based on a Tony Hillerman novel. According to leaders, the movie violated sacred rituals and diluted their beliefs. Redford's crew reportedly trampled their land and entered sacred kivas. Tourists who came to watch the movie being filmed reportedly swarmed through Hopi villages. Filmmakers left, but resumed filming on nearby Navajo land. Even so, tribal spiritual leaders claimed the movie revealed too much sacred information and pressured Redford to cease filming.[32]

Native Americans have found their religious beliefs commercialized in other ways as well. In some instances, their burial grounds have been ransacked and religious objects stolen. Pot hunters over the past hundred years or so have vandalized archaeological sites and taken objects for their private collections or museums, usually without tribal consent. AIRFA has not proven very useful in such cases since it is not binding upon federal museums and is easily ignored by private citizens. The Native American Graves Protection and Repatriation Act of 1990 and the 1979 Archaeological Resource Protection Act have helped, but tribes often lack the financial resources to fight for their stolen artifacts in court or to travel to where they are located and retrieve them.

In addition, tourists sometimes film sacred dances and ceremonies and sell them to the media. Collectors take religious stones and conduct a lucrative black market in sacred eagle feathers. Since eagle feathers are regulated by the federal government, they are even difficult for tribes to obtain. Libraries abound with works that painstakingly detail rituals, dances, and chants that Native Americans would prefer remain private. In many cases these were written by anthropologists who were invited to ceremonies, recorded them in great detail, and later published their reports. Such intrusions are difficult to control, and laws provide little assistance. Furthermore, they leave Native Americans feeling vulnerable and exploited.

Commercialization of Native religions in New Mexico so far has fallen short of that directed at the Lakota of the Black Hills region of South Dakota. "An observation deck—complete with telescope—so tourists can gawk at the Indians praying on the mountain" has turned Lakota religious practices held in sections of the Black Hills into a circuslike attraction.[33] Even so, New Mexico has attracted alternative religious groups during much of the twentieth century, some of whom have apparently come to "play Indian." New Agers have assumed that Native religions were free for the asking and appropriated their outward trappings. Wendy Rose, associate professor of anthropology at Fresno City College, calls the phenomenon "whiteshamanism," which reduces Native beliefs to a trivial assortment of chants, drumming, sage burning, and peyote use. Ironically, such appropriations have generally been intended as compliments, yet they intrude into the lives of people who already practice some of their religion underground.[34]

Forces of Fragmentation

As this essay has noted, the issue is far from simple. For example, Native Americans by no means adhere to any single set of religious practices, and some, in fact, oppose attempts to legalize their traditional ways. Some prefer to raise their children within the mainstream society, although one could argue that this has resulted from years of outside pressure. On the other hand, Christian organizations have often supported legal and Constitutional protection of Native religions. Although many Protestant missions to the Navajos in the late nineteenth and early twentieth centuries fared poorly, some made dramatic advances by the 1950s. In 1934, BIA Commissioner John Collier asserted that "no interference with Indian religious life will be tolerated."[35] Yet, in the 1930s, when the Native American Church became popular on the reservation, it was often Navajos, not Anglos, who opposed it. Traditional Navajos frequently associated the Native American Church with a decrease in Native ceremonies and syncretization with Christian beliefs.[36] In 1940, the Navajo Tribal Council under J. C. Morgan, an ordained minister of the Christian Reformed Church, passed a resolution prohibiting the sale, use, and possession of peyote, a sacrament essential to worship services held by members of the Native American Church. Taos Pueblo and the White Mountain Apaches passed similar ordinances.[37]

Anthropologists on the Navajo reservation in the early 1940s reported few true Christians despite the proliferation of denominations.[38] Nevertheless, the late 1940s marked a period of intense activity by the Latter-day Saints, and by the early 1950s several evangelical Protestant denominations began to attract converts. Faith healing was apparently quite prevalent.[39] Thus, a visitor might have been as likely to encounter a tent revival on the Navajo reservation as to meet a traditional medicine man. Also in the 1950s, a multitude of independent, unaffiliated Christian congregations began to appear, representing, it seems, the conversion of entire kinship groups.[40]

This evangelical fervor of the 1950s has perhaps been blamed for undermining tradition. For one thing, these denominations are less likely to permit syncretization. They have a greater tendency to tell Native people to "throw away or burn your pollen bags" than to accept the combination of Christian and non-Christian.[41] However, other elements in the past forty or so years have contributed as well. More young men and women attend colleges and universities. This has left fewer candidates available to learn the songs and stories. There has also been a dramatic loss of Native languages. Nineteenth-century Anglo-Americans believed that Indians must drop their old tongues to assimilate fully. White BIA teachers seldom spoke Indian dialects, and instruction was conducted exclusively in English. Culture and language, it was believed, went hand in hand. Thus, children carted off to boarding schools had their mouths washed out with soap for speaking their Indian languages. As late as 1963, some students still spoke no English when they began primary grades, and teachers reported that youngsters sat immobile and terrified at their desks, unable to communicate. It was apparently not uncommon for teachers to search the bushes after recess to locate the frightened children.[42] The turnabout has been rapid and complete in recent years, and many now fear that soon no children will be fluent in their Native languages. Without them, chants will be lost and songs forgotten.

Language originally created a barrier between Native Americans and Christians as well. The Reverend Charles Bierkemper, a Presbyterian missionary to the Navajo from 1901 to 1912, found language the single, herculean barrier to evangelizing. Language, he claimed, was the primary reason why after eleven years of work among the Navajo, he could count only 508 professing Christians on the main reservation.[43]

Presbyterian missionary Faye Edgerton, who arrived in Ganado on the Navajo reservation in 1924, discovered that the people had trouble associating a supreme deity with the English word "God," which they often pronounced "Gah," meaning "rabbit" in Navajo. Neither could they translate Bible passages from English to the subtleties of their Native language. It would be two more decades before linguists and anthropologists put the Navajo language into written form so that educators and others might use it. In 1956, Edgerton helped translate the New Testament into Navajo, and it was published by Wycliffe Bible Translators of Huntington Beach, California. In 1965, an Apache New Testament was also published.[44] As historian Ferenc Szasz ironically points out, although "missionaries were engaged in trying to undermine Indian culture, they also provided one means of saving it from extinction."[45] Still, the same might not be true of traditional religious practices.

Christian denominations also began to bridge the cultural and linguistic gap by recruiting Native clergy. Native clergy have served several purposes. First, they were more likely to understand the needs of their people and attract greater numbers into the Christian fold. Moreover, Native clergy have actively encouraged use of Native languages by incorporating the Navajo Bible into their worship services.

The Economic Impacts

Widespread unemployment on reservations has also tended to fragment tribal unity and responses to religion in twentieth-century New Mexico.

The factories that machine-produce Hopi kachinas, for example, have been largely staffed by Navajo workers trying to earn a living. Collectors willing to pay high prices for eagle feathers have too frequently discovered that they can purchase items directly, albeit illegally, from Indians.[46] Before condemning these actions, however, one should consider the problems faced by Native Americans on and off the reservations. Lutheran minister Jon Magnuson accurately stated that the fusion of the spiritual life with the "gritty problems of political survival, alcoholism, and poverty is the real face and heart of the Native Soul" today.[47]

Conclusions

Competition for the Native American soul over the centuries has had many faces, some benevolent and some not. Most outsiders sought to erode traditional Indian spiritual views rather than understand or respect them. Non-Indian Americans may also suffer for this short-sighted view. For one thing, Native Americans tend to believe that all people benefit from their worship, and few can afford to turn down such assistance so freely given. Furthermore, those who see land and resources only as commodities for personal gain often pollute the environment, diminish animal species that inhabit it, and then move on, their pockets full of profit. This leaves the rest of us to clean up the mess. Something can be learned from a people who have occupied a specific piece of land for centuries and intend to remain there forever. Also, if Christianity had answered all of the questions that its missionaries claimed, perhaps fewer non-Indians would be seeking spiritual answers among Indians. Finally, centuries of assimilation attempts, land confiscation, and rampant misunderstanding have fragmented Indian communities, thus creating added problems of unemployment, alcoholism, land disputes, and political exclusion. Many Americans are surprised to discover that after more than two hundred years, Indians still lack First Amendment protection for their religious freedoms. As events in New Mexico show, tribes must press hard for what most Americans take for granted.

Although some might be eager to ring the death knell for Native beliefs, that position is obviously premature. To assume that Native American spiritual views will crumble in the face of modern New Mexico is to see these beliefs as static and unchanging. Robert S. Michaelsen, professor of religious studies at the University of California, Santa Barbara, claims that literature on the subject often assumes that Native American religions are artifacts from some prehistoric time.[48] Yet nothing could be further from the truth. If anything, Native values have been ever flexible and accommodating. Moreover, Indian citizens have begun more frequently to speak out on issues that concern them. On January 5, 1993, a blue ribbon panel of experts met at Sandia Pueblo to discuss how the Albuquerque Petroglyphs might be preserved.[49] Just as Taos Pueblo campaigned for return of Blue Lake, so pueblos have protested destruction of this sacred place. Hundreds of New Mexico Indians spoke at hearings concerning AIRFA amendments. The Navajos have begun to teach their native language in their schools and at Navajo Community College, and many hope that more young people will prove willing to learn it as well as traditional rituals and stories.[50]

The growth of Christianity among urban and reservation Indians does not necessarily preclude a belief in Native traditions. After the Pueblo Indian Revolt of 1680 drove the Spanish out of New Mexico, Franciscan friars learned that Catholicism and traditional faith could coexist. Today Pueblo people practice both, and although it probably occurs less among converts to evangelical Protestant denominations, similar syncretization has occurred among Apaches and Navajos as well.

Many non-Indian Americans view their history as an upward progression, with the present generation a bit more educated and enlightened than those who came before. Keeping in that vein, if there are solutions to these very complex problems—and one must believe that there are—they will not be easily come by. The solution to any problem usually requires meaningful dialogue between the parties involved. In this case, perhaps the dominant society has done enough talking over the past five hundred years. Now, it needs to do some listening.

Notes

1. Alfonso Ortiz, "Indian/White Relations: A View from the Other Side of the 'Frontier,'" in *Indians in American History*, ed. Frederick E. Hoxie (Arlington Heights, Ill.: Harlan Davidson, 1988), 12.

2. David J. Weber, *The Spanish Frontier in North America* (New Haven: Yale University Press, 1992), 118. Also, see Edward H. Spicer, *Cycles of Conquest: The Impact of Spain, Mexico, and the United States on the Indians of the Southwest, 1533–1960* (Tucson: University of Arizona Press, 1962), 537–38.

3. Ruth M. Underhill, *The Navajos* (Norman: University of Oklahoma Press, 1956), 170. Also, see C. L. Sonnichsen, *The Mescalero Apaches* (Norman: University of Oklahoma Press, 1973), 149.

4. Ralph H. Ogle, *Federal Control of the Western Apaches, 1848–1886* (Albuquerque: University of New Mexico Press, 1970), 87.

5. Ferenc Morton Szasz, *The Protestant Clergy in the Great Plains and Mountain West, 1865–1915* (Albuquerque: University of New Mexico Press, 1988), 177.

6. Michael J. Warner, "Protestant Missions among the Navajo, 1890–1912," *New Mexico Historical Review* 45 (July 1970): 209–32.

7. Clyde Kluckhohn and Dorothea Leighton, *The Navajo* (Cambridge: Harvard University Press, 1946), 81.

8. Joe S. Sando, *The Pueblo Indians* (San Francisco: Indian Historian Press, 1976), 75–77.

9. John Collier, "Our Indian Policy," *Sunset Magazine* 50 (March 1923): 13.

10. Robert S. Michaelsen, "'We Also Have a Religion': The Free Exercise of Religion among Native Americans," *American Indian Quarterly* 7 (Summer 1983): 113.

11. Ward Churchill and Glenn T. Morris, "Key Indian Laws and Cases," in *The State of Native America: Genocide, Colonization, and Resistance*, ed. M. Annette Jaimes (Boston: South End Press, 1992), 17.

12. Michaelsen, "'We Also Have A Religion,'" 113.

13. Warner, "Protestant Missions," 214.

14. Sando, *Pueblo Indians*, 23.

15. Roland H. Bainton, *Christianity* (Boston: Houghton Mifflin, 1964), 221.

16. Alfonso Ortiz, "The Tewa World View," in *Teachings from the American Earth: Indian Religion and Philosophy*, ed. Dennis Tedlock and Barbara Tedlock (New York: Liveright Publishing, 1975), 187.

17. R. C. Gordon-McCutchan, *The Taos Indians and the Battle for Blue Lake* (Santa Fe: Red Crane Books, 1991), 19.

18. Dean M. Kelley, "Guest Editorial: The Impairment of the Religious Liberty of the Taos Pueblo Indians by the United States Government," *Journal of Church and State* 9 (Spring 1967): 163.

19. Gordon-McCutchan, *Taos Indians*, 91.

20. Ibid.

21. *Congressional Record*, Senate, 91st Cong., 2d Sess., 30 November 1970, 39140.

22. Ibid., 1 December 1970, 39332.

23. Gordon-McCutchan, "The Battle for Blue Lake: A Struggle for Indian Religious Rights," *Journal of Church and State* 33 (Autumn 1991): 785.

24. Jim Carrier, "Law of the Land: Bill Would Help Save Indian Sites," *Denver Post*, 14 February 1993, C1.

25. Press Release, "Conservation Groups Seek Court Ruling to Protect New Monument from Highway" (Albuquerque: National Parks and Conservation Association, National Trust for Historic Preservation, Sierra Club, Friends of the Albuquerque Petroglyphs, The Wilderness Society, 1 May 1991).

26. "Pueblo Indian Religious Significance," *Proceedings of the Blue Ribbon Panel of Experts for the Petroglyph National Monument Alliance* (Albuquerque: Albuquerque Museum, 6 March 1993), 1.

27. Harrison Fletcher, "Road through Ancient Church? Please Don't, They Plead," *Albuquerque Tribune*, 31 January 1994, A3.

28. Sando, *Pueblo Indians*, 23.

29. Carrier, "Loophole Threatens Religious Freedom, Indians Say," *Denver Post*, 10 February 1993, B2.

30. Carrier, "Few Indians Cashing In on Tourism," *Denver Post*, 31 May 1992, C10.

31. Carrier, "Hollywood vs. the Sacred," *Denver Post*, 31 May 1992, C1.

32. Ibid.

33. Mordecai Specktor, "American Indians, Panel Discuss Religious Law," *National Catholic Register* 29 (March 26, 1993): 4.

34. Wendy Rose, "The Great Pretenders: Further Reflections on Whiteshamanism," in Jaimes, *State of Native America*, 406.

35. Mary Shepardson, "Changing Attitudes toward Navajo Religion," in *Navajo Religion and Culture: Selected Views*, ed. David M. Brugge and Charlotte J. Frisbie (Santa Fe: Museum of New Mexico Press, 1982), 201.

36. David F. Aberle, "The Future of Navajo Religion," in Brugge and Frisbie, *Navajo Religion*, 225.

37. James S. Olson and Raymond Wilson, *Native Americans in the Twentieth Century* (Provo, Utah: Brigham Young University Press, 1984), 90.

38. Kluckhohn and Leighton, *Navajo*, 81.

39. Aberle, "Future of Navajo Religion," 225.

40. Ibid.

41. Ibid., 226.

42. Richard J. Perry, *Apache Reservation: Indigenous Peoples and the American State* (Austin: University of Texas Press, 1993), 144.

43. Warner, "Protestant Missions," 209–32. For early missionary efforts on the Navajo, see Edgar W. Moore, "The Bierkempers, Navajos, and the Ganado Presbyterian Mission, 1901–1912," *American Presbyterians* 64 (Summer 1986): 125–35.

44. Ethel Emily Wallis, *God Speaks Navajo* (New York: Harper and Row, 1968), 129.

45. Szasz, *Protestant Clergy*, 189.

46. Carrier, "Hollywood vs. the Sacred," C5.

47. Jon Magnuson, "Selling Native American Soul," *Christian Century*, 22 November 1989, 1087.

48. Robert S. Michaelsen, "Red Man's Religion/White Man's Religious History," *Journal of the American Academy of Religion* 51 (December 1983): 679.

49. "Interim Management," *Proceedings of the Blue Ribbon Panel of Experts for the Petroglyph Monument Alliance*, 5 January 1993. A second meeting held on 6 March 1993 at the Albuquerque Museum also included representatives of five Indian pueblos.

50. Magnuson, "Selling Native American Soul," 1086.

5

Mormons in Twentieth-Century New Mexico

Leonard J. Arrington

THE MORMON OR LATTER-DAY SAINT EXPERIENCE IN NEW MEXICO can be divided into three periods: the 1846 journey through the region of the Mormon Battalion; the founding of several settlements in the 1870s, 1880s, and 1890s; and the period of maturing communities that lasted from the pioneering period to the present.[1]

The Mormon Battalion

When the Mormons decided in the fall of 1845 to leave Nauvoo, Illinois, the following spring and go to the Salt Lake Valley, Brigham Young instructed his nephew, Jesse C. Little, the church's ambassador in the eastern states, to try to get assistance from the federal government for the migration west. The United States had just declared war against Mexico, and when Little met with President James K. Polk, Polk proposed the enlistment of five hundred LDS soldiers to go by land to California in support of the army of General Stephen Watts Kearny. Brigham Young approved this arrangement because it would provide "hard cash" income to the Saints, guarantee government permission to camp on Indian lands and use grass and timber, and assure the transportation, at government expense, of five hundred men to the West Coast.[2]

Confident that the Battalion would be a help, Brigham moved from camp to camp, speaking before campfires and from wagon tongues, and managed to induce five hundred young men to leave their families and enlist. They moved out from Mormon camps at Council Bluffs, Iowa, on July 20, 1846, and marched to Fort Leavenworth, Kansas, on the Missouri River just north of Independence. There, they were outfitted and began what was regarded as the longest march of infantry to that date in American history. Their arms consisted of United States flintlock muskets, with a few cap-lock yaugers for sharpshooting and hunting purposes.

They marched across Kansas, following the Arkansas River into Colorado, and then cut across the southeastern corner of Colorado into New Mexico, heading for Santa Fe, where they arrived early in October—an advance group arriving there on October 9 and the rest on October 12. A small detachment never reached Santa Fe but, because of sick personnel, was diverted to Fort Pueblo, in present-day Colorado.

The reaction of the soldiers as they arrived in Santa Fe was suggested by the October 29, 1846, diary entry of Henry S. Boyle: "We had always expected [that Santa Fe] was some great place [but] the city looked desolate and barren, with miserable looking Spanish dwellings made of adobe and covered with earth."[3]

There were five companies in the Battalion, each with about one hundred soldiers. Each company was permitted to employ four laundresses, so about twenty women, wives of officers, were employed in that capacity. Other women were employed as cooks, so that thirty-eight wives and sixty-nine children, including several babies, accompanied their husbands on the march. Most of these were detached with eighty-six disabled members of the Battalion at Santa Fe and went from there to Fort Pueblo, Colorado, where they remained for the winter of 1846–47 and later joined their fellow-religionists in July 1847 in the Salt Lake Valley. Some of the teenage boys were employed as servants of the officers. All of the families were presumably taken at the expense of the army. As many as four women, some historians say five, marched all the way to San Diego and were thus with their husbands when they were discharged there in the summer of 1847.

At Santa Fe the Battalion was overjoyed to get a new commanding officer, Lt. Colonel Phillip St. George Cooke, whom the soldiers and their wives welcomed. He was a friend.

Colonel Cooke and the remainder of the Battalion—some 360 men and 4 or 5 women—left Santa Fe for California on October 21. They marched down the Rio Grande, passing Bernalillo, Albuquerque, Socorro, and other New Mexican villages. On November 13, near the present village of Hatch, the Battalion turned southwest from the Rio Grande, cutting a wagon trail past Cooke's Peak (which was named for the Battalion commander), past present-day Lordsburg to Tucson, now in Arizona, and on to San Diego. Their guide was none other than Jean Baptiste Charbonneau, the son of

Toussaint Charbonneau and his young Shoshoni wife, Sacagawea, who had helped to guide Lewis and Clark on their epoch-making journey of exploration of the Rocky Mountains and the Northwest in 1805–6. Jean Baptiste, called "Pomp" by the explorers, had been born just two months before his parents were employed by Lewis and Clark and had ridden on cradleboard on the back of Sacagawea all the way from the Missouri River to the Pacific Coast and back. After the journey, he was educated at a Catholic academy in St. Louis, then accompanied Prince Paul of Wurttemberg, who was in the West on a scientific expedition, and eventually lived at his castle near Stuttgart for several years. Returning to the states, he served with the American Fur Company, worked with the Robidoux fur brigade in the Utah–Idaho region, attended the great fur rendezvous of 1833 on the Green River, and accompanied Sir William Drummond Stewart, a Scottish nobleman, on a pleasure trip to the Rockies via South Pass to the Green River and then north into Yellowstone country.[4]

The march from Santa Fe to San Diego, which required three months, was marked by days of thirst, fear of envelopment by grass fires, and fear of Indians, Mexicans, and wild bulls. The Battalion occasionally ran across wild turkeys, which they killed and roasted. Two members of the Battalion, Elijah Freeman and Richard Carter, died and were buried along the trail south of Socorro.

Upon their arrival in San Diego, Colonel Cooke reported to U.S. Army officials: "Everything conspired to discourage the extraordinary undertaking of marching this Battalion 1100 miles, the greater part through an unknown wilderness, without road or trail and with a wagon train. It was enlisted too much by families; some were too old and feeble, and some too young; it was embarrassed by many women, it was undisciplined; it was much worn by traveling on foot, and marching from Nauvoo, Illinois; their clothing was very scant; there was no money to pay them or clothing to issue, their mules were utterly broken down; the quartermaster department was without funds, and its credit bad; and animals scarce. Those produced were inferior and were deteriorating every hour for lack of forage and grading." But, he added, "history may be searched in vain for an equal march of infantry, half of it through a wilderness where nothing but savages and wild beasts are found, or where, for want of water, there is no living creature. There, with almost hopeless labor, we have dug deep wells which the future traveler will enjoy. In several marches with crowbar and pickaxe we have worked our way over mountains which seemed to defy aught but wild goat. We have hewed a chasm through solid rock, more narrow than our wagons, to the Pacific. Thus, marching half naked and half fed, and living upon wild animals, we have discovered and made a road of great value."[5]

Most members worked their way back to the Salt Lake Valley, where they joined their relatives and friends. In the meantime, they had learned something about making adobe buildings, about inaugurating an irrigation system, and about the country and peoples of New Mexico, Arizona, and California.

The Founding of Settlements

Although the Mormons called various persons to work with Indians of the Southwest in the 1850s, including Daniel W. Jones, Jacob Hamblin, and James S. Brown, each of whom spent time in New Mexico, the first permanent Latter-day Saint settlement in the territory occurred in 1875, when Daniel W. Jones was assigned to be president of what was called the Mexican Mission.[6] He and his companions left Nephi, Utah, in September 1875, then went south to Kanab, where they were joined by Ammon M. Tenney. They crossed the Colorado at Lee's Ferry, went to Moencopi and north-central Arizona, then down to Mesa, on to Tucson, and then backtracked on the old Mormon Battalion trail until they turned southeast to go to El Paso, which they reached in January 1876. Most of the missionaries then went on into northern Mexico, but Ammon Tenney and Robert H. Smith turned north up the Rio Grande Valley to work in New Mexico. They spent several months visiting with the Isleta, Laguna, and Acoma Pueblo Indians. They were not successful in converting these Indians. They reached Zuni Pueblo, near the Arizona border, in the early summer of 1876, and they had phenomenal success, baptizing more than one hundred Zunis. When Brigham Young became aware of this achievement, he telegraphed a call to Lorenzo H. Hatch and John Maughan to settle with the Zunis; so, in December 1876, the first permanent Mormon settlers arrived in New Mexico and founded the community originally called Savoia (later, Ramah). Early in 1877, Luther Burnham and Ernest Tietjen and their families joined the community. A few months later five additional families joined them. By October the branch numbered, in addition to the whites, 116 Zunis and 34 Navajos.

Elder Hatch described their situation in a letter to the *Deseret News* for March 18, 1877:

> The Zunis are hardworking, self-sustaining, law-abiding Indians having many sheep, goats, horses, donkeys, and good work cattle. They have plenty of wheat and corn and produce a good article of peaches. They number 3 or 4 thousand, live in towns, with houses

built in the Mexican style. Many of them speak Spanish. . . . We have warm friends among them.

Late in the fall of 1877 nearly one hundred converts from Arkansas arrived at Savoia, but the community couldn't feed them for the winter, so Lorenzo Hatch sent most of them on to Joseph City, Arizona. Unfortunately, the Arkansas converts brought smallpox, which one of their members had become infected with while passing through Albuquerque. The disease spread from the Mormons to the Zuni, and hundreds of Indians became ill. Their only remedy lay with spiritual healing, and one elder, Llewellyn Harris, soon began to bless the Indians. Throngs came to him, and he blessed for many hours until he had blessed more than four hundred. He reported that all but one of those he blessed recovered. A Protestant missionary doctor, upon hearing the news, declared that Elder Harris had healed by the power of the devil. The circulation of this rumor hurt LDS proselyting efforts among the Indians.

In 1877 the land along the San Juan River in northwestern New Mexico was opened for settlement. The next year, Jeremiah Hatch and his family settled Fruitland, the second LDS community in New Mexico (later, Burnham). Several of the Arkansas families passed through there that year on their way to the San Luis Valley in southern Colorado, where several settlements were founded.

In the late 1870s and early 1880s, during the national crusade to stamp out polygamy, many of the church's leaders had to go into hiding, and several of them chose eastern Arizona and New Mexico as places to hide. There they were able to move about quite freely and openly, as did Wilford Woodruff, soon to become president of the church, who spent most of 1870 doing missionary work in Isleta and Zuni. Ammon Tenney was his guide and missionary companion. Elder Woodruff, for instance, wrote a report to the *Deseret News* of his travels in eastern Arizona and western New Mexico in April and May 1879. He told of crossing the Colorado River at Lee's Ferry and ascending what he called the hog's back, which he said was "the most difficult and dangerous road for loaded teams to pass over I ever saw," and then went on to Moencopi and Tuba City. Elder Woodruff said that he had an interview with Llewellyn Harris concerning his administrations among the Zuni sick with the smallpox, and he confirmed the account of his healing the Zunis.

Elder Woodruff went on to Woodruff, Snowflake, and St. John, then over to Zuni in New Mexico. He referred to the Isletas, Lagunas, and Zunis as "Nephites"; that is, a very righteous people. He thought they were "a different race of people altogether from most Indians in the area." He was impressed with their beauty and cleanliness, the order in their homes, the adornment of their dwellings, their industry and indefatigable labors, and their virtue and the purity of their national blood. "Their bearing and dignity in their intercourse with strangers, and, above all else, the expansion of their minds and their capacity to receive any principle of the Gospel, such as endowments or sealing powers," he wrote, "is fully equal to that among the most civilized peoples." He referred to them as noble-minded people. Of the three groups, the Isletas, a pueblo of three thousand, lived in a village twelve miles below Albuquerque, on the Rio Del Norte. All in all, there were forty villages of "Nephites," with thirty-two thousand persons. Albuquerque at the time, he wrote, had three thousand persons.

In 1879 a group of Mormon pioneers settled Blanding and Bluff in southeastern Utah, so a San Juan Stake was created that included both Utah and New Mexico settlements. About that time other settlements were made in New Mexico's San Juan Valley–Kirtland, Waterflow, and La Plata. The Fruitland Branch was organized as Burnham Ward, named after the Savoia pioneer called to be its bishop.

In 1880 a son of Brigham Young, John W. Young, participated in the early settlements in eastern Arizona. He contracted to prepare the grade for two hundred miles of the Atlantic and Pacific Railroad, which later was known as the Santa Fe. Most of the grading crews were Saints from Arizona and Savoia. When the projects were finished, most of the workers went to Mormon settlements in eastern Arizona. In 1882 one of the Arizona settlements, Sunset, was dissolved, and many of its settlers moved to New Mexico to join the Savoia settlement. Under the leadership of Ernest Tietjen and John Hunt, who had remained at Savoia, they moved the settlement a few miles south to its present location. They also changed the name of the community to "Navajo," but the U.S. Postal Service rejected that name because there was already a "Navajo"; so they chose the Book of Mormon name "Ramah." In 1883, apostles Brigham Young, Jr., and Heber J. Grant organized the ward with Ernest Tietjen as bishop.

Bishop Tietjen, who had moved his family to Savoia in 1876 as an Indian missionary, lived in a small log house that consisted of one room, with an inside measurement of 14' by 16'. It had a door and small window on the east side and a small window on the south side and a large fireplace on the north. The chimney was built on the outside so as to avoid taking up too much space. The roof was covered with dirt, and the floor was made of common rough lumber of varying widths. This house provided shelter from rain, snow, and cold blasts of winter and cooled the hot burning rays of the summer sun. School was held in a one-room log house that was used by the ward for all meetings and dances.

A few years later, in 1894, Bishop Tietjen bought a ranch near Bluewater and invited family and friends to join him there. At the same time his son Joe bought a ranch at Prewitt, east of Gallup, which was along the route of the railroad.

In 1879 Mormons settled in Williams Valley, in what is now southwestern Catron County, on the drive route from the eastern Arizona communities (St. Johns, Thatcher, and Safford), to the colonies that were being settled in Chihuahua, Mexico. There were also rumors that a railroad was about to be built through the valley.

In 1881 two brothers, William and Melvin Swapp, drove a herd of cattle to Mexico over the route and became interested in an area about thirty-five miles to the north. In 1883 they returned, having purchased the property from prospectors. They brought with them their families, that of a brother, John, and four or five other families. In 1884 the Luna Ward was organized.

Shortly after settlement, the settlers in Pleasant Valley were visited by apostles Brigham Young, Jr., and Heber J. Grant. After the visit, which lasted several weeks, young Heber J., only twenty-six and a newly appointed apostle, sent a letter to the *Deseret News*, dated Albuquerque, December 2, 1883. His letter indicated that the apostles were the ones who had named it "Pleasant Valley." He declared, "Pleasant Valley, although it does not compare with our large valleys in Utah, is nevertheless a nice spot, and will, no doubt in the future, have a large and prosperous settlement of our people established in it. There are at present between twenty and thirty families located in the valley." Pleasant Valley later became Luna Valley.

At Savoia, in April 1883 (which at that moment was named Navajo), Elder Grant and Brigham Young, Jr., counseled with a Navajo chief named Manuelito. "He was a fine-looking Indian," wrote Heber, "stands about six feet high and is remarkably well built." Manuelito willingly granted permission for the Latter-day Saint missionaries to proselytize among his people.

In 1883, with settlements being made in several areas across the Arizona border into New Mexico, Jacob Hamblin, the famed Mormon Indian missionary, and others were asked to go to Pleasanton, on the San Francisco River. There were soon nice homes, young orchards, and many fields of grain. Jacob's last child was born there. His granddaughter remembered Pleasanton, which has since disappeared, because in 1885, at the time of an Indian uprising in the southern end of Pleasant Valley, General John Pershing was wounded in a fight while trying to capture the noted Indian chief Geronimo. He had driven his rattling buckboard into the valley and asked her to bring him a drink of water.

Hamblin came down with malaria in 1886 and died after a month's illness. In poverty and obscurity, thus ended the life of the Latter-day Saint who left the greatest imprint on the desert Southwest. As Juanita Brooks wrote: "He worked for peace with the tools of peace—with understanding and tolerance and love." Two years after his death, his body was moved from the deserted village to Alpine, Arizona, where a simple shaft marks his grave, bearing the inscription "Peacemaker in the Camps of the Lamanites." When his family sold their holdings to non-Mormons and moved south to Mormon colonies in Mexico, his final homestead was left to the bitter judgment of the New Mexico desert.

Life in all these New Mexico Mormon villages was hard—farming, building homes, building schools and meeting houses, protecting families against marauding groups, flash floods, drought, and so on. But there were also compensations. For one thing, they worked together to put in dams and canals, erect fences, build roads, construct schools and churches, and establish community enterprises like tanneries, woolen factories, and sawmills. The less fortunate victims of disease, death, or natural disasters were assisted by those who had done better. But their life was also enriched as they jointly established and maintained cultural facilities and activities: they put on plays, held dances and "sings," and sought to enjoy themselves.

Third, they felt a deep satisfaction in their efforts to establish friendly relations with Indians, helping them in the arts of agriculture and, especially, trying to improve the lot of Indian women and children.

Fourth, the Saints were able to accord pioneering women a richer, more emotionally satisfying life than was possible for many other western women. They did this partly by locating in villages, where the families would have close neighbors and would thus find it easy to participate in many village activities, and partly by organizing in each village a branch of the Women's Relief Society. The Relief Society held weekly meetings where they sang songs, made clothing and quilts for Indian women and children and other needy persons, held classes in hygiene and nursing, and discussed literature and art. These meetings provided opportunities, not only to do worthwhile things for the village but for self-expression and self-fulfillment as well. These women lobbied for the right of suffrage in New Mexico and Arizona, as they had successfully done in Utah in 1870; they had their own magazine, *The Woman's Exponent*. Several wrote novels and poetry, and, of course, led in building schools and promoting programs to improve health. The New Mexico Relief Societies were similar to those in early Arizona. Based on a study of the minute books of their meetings, one learns that their official songbook was an LDS Suffrage Songbook and contained the following song that they often sang. The words were composed by Lula Greene Richards, the founding editor of *The Woman's Exponent*. One can picture the sisters in their own Relief Society hall, singing this, directed by Mary Jane West. It is sung to the traditional Mormon tune of "Hope of Israel."

> Freedom's daughter, rouse from slumber;
> See, the curtains are withdrawn
> Which so long thy mind hath shrouded;
> Lo! the day begins to dawn.
>
> Chorus:
>
> Woman, 'rise, thy penance o'er,
> Sit thou in the dust no more;
> Seize the scepter, hold the van,
> Equal with thy brother, man.

This song gives a little of the flavor of the "raising of consciousness" that occurred in Mormon villages in the Southwest in the 1880s.

The Mormon village was a function of irrigation agriculture, of the need for protection against Indians, and of the Mormon belief that they must prepare a dwelling place for the Savior at His Second Coming. Despite the shifting of the Mormon subsistence pattern toward cattle raising, the basic "bunched up" village plan is still being maintained.

The Mormon economic system in New Mexico was a modification of private enterprise. There were several extended family enterprises. The irrigation, town water, and cattle companies were operated on a cooperative basis. Insistence upon cooperative solutions was supported both by strong kinship connections and by the church. The cooperative bias was also evident in the operation of the individually owned businesses. There were also elaborate community-wide economic enterprises—irrigation and cattle companies.

Finally, and most importantly, Mormon settlers were supported and encouraged by rich spiritual experiences. For example, the following is from the journal of Samuel C. Young, who lived in Fruitland. (Samuel had married Laura Tietjen, daughter of Bishop Ernest Tietjen of Ramah.) The entry is for June 1899:

> I was mowing hay when one of bro. Evans little girls came running to me crying "Sammie, get some elders and come at once and administer to Mama, she is dieing." Sister Evans was suffering from a very bad case of lung trouble. I unhitched my team from the mowing machine and hitched them to a heavy freight wagon and started up the street, letting my team go in a run. I overtook Ira Hatch, an old Indian missionary. I stopped the team and told him to climb in, he was wanted. He asked no questions but climbed into the wagon.

I let the team go into a run. I soon saw two other elders and got them into the wagon....

We drove up to the house. As I entered the room Aunt Clarissa said, Sammie I am so glad you have come, but you are too late, she has gone. I asked if she was dead. As long as there are signs of life there is hope. "Let us kneel and pray." The five of us kneeled down and bro. Hatch prayed. The sentences may have been disconnected and broken as bro. Hatch had spent so much of his life among the Indians that it was hard to speak his own language, but he prayed. The prayer was short, possibly not more than 20 words were spoken.

Sister Evans body lay there as lifeless as the wood in the door of the house. We arose and bro. Hatch took the little bottle of oil and anointed her head and turned to me and said "Sammie, you seal the anointing."

I had said but a few words when I heard the voice of a person who was just behind and above me say "in the authority of the Holy Priesthood which we hold and in the name of Jesus Christ we command death to depart and for health and strength to return and you shall live to see your son, who is now in the Eastern States mission." I repeated the words as I heard them spoken. In a very short time she was breathing naturally and she spoke saying "I am so tired but I feel much better." In a few days she was assisting with housework and walking a mile to attend our Sunday afternoon sacrament meeting."

The son who was on a mission came home in eight months, and "Sister Evans died from the effect of the same ailment about two months after his return home."

A dozen years later, in 1912, when the Mexican Revolution was at its height, most of the Latter-day Saints in Chihuahua were forced to leave. Many of them settled in New Mexico. Refugee camps were established in Chamberino of Doña Ana County, in Hatchita, south of Deming, and elsewhere along the border. In 1915 the Chamberino refugees were able to buy a tract of land east of the New Mexico–Arizona border on the Gila River, where they founded Virden, the last of the Mormon settlements in New Mexico. Refugees from Hatchita later joined the community. With more than five hundred settlers, it became the largest settlement of ex-colonists, and, as one person suggested, the only community founded expressly for the purpose of reestablishing a close LDS lifestyle.

The town was isolated, had neither post office or phone system, and found all communication funneled through Duncan, Arizona. Exemplars of the pioneer LDS lifestyle, the Saints had their own dance band, and dances were regularly scheduled, including dance instruction in young peoples' classes and dances. They raised potatoes, alfalfa, and grains until the 1950s, when they began to grow cotton. They have exhibited the LDS heritage of cooperation, working together for church, school, and community. They won basketball, girls volleyball, and tennis championships, and were active in 4-H clubs, scouting, and other youth activities. In recent years the population has declined to about 250, and they are a part of Duncan Stake. But the old spirit of love and sharing still exists. From the ward have come patriarchs, stake presidents, mission presidents, a temple president, and many other leaders.

The early years in the twentieth century witnessed some migrations into New Mexico and some out of it, and some missionary work but few convert baptisms. The journal of James W. Huish, who went on a short-term mission to New Mexico for six and one-half months in 1927, reported that he visited 1,141 homes, baptized 905 persons, held 21 meetings in halls, and 17 meetings in cottages.

The first Latter-day Saints to move into the Mesilla Valley, where Las Cruces is located, appear to have been the Smith Skousen family, who came from the Mexican colonies in 1912. Brother Skousen was a Singer sewing machine salesman. With ten children, their family consisted of a third of the Las Cruces Sunday school. When they moved to Mesa, Arizona, in 1940, they cut the LDS population by one-third.

The Maturing Communities

Nearly every sizable community in New Mexico now has a ward or branch. In nearly every case, growth of these wards has been through separate family immigration into the area, plus occasional conversions. There are LDS stake centers at Farmington, Albuquerque, Las Cruces, Gallup, Bloomfield, Roswell, Santa Fe, Grants, Kirtland, and Silver City. All told, there are now 12 LDS stakes in New Mexico, with 112 wards and branches consisting of about 50,000 members. One person in thirty-three New Mexicans is a Mormon. Of the early settlements, there continue to be Mormon communities in Luna, Ramah, Fruitland, Kirtland, and Bluewater.[7]

A considerable proportion of the Latter-day Saints in New Mexico are Native Americans—some Zuni, some Hopi, but mostly Navajo.[8] Mormons have always had a special relationship with Indian peoples. This is a product of the church's belief that the Book of Mormon is an inspired record of God's people in this hemisphere in precisely the same sense that the Bible is an inspired record of God's people in ancient Israel. Indians, Mormons believe, have a glorious heritage, just as do the Jews and Christians, and the Mormons have always felt a special kinship with these people. Their traditions and customs, the Mormons believe, are inherited from a "true gospel" preached by ancient prophets, and Latter-day Saint officers and members make every effort to accommodate the "true principles" the Indians possess. Mormons do not seek to destroy the faith of the Indians but to update it by restoring the true principles taught by their early prophets. Indians are permitted to practice their own ceremonies. Under the Mormon placement program, many Indians have lived in "white" LDS homes for extended periods, which produces a familial as well as religious tie.

Because of the substantial number of Native Americans and Spanish-speaking members in New Mexico, the church has vacillated between a policy of integration and one of having separate-culture wards and branches. Should Indian and Mexican-American members be assimilated into the mainstream church, or should they be segregated into separate congregations to maintain their separate languages and cultures? Where there are many new members, one argument holds, Natives feel a source of strength and encouragement in holding their own services. They obtain social contact, retain and enjoy their own cultural distinctions, and are able to worship in a setting where they feel comfortable. It also gives them opportunities for leadership in a church that features lay leadership. On the other hand, an integrated ward, incorporating Anglos, Indians, and Hispanics, trains new members by letting them watch how other members conduct themselves in church and perform their church callings.

Just as in pioneer times, when the church established separate congregations for Danes, Germans, Swiss, and Hawaiians, the church in recent years has established special wards for Blacks, Poles, Tongans, Samoans, Chinese, Hmong, Vietnamese, and Laotians. Should it do the same for Zunis, Navajos, and Mexican Americans? Obviously, the church's membership contains many peoples and cultures. Where wards are integrated, should choirs sing songs from each culture; should persons give prayers and sermons in their own language; and should church dances include those of the various cultures present? How can wards and branches best serve the needs of people whose language, culture, and life experiences are different from those of the majority? During the 1960s, Apostle Spencer W. Kimball was active in organizing Indian congregations, sometimes called Lamanite branches. Designed to help preserve Native American culture, the arrangement was favored by the Council of Twelve Apostles and First Presidency; they reflected a view that it was not right to force every "nation" to adopt Anglo ways.

Ethnic branches continued until the early 1970s, when some church leaders questioned the utility of the separate branches. This retreat was again reversed in 1977, when the church introduced the Basic Unit plan—an effort to provide the essential church programs for small groups that might not have all the leadership or membership to conduct the regular, complete church programs. In the view of some, these should be temporary. As one church leader declared, "When we get to the other side of the veil, the Lord won't care whether we come from Tonga, New Zealand, Germany, or America. We are in an eternal family. The color of skin, the culture we represent, the interests we have are all quite secondary to the concept of the great eternal family."[9]

Ernesteen Lynch, a prominent Navajo teacher in Window Rock, "loved" her Alma Branch in Upper Fruitland, New Mexico. "We were all Navajo and we just understood where the other was coming from. We didn't have to feel uncomfortable about what we did because we were all Navajo and we knew our Navajo-ness."[10] As another Navajo explained, "If you don't find good LDS Indian people [in your ward], then you lose your culture, get off track, and become more non-Indian. You lose your Indian point of view. You lose interest in being who you are and where you came from. You lose everything about your whole family as an Indian."[11] In Alma Branch, everyone was Navajo—the bishop, the Relief Society president, all the teachers. There was a sense of pride in their callings and in their arrangements, as they strove to "grow in the church." They planned activities appropriate for their culture—socials, funerals, skits, and foods.

Many Native Americans interviewed by the Charles Redd Center at Brigham Young University took the position that the eventual goal must be an integrated ward, but one that would permit them to retain their heritage:

> I'd like the Indians to be proud of themselves. I wouldn't want them to hide that. I'd like them to blend in, but at the same time be individuals. . . . I just think that we don't need to bury our heritage, bury our skin color. We don't need to raise it on a flagpole either. We just need to be somehow more aware of who we are but it's not a big deal to anybody. I don't think we need to glorify it, just be content. I don't know what a program like that would be.[12]

The same difficult choice faces most churches and American society as a whole. Hispanics want to maintain their language and culture; most Americans (according to polls) want them to learn to speak English, to "Americanize."[13] Can a multicultural society be developed that can still maintain a minimal level of common understanding and values? What is the basic gospel to which all should adhere, and what is the Anglo culture in which it is embedded, that can be replaced by symbols and portions of another culture?

The growth of the LDS Church in the past twenty-five years in Mexico, Central and South America, Asia, Africa, and areas of the United States far removed from Utah and the Mountain West has been accompanied by a broadening of tolerance. Particularly after June 1978, when the church extended the priesthood to worthy males of all races, church sermons, periodicals, and lesson manuals have sought to eliminate color as a factor in socialization. There are now many Black members, a substantial number of Blacks in administrative positions, and Blacks are welcomed in temple ceremonies. Tolerance, mutual love, and understanding are now key elements in official messages and policies.

If the growth of the church has brought increasing tolerance, the spread of young missionaries around the world—forty-five thousand men and women, mostly from ages nineteen to twenty-six at this date, with each spending about two years in an assigned location—vastly improves the lay Mormon understanding of other nations and cultures. The missions allow young Latter-day Saints to develop language skills that far exceed those of most Americans. They also develop speaking and organizational skills.

A third constituent of LDS values is the remembrance of a pioneer heritage, one that emphasizes industry, frugality, and a heightened sense of community.

Finally, the Mormons, with their large families and family-centeredness, maintain a heavy stress on family values. They seek to perpetuate these values by marriages in the sacred temple, by discouraging divorce, and by teaching family loyalty and obedience to their children.

As with all faiths and churches, there are many problems. The spread of the LDS Church around the world means fewer visits by central church authorities and more government by manuals and guidebooks. This isolation means more conformity, more going by the letter, more direction by the Central Church Correlation Committee that commissions and approves the manuals and all articles and books published by the church. One may say this but must not say that; one may do this but must not do that; and so on. These instructions are accepted, but they irritate a few, and there is seldom any opportunity to appeal.

Along with this stringency in regulations are the manuals themselves. Rather than depending on professionally trained people to write up-to-date manuals, the church has settled into a policy of using the same manuals year after year. The pattern of Sunday school, for example, is to study the Book of Mormon one year, church history and doctrine the following year, Old

Testament the next year, and New Testament the fourth year, each year with an appropriate manual, always the same one. Thus, every fourth year, Sunday school classes go back to manuals used before. This is no problem for new converts, who have never been exposed, but those who have been members for many years find themselves repeating a manual every four years. This is not only repetitive but tedious.

A second problem is the advanced age and infirmity of some of the key policymakers, the First Presidency and Council of the Twelve. President Howard W. Hunter is eighty-seven, and his counselors, Gordon Hinckley and Thomas Monson, are eighty-four and sixty-seven. The average age of the members of the Council of the Twelve Apostles is seventy-two, with ages ranging from sixty-one to eighty-seven. Inevitably, policies are made by men who were born well before World War II; four of them were born before World War I.[14] Despite his age, President Hunter is popular with both "liberals" and "conservatives."

Because all of these are men—because all general authorities, regional representatives, stake presidents, and bishops are men—there is no feminine voice in the centers of power, either locally or churchwide. Mormon women have their own organization, the Relief Society, but even this group is subject to the authority of the men, from the local bishops to the First Presidency. Yet half the members of the church—perhaps more than half—are women. Many women would like a wider role. They may pray in church, they may teach Sunday school lessons, they may give talks in Sacrament meetings. But they may not assist their husbands in blessing babies, and with the exception of token invitees, they may not speak in general church conferences.[15]

Another dilemma also faces the church. Because of the age of leading authorities, and perhaps because few of the leaders are from academe, they do not encourage intellectual speculation. Young people who advance in university training face intellectual challenges because, in part, the stance of authorities tends to be conformist. With so many biblical literalists, harmonizing high school and university classes in science, social science, and the humanities with those in religion is not always easy. Once there was a way of doing this, with classes at the LDS Institute of Religion adjacent to colleges and universities. Recent policies have seen the appointment not of distinguished scholars, as was once the case, but of recent graduates in Religious Education at Brigham Young University, to teach these classes. Far from attempting to harmonize secular and church learning, many of these instructors now insist upon the Religious Education approach, which tends to be dogmatic and anti-secular.[16]

A final result of the continued growth of the church is the adoption of a consolidated meeting schedule. Those over forty had many opportunities for interaction as they grew up: priesthood meetings for men on Friday evening, young people's meetings on Tuesday evening, Primary Association for children on Wednesday afternoon, Relief Society meetings for women on Tuesday afternoon, Sunday school on Sunday morning, and Sacrament service on Sunday evening. At each meeting one would find people to chat with and thus maintain friendships. A few years ago, to limit the number of meeting times so as to avoid excessive travel for those in metropolitan or outlying areas, the church adopted the consolidated meeting schedule. All meetings were to be held on Sunday morning or afternoon—for example, Priesthood and Relief Society at the same time on Sunday, at 9:00 A.M., Sunday school at 10:00 A.M., and Sacrament service at 11:00 A.M. One meeting after another and one is through for the week. The enormous advantage is that this means less time at church and leaves more time for the family and for neighborhood and civic activities.[17]

Finally, one should mention the unrest among Indian members caused by the excommunication in 1989 of Elder George P. Lee, the only full-blooded Indian among the general authorities of the church. As a college graduate, college president, doctoral candidate, and mission president, Lee was Mormonism's example of success in its Indian program. Ordained a general authority in 1975, when he was thirty-two, Lee was a role model for many Native Americans, especially for the tens of thousands of Navajos who were Mormons. As predicted in the Book of Mormon, the story of their "Lamanite" grandfathers, the day of the Lamanite was coming. The Indians would lead; they were the harbingers of the "last days." George Lee believed this, possibly too fervently, but while pleading for love and understanding, he saw racism and materialism and perceived what he called "the spiritual slaughter" of his people. He sometimes offended people in denouncing materialism; his interpretation of doctrine was not always orthodox; he went far in defending and promoting his own concerns, his own people, but he often criticized his brethren for their decisions on inspired programs and policies. His excommunication for "apostasy" caused many Navajos and other Native Americans to curtail or abandon their support of the church. Little of that feeling still persists today among Native Americans in New Mexico; several dozen Indian branches and wards in New Mexico are making what church authorities regard as satisfactory progress.[18]

Overall, Mormons represent only 3 percent of the 1.5 million people in New Mexico. They are not a minority with any power, and they do not represent any significant threat to other denominations. By and large, they are peaceful, law-abiding, hardworking families, interested in the life of the community and making positive contributions toward their professions and businesses. They have made positive contributions in raising Mexican and Spanish Americans and Native Americans to middle-class status and in encouraging their loyalty to American institutions. Their talented young people who remain in the state are good taxpayers and, by and large, good farmers, businessmen, teachers, and citizens.

During their history, the Mormons attempted to retain some of the essential structure of the Elizabethan family, with patriarchal authority, limited status of women, and complete filial obedience. A dominant value was success—achievement. There remains considerable emphasis on extended kinship. Family reunions are common. Family solidarity is emphasized, "sealing" marriages for all eternity and expecting the ties of kinship to last forever. Family members are enjoined to adopt a measure of responsibility for joint salvation, and arrangements are made for the consecration of deceased relatives of any known degree. This doctrine has led to an unparalleled interest in genealogy.

New Mexico is one of the leading arts-producing areas in the world, and Indian artists, building on the best of their tribal and cultural heritages, have created an enduring art that represents a direct link with the earth, its plants, and its animals. Among the finest of New Mexico's Indian artists are Latter-day Saints. They are prominent in virtually every field of Indian arts.[19]

Perhaps one should begin with the nearby Hopi artists. One of the heaviest concentrations of LDS Indian artists lives in the Hopi village of First Mesa. Their LDS roots begin with the missionary expeditions of Jacob Hamblin in the 1850s, 1860s, and 1870s. The descendants of Tom Polacca, a major Hopi leader, and of Fannie Nampeyo Polacca inaugurated a renaissance of Hopi pottery. Their work has been displayed widely and exhibited in many parts of the world, including China. One of the Polacca sons, Howella, married a Navajo woman named Ruth and lived with her at Crystal, in eastern New Mexico, also the location of the first permanent chapel that the LDS Church built on a southwestern reservation. Ruth was a weaver and for many years demonstrated traditional Navajo weaving at Mesa Verde National Park in southwest Colorado. Her rugs are in many private collections, including the Rockefeller collection. Fannie Nampeyo Polacca paints hauntingly beautiful pots using the traditional yucca brush and boiled plant juices and crushed minerals. Other Hopi and Navajo potters in the area include Feather Woman (Helen Naha), Frog Woman (Joy Navasie), and Carol Namoki. Hopi pottery is subtle and rich; the clay is carefully dug from certain places on the reservation, then kneaded by hand. Pots are fashioned without the use of a potter's wheel, scraped smooth with a piece of gourd, and polished with a smooth stone.

In north-central New Mexico are the Jicarilla Apaches. As a nomadic people, they lavished their best craftsmanship on items easily transported and unbreakable: baskets, beadwork, and buckskin. One of the Jicarillas, Lassie DeDio of Dulce, despite arthritis in her hands, has done beautiful and intricate beadwork.

South of the Jicarilla Apache are the Pueblos. At Santa Clara Pueblo, Isabelle and Eugene Naranjo, from Española, thirty miles north of Santa Fe, make pottery that is typically heavy, black, and carved, having the appearance of hand-rubbed ebony. Teresita Naranjo is one of the finest potters, not only of Santa Clara, but of all the Rio Grande Pueblos. Her pottery has been exhibited in the Smithsonian Museum in Washington and has been featured in every publication on Pueblo pottery; along with Joy Navasie, she was honored at a White House reception as one of America's leading Indian artists.

On the Laguna reservation, west of Albuquerque, are rich deposits of uranium ore that furnish employment for many Laguna Pueblos, causing them to neglect their pottery. But Carolyn Browning has kept that tradition alive; in tribal tradition, she makes tiny pots to leave near the site from whence the clay is dug as an offering to show respect to the mother earth that yields the clay.

About thirty miles south of Gallup is Zuni Pueblo, near where Ramah was established. Zuni art fame results from its excellent jewelry, including both inlay and petit point. Using mother-of-pearl as a background, the artist, Bowman Paywa, one of the finest, creates an intricate inlaid mosaic of turquoise, coral, and silver. The Heard Museum of Phoenix also exhibits the work of Brenda Paloma, a Zuni, as well as that of Daisey Hooey, a Hopi potter from the Nampeyo family who studied art in Paris, toured the world, married a Zuni, and now teaches traditional pottery there.

Navajo Mormons also include weavers, jewelers, and silversmiths. Weaving from wool sheared from their own sheep, and cleaned, carded, and spun themselves, women weavers make several styles, all lying flat, with straight parallel edges, woven very tightly, and having a warp of wool. A member of Shiprock Ward, Ora Jim, has won many ribbons with her rugs featuring Yeis, mythological figures of healing and rain originally copied from sandpaintings. Lily Tachane of the Farmington area weaves the Storm Pattern style. In addition, Mormon Navajos in the Two Grey Hills area, halfway between Gallup and Farmington, make exquisite rugs that sell for ten thousand dollars or more. No dyes of any kind are used, just wool from white, brown, and black sheep. The intricate patterns are woven as fine as

180 strands to the inch, from yarn spun on a simple hand spindle rolled on the thigh. Because of tight weaving, the rugs are strong and durable. A single rug can take up to a year to make. Among the weavers are Cora Curley and Ruth Polacca.

Jimmy Abeyta, a young Navajo artist living in Crown Point, northeast of Gallup, is one of the best oil painters of the Navajo, important enough to warrant a published biography. Having studied at the Art Institute of Chicago, he paints scenes on the reservation and portraits of his people with a rich, glowing impressionist style.

A number of other artists have been outstanding contributors. Lee Yazzie, another Navajo, is one of the best living Navajo silversmiths and jewelers and has won blue ribbons at every major Indian art competition in the Southwest. Wilbert Hunt, an Acoma Pueblo now living in Albuquerque, has traveled through Europe demonstrating silversmithing and has served as an LDS missionary teaching traditional arts among the peoples of the Southwest. Paul Enciso, an Apache/Pueblo who teaches at an LDS seminary in New Mexico, is a gifted weaver, potter, and silversmith and has taught traditional Indian art classes in government schools on the reservations. Agnes Dill, from Isleta Pueblo near Albuquerque, has been a leader in the creation and operation of the Pueblo Cultural Center.

In short, Latter-day Saints from Native American backgrounds are representative of one of the finest art-producing groups in the world. They create masterful works of art for collectors and museums throughout the world and are making major contributions to the artistic heritage of their cultures. They demonstrate that Mormonism has not annihilated Native cultures but, rather, has encouraged and promoted them.

About two miles northeast of San Juan College in Farmington lies an outdoor amphitheater that each summer provides a rendezvous with history, music, and legend. This outdoor musical pageant, staged among sandstone cliffs dotted with sagebrush and piñon pine, with a starry dome overhead, tells the story of Ira Hatch, Mormon missionary, and an orphaned Navajo-Paiute girl, Sarah-Mara Boots, whom he eventually married. The playwright was Sharon French, born in Shiprock, not far from the pageant site, and her work portrays Black Shawl, her own Navajo great-great-great grandmother. The pageant, entitled *Anasazi, the Ancient Ones*, entertains, but it also carries the message that all of us are cut from the same divine pattern. The pageant has now been presented to about twelve thousand persons in five summers. Most observers have gone away with a greater understanding of Indian history and legend and a greater respect for Indian people.[20]

One is struck by the insights of the "New Western History" in providing a fresh look at our past. Although the New Western Historians examine common people's devotion to family and community, they often exclude their activity on behalf of their religion and church. Yet religion, whether Pueblo, Navajo, Roman Catholic, Protestant, or Mormon, has long been an important part of the social and intellectual world of the Southwest. Frontier and modern New Mexico has nurtured many religious communities. Among these, the Mormons have maintained homogeneous social orders and continue to maintain religious neighborhoods and residential networks in metropolitan areas. Study of the faiths of New Mexico helps us remember the important role religion has played in the past and its equally important role today.

Notes

1. General Mormon history is treated in James B. Allen and Glen M. Leonard, *The Story of the Latter-day Saints*, 2d ed. (Salt Lake City: Deseret Book Company, 1992); Leonard J. Arrington and Davis Bitton, *The Mormon Experience: A History of the Latter-day Saints*, 2d ed. (Urbana: University of Illinois Press, 1992); and Jan Shipps, *Being Mormon: The Latter-day Saint Experience, 1941–1991* (Bloomington: Indiana University Press, forthcoming).

General New Mexico histories include: Warren Beck, *New Mexico: A History of Four Centuries* (Norman: University of Oklahoma Press, 1962); Frank D. Reeve, *History of New Mexico*, 3 vols. (New York: Lewis Historical Publishing Co., 1961); Erna Fergusson, *New Mexico: A Pageant of Three Peoples* (New York: Alfred A. Knopf, 1951); and George I. Sánchez, *Forgotten People: A Study of New Mexicans* (Albuquerque: Calvin Horn, 1967).

2. For background on the Mormon Battalion, see: Daniel Tyler, *A Concise History of the Mormon Battalion in the Mexican War* (n.p., 1881); Brigham H. Roberts, *The Mormon Battalion: Its History and Achievements* (Salt Lake City: Deseret Book Company, 1919); Brigham H. Roberts, *A Comprehensive History of the Church of Jesus Christ of Latter-day Saints*, 6 vols. (Salt Lake City: Deseret Book Company, 1930), 3: 60–122; Frank A. Golder et al., *The March of the Mormon Battalion* (New York, 1928); John F. Yurtinus, "A Ram in the Thicket: A History of the Mormon Battalion in the Mexican War" (Ph.D. diss., Brigham Young University, 1975).

3. Journal of Henry G. Boyle, 1824–88, typescript, Harold B. Lee Library, Brigham Young University, Provo, Utah.

4. Howard R. Lamar, "Jean Baptiste Charbonneau," in *The Reader's Encyclopedia of the American West*, ed. Lamar (New York: Thomas Y. Crowell, 1977), 190–91; and Ann W. Hafen, "Jean Baptiste Charbonneau," in *The Mountain Men and the Fur Trade of the Far West*, ed. Leroy R. Hafen, 10 vols. (Glendale, Calif.: Arthur H. Clark Co., 1965–70), 1: 205–24.

5. Cooke letter of 30 January 1847, in *Heart Throbs of the West*, ed. Kate B. Carter, 12 vols. (Salt Lake City: Daughters of Utah Pioneers, 1936–48), 1: 186–87.

6. Mormons in New Mexico are discussed in: Evon Z. Vogt and Ethel M. Albert, eds., *People of Rimrock: A Study of Values in Five Cultures* (Cambridge, Mass.: Harvard University Press, 1966); Gary Tietjen, *Mormon Pioneers in New Mexico* (Los Alamos, N.Mex.: Duplicated by the Author, 1980); *Do You Remember Luna? 100 Years, 1883–1983* (Luna, N.Mex.: Luna LDS Ward, 1983); H. Mannie Foster, "History of Mormon Settlements in Mexico and New Mexico" (master's thesis, University of New Mexico, 1937); and John F. Palmer, "Mormon Settlements in the San Juan Basin of Colorado and New Mexico"

(master's thesis, Brigham Young University, 1967).

7. The following professional and semiprofessional articles provide helpful background: Evon Z. Vogt and Thomas F. O'Dea, "A Comparative Study of the Role of Values in Social Action in Two Southwestern Communities," *American Sociological Review* 58 (December 1953): 645–54; Thomas F. O'Dea, "Mormonism and the Avoidance of Sectarian Stagnation: A Study of Church, Sect, and Incipient Nationality," *American Journal of Sociology* 60 (November 1954): 285–93; Thomas F. O'Dea, "The Effects of Geographical Position on Belief and Behavior in a Rural Mormon Village," *Rural Sociology* 19 (December 1954): 358–64; Irving Telling, "Ramah, New Mexico, 1876–1900: An Historical Episode with Some Value Analysis," *Utah Historical Quarterly* 21 (April 1953): 117–36; D. Michael Quinn, "Religion in the American West," in *Under an Open Sky: Rethinking America's Western Past*, ed. William Cronon, George Miles, and Jay Gitlin (New York: W. W. Norton, 1992), 145–66; and Robert T. Divett, "New Mexico and the Mormons," *Southwest Heritage* 6 (Spring 1976). I have also benefited from reading several interviews in the Oral History Collection of the Charles Redd Center for Western Studies at Brigham Young University and from correspondence with Howard F. Wolfgramm, Lyle and Wilma Porter, and Farrell and Lucintha Lines, but they are not to be held responsible for anything in this essay.

8. Specialized treatments of Mormon and other Native Americans include: Jerry and Lois Jacka, *Beyond Tradition: Contemporary Indian Art and its Evolution* (Flagstaff, Ariz.: Northland Publishing, 1988); Russell P. Hartman and Jan Musial, *Navajo Pottery: Traditions and Innovations* (Flagstaff, Ariz.: Northland Publishing, 1987); Jessie L. Embry, "Ethnic Groups and the LDS Church," *Dialogue* 25 (Winter 1992): 81–97; and Jessie L. Embry, "Separate but Equal? Black Branches, Genesis Groups, or Integrated Wards?" *Dialogue* 23 (Spring 1990): 11–37.

9. Paul H. Dunn in Oakland Stake, as quoted in Embry, "Ethnic Groups and the LDS Church," 84.

10. Oral History Interview with Jessie Embry, 78, transcript in Charles Redd Center for Western Studies, Brigham Young University.

11. Quoted in Embry, "Ethnic Groups and the LDS Church," 86.

12. Robert Hatch, interview with Ernesteen Lynch, 1989, 9, 11–12, Charles Redd Center.

13. Dr. Clark Knowlton, a professor of sociology at New Mexico Highlands University in Las Vegas, 1958–62, became president of the Las Vegas branch of the church, which at the time had about 170 Spanish-Americans and 130 Anglo-Americans. He established a Spanish-speaking Sunday school and "cottage meetings." In 1960 he was notified that all Spanish-speaking church meetings would be discontinued. Many Spanish-Americans became inactive; the all-English church policy destroyed a once-promising Spanish-

speaking branch. The policy was later reversed, but the Las Vegas branch never recovered. See Clark S. Knowlton, "Cultural Imperialism," *Dialogue* 21 (Winter 1988): 7–8.

14. The evolution of LDS organizational structure is traced in D. Michael Quinn, *The Mormon Hierarchy: Origins of Power* (Salt Lake City: Signature Books, 1994).

15. A recent compilation of contemporary essays about how Mormon women interact with church, family, and society is Maxine Hanks, ed., *Women and Authority: Re-emerging Mormon Feminism* (Salt Lake City: Signature Books, 1992). See also Jill Mulvay Derr, Janath Russell Cannon, and Maureen Ursenbach Beecher, *Women of Covenant: The Story of Relief Society* (Salt Lake City: Deseret Book, 1992).

16. A recent publication representing a typical view of many Mormon educators is Robert L. Millet, ed., *"To Be Learned Is Good If . . . "* (Salt Lake City: Bookcraft, 1987). This is characterized as "a response by Mormon educators to controversial religious questions."

17. For a discussion of this and other recent church policies, see Armand L. Mauss, *The Angel and the Beehive: The Mormon Struggle with Assimilation* (Urbana and Chicago: University of Illinois Press, 1994); and Marie Cornwall, Tim B. Heaton, and Lawrence A. Young, eds., *Contemporary Mormonism: Social Science Perspectives* (Urbana and Chicago: University of Illinois Press, 1994).

18. Several interviews and papers at the Charles Redd Center, Brigham Young University deal with this problem. See especially Jessie L. Embry, "Reactions of LDS Native Americans to the Excommunication of George P. Lee," typescript. See also George P. Lee, *Silent Courage: An Indian Story* (Salt Lake City: Deseret Book, 1987).

19. The following is based on Richard G. Oman, "LDS Southwest Indian Art," *The Ensign* 12 (September 1982): 33–48; Jacka, *Beyond Tradition*; Hartman and Musial, *Navajo Pottery*.

20. Margaret Cheasebro, "Journey into Anasazi Country," *This People* 10 (Summer 1989): 37-38, 41.

6

A Rhetorical Approach to Protestant Evangelism in Twentieth-Century New Mexico

Janice E. Schuetz

NEW MEXICO PROTESTANTS ADAPTED FORMS AND STYLES OF RHETORIC suited to the state's unique geographic and cultural environment. Rhetoric refers to the theory and practice of public discourse. An analysis of the form, content, and style of discourse of different evangelists involved in the prominent religious practices and events identified here showcases Protestant rhetoric in twentieth-century New Mexico. Rhetorical analysis seeks answers to several questions. How does social change occur, and what are the contributions of public discourse to this change? How do persuaders creatively use symbols to influence their audiences? How do persuaders overcome cultural obstacles to social influence?

Two prominent goals of New Mexico Protestants have been to convert others to religious belief and to influence public policy. Achieving these goals has been complicated. New Mexico audiences often have resisted religious persuasion because it clashed with their cultural norms, existing religious practices, and the complexities of the rural way of life.

This essay (1) investigates the evangelical goals of Protestant communicators by looking at conversion narratives and rural evangelism and (2) examines how Protestants changed public policy by legal action. New Mexico Protestants in the first half of the twentieth century borrowed from traditional modes of persuasion and devised forms uniquely suited to the multicultural and rural environment of the state. After 1950, Protestant rhetoric in New Mexico lost some of its cultural and rural character and became part of the institutional rhetoric of denominations and of the religious mass media.

Evangelical Goals

Evangelism means "any type of conversionary activity that tries to effect an authentic change in someone from one state of thinking and feeling to another."[1] Protestants in New Mexico sought individual converts who accepted Jesus as their Savior. Jon Alexander claims that the emphasis on personal conversions is "an essential feature of authentic [American] religion" resulting from the early colonists' values about representative government and religious freedom.[2]

From the beginning, the goals of New Mexico Protestant evangelists were ambitious, considering the domination of the state by Hispanic Catholics and Indians. Evangelists tried to convert Indians to Christianity, to make Hispanics into Protestants, and to bring the unchurched to Christian baptism. Additionally, they wanted all converts to adopt the values of cleanliness, efficiency, and hard work.

The rhetorical practices of evangelists changed as the century evolved. From 1900 to 1920, religious rhetors stressed education through missionary schools and distribution of Bibles and tracts. From 1920 to 1950, evangelists expanded their missionary efforts to include social, economic, and health assistance to Hispanics and Indians; made conscious efforts to ordain and train Hispanic and Indian clergy; and expanded their concept of ministry by emphasizing the needs of rural New Mexicans. From 1950 to 1990, many mainline Protestant churches abandoned aggressive personal evangelism and engaged in ecumenical cooperation. Active efforts to convert others continue in New Mexico today, especially as part of the evangelism of fundamentalist, Pentecostal, and Assemblies of God churches. These denominations are particularly active in training Navajo preachers to work on the reservation and to establish multicultural ministries in urban settings.[3] Other evangelism is carried out through mass media—paperback books, radio, television, audiotaped messages, and religious music.[4] Contemporary evangelism is so diffuse, however, that the secular public often pays little attention to evangelistic communicators until they enter the secular sphere by advocating prayer in schools, speaking out against abortion clinics, leading rallies against pornography, or lobbying for public policies opposing alcohol use and abuse.

Conversion Narratives

During the twentieth century, the conversion narrative has been a central rhetorical form for demonstrating the positive consequences of evangelism.

A conversion narrative is a simple story about how a person came to the Christian faith.

The content of the conversion narratives prior to 1950 drew upon themes used by revivalists of the turn-of-the-century Third Great Awakening led by Wilbur Chapman, Aimee Semple McPherson, and Billy Sunday. This type of evangelism mixed patriotism with religion, stressed separate spheres of religious activity for men and women within families and in religious contexts, and emphasized how converts could overcome sins caused by alcohol use, gambling, and sexual promiscuity by turning to the Bible and accepting Jesus.[5] Evangelists used many of these same themes to convert New Mexicans to Protestantism. For example, early New Mexico Baptists claimed that "evangelism means bringing the gospel to bear on unsaved humanity."[6] The conversion story played an important part in this message since it provided the verbal proof that the Bible could change people's lives.

Conversion narratives have several common features.[7] Not all narratives contain each feature, but they do share a common logical development. First, they show how the convert lacks knowledge, shows disinterest, or expresses hostility toward religion. Second, they indicate how the Bible makes potential converts aware of problems with their lack of religion, forces them to see their own sinfulness, and leads them to despair. Third, they make converts recognize that the Bible message of Jesus Christ will alleviate their despair. Fourth, they demonstrate how converts accept Jesus, seek forgiveness, and change their perspective. Instead of centering their lives on self, they center on God. Finally, they show the convert's experience of joy and renewal as the result of the conversion.

Traditionally, accounts of New Mexico conversion stories differed from this formal conceptual scheme in that they usually were truncated; that is, they contained only one or two facets of the complete conversion story. They functioned rhetorically like enthymemes; they expressed only part of the logic of the conversion scenario, and the reader or hearer had to fill in the missing premises and conclusions. Additionally, the storytellers often edited the narratives to prove the success of their evangelism to reflect positively on their work by taking credit for the conversions.

New Mexico conversion stories were of three types. The first type included stories about conversions from sin and unbelief to belief. Baptist, Methodist, Seventh-day Adventist, and Pentecostal literature provide many examples of converts addicted to alcohol who read the Bible and then turned to God. These conversion stories served both the denominational purpose of discouraging drinking and the political purpose of demonstrating the evils of the liberal alcohol policy in New Mexico.

A typical conversion of this kind was reported by Baptists in southern New Mexico in 1915.[8] An evangelist visited a "saloon man." The saloon man complained that he didn't like preachers because they emphasized unrealistic deathbed confessions. The evangelist refuted this claim and invited the saloon man to a revival. When the saloon man came, the preacher pleaded with him: "Give me your hand and God your heart." Later in the service, the saloon man joined the church, accepted baptism, and swore off liquor forever. In his explanation the evangelist edited this story so that it stressed how he made the saloon man become aware of his own sinfulness, accept Jesus, and reform his life.

In another instance, William H. Hodge recorded the conversion story of a Navajo, Joe Sandoval, who became a member of an Albuquerque Pentecostal church in 1963.[9] Sandoval's family was plagued by witch attacks. These misfortunes drove him to drink whiskey and use peyote. Eventually, Sandoval recalled how he was stricken with tuberculosis and spent nine years in a sanitarium. During his stay at the sanitarium, he read the Bible and prayed that if he were cured of tuberculosis he would convert to Christianity. His illness was cured; he then accepted Jesus and transformed his life. This personal story emphasized Sandoval's sinfulness, despair, acceptance of Jesus, and reward of a better life.

A second type of story showed the conversions of Catholics to Protestantism. These stories were especially prevalent prior to 1920 in the literature of Protestant missionaries who believed that Roman Catholicism was anti-Bible, superstitious, Romanist, pagan, authoritarian, and idolatrous.[10] This anti-Catholic conversion story became less common among mainline Protestants after 1940, but it often was replaced with anti-Mormon, anti–Seventh-day Adventist, and anti–Christian Science stories. One contemporary Church of Christ pastor claims that he now uses conversion stories to show his church's opposition to cults, gangs, and devil worshipers—groups that lead people away from the Bible.[11]

The conversion of a successful Presbyterian pastor and convert, Gabino Rendon, typified the anti-Catholic conversion story. Rendon recalls his conversion in his memoirs.[12] He tells how he heard about Bendito, a Catholic who sold vegetables to a Protestant grocer owning a Bible. Bendito eventually got up enough courage to ask the grocer to borrow the Bible even though his mother thought it a sin. Upon reading the Bible, one verse continued to hound Bendito; the verse was "I am the way, the truth and the life." This verse made Bendito realize that salvation was not gained by saying "Hail Marys," by praying to the saints, or by attending Mass. Bendito eventually lost his family but "gave his life to Jesus Christ." Rendon recalled, "By the time I read this story, I was no longer reading about Bendito, I was Bendito."

This story had rhetorical power because it ridiculed Catholic beliefs and practices, elevated the Bible to a central position in faith, and showed how the narrator succeeded in overcoming the ethnic-religious indoctrination of his youth. This narrative also expressed the joy and success of the conversion because Gabino Rendon eventually became an evangelist and a prominent Presbyterian pastor.[13]

One Baptist story went even further in renouncing Catholicism. It claimed that a Catholic husband abused his wife because she was Protestant. The story noted that "there have been times when he would string her up by the neck until her toes would barely touch the floor. This was his method of trying to make a Catholic out of her." She remained a converted Protestant and refused to go to the priest for confession.[14] This narrative differed from other conversion narratives because it stressed the pain and suffering that some converts endured as the result of their conversions, at the same time as the story ridiculed the Roman Catholic practice of confession. As an enthymeme, the story led Protestant readers to conclude that not only is the Catholic church undesirable but that its devout church members may be abusive even to their own family members.

A third kind of narrative emphasized the conversion of Indians, especially members of the Navajo Nation. The conversion of Navajos was problematic prior to 1920 because Protestant churches gained so few members, even though they spent a great deal of time and money on this missionary goal. Historians claim that from the time of the Great Awakening to the present day, missionaries were eager to convert Indians because they considered it their duty to bring the Gospel and to impose sectarian behavioral norms of cleanliness, sexual purity, and the Protestant work ethic on Indians.[15]

This explicit statement of New Mexican Protestants' goals regarding the Indian appeared in the Presbyterian journal *La Aurora* at the beginning of this century:

> To Christianize the Indian is to make a loyal citizen of him. . . .
> Christianity is the only hope of the Indian educationally. . . .
> Christianity is the only hope of the Indian morally and socially. . . .
> Christianity is the only hope of the Indian spiritually.[16]

After decades of missionary work to the Indians, Pastor R. A. Pryor reported in 1937 that his Baptist mission distributed food, taught sewing, and brought medical care to Navajos. He claimed that sixty-two "have come forward and have given us their hand as an indication of their acceptance of God. . . . Many have shown a change of heart while others go on living the same way."[17] Even though this tentative account suggested hope for conversions, it presented no conversion narrative. This type of information, however, provided evidence to mission supporters that missions were successful and warranted additional financial support.

Actual conversions depended on a change of heart, and evangelists on the reservation sometimes may have been deceived by Navajos who came forward during altar calls for reasons other than their acceptance of Christianity. While attending services of evangelists on the Navajo reservation in the 1970s, Wendy Grayson recalled that she and members of her family often went forward to the altar call because they expected to get clothes and other material rewards from the evangelists. She had no recollection of what denomination had "converted" her or any religious obligations she incurred.[18]

Since the 1960s Pentecostal and Bible-based denominations have demonstrated success in converting Navajo Indians and in keeping them as active members. When in 1963 Herman Sanchez converted to a Pentecostal denomination, he recalled that he had been very ill from infections that forced him to use peyote to relieve the pain. His brother, a member of an Albuquerque Pentecostal denomination, urged him to give up peyote and attend church. His church attendance forced him to read the Bible, understand himself, and accept Jesus. He accepted Jesus and expressed a desire to return to the Navajo reservation and preach the gospel to his people.[19] This conversion story fits well with the traditional genre of conversion narratives; it begins with sin and despair, notes the conditions of finding Jesus, and indicates the positive effects of conversion. These types of conversion narratives have become part of the contemporary Pentecostal church on the reservation, where most of the services are conducted by Navajo preachers who understand the needs of the people. Such narratives commonly appear as part of testimonials and in healing services.[20]

Between 1900 and 1940, the conversion story was an integral part of the report of missionaries to the boards who supported them and to potential converts attending religious services. After 1940, the conversion story appeared less in the rhetoric of mainline churches but retained a central place in the preaching, media, and services of Pentecostal and conservative churches. Currently, conversion stories symbolize the growth and vitality of individual ministries, the power of emotional outreach, and the success of conversions among Indians, dissatisfied Hispanics, and the unchurched. Most conversion stories operate like self-fulfilling prophecies; they prove that evangelist's goals are worthwhile and achievable.

Contemporary media feature conversion narratives involving public figures in best-selling paperback books. For example, in the 1970s the conversion stories of Watergate accomplice Charles Colson and of paralyzed athlete

Joni Eareckson were best-sellers nationwide. The religious talk shows, such as 700 Club, broadcast throughout the state, typically feature a story about someone who converted to Jesus following a life of stress or sin. Contemporary religious radio stations in New Mexico feature talk formats encouraging callers to tell their conversion stories to the listeners. Since the 1940s, radio evangelists have broadcast in the Spanish and Navajo languages.

Colporters and Circuit Riders

The preaching of the ordained and lay evangelists spread Protestantism into rural New Mexico. These evangelists sought conversions through preaching in churches, visits and literature dissemination, education and social work, and interdenominational revivals and camp meetings. What made New Mexico preaching unique was not the content as much as it was the context for the evangelism. This context featured vast distances between towns; boom or bust occupations of mining, cattle raising, and farming; and populations composed of diverse ethnic backgrounds and languages. This preaching context demanded tremendous energy and commitment from evangelists who struggled to bring the Bible to locations where people lived and worked.

A major difficulty of delivering evangelism in New Mexico involved the sparse population and long distances. This challenge was met by the colporter and the circuit rider, evangelists who served rural New Mexico until the 1960s.

"Colporters" are distributors of tracts and devotional literature. Colporters in New Mexico, however, did much more than disseminate Bibles and tracts. A report of a Baptist colporter in 1914 revealed the following list of accomplishments for nine months: traveled 1,770 miles, delivered 150 sermons, made 387 religious visits, baptized 9, baptized 21 by letter, distributed 7,095 pages of tracts, sold 92 Bibles, and gave away 85 Bibles.[21] Baptist colporters recommended that their people read the work of these popular American evangelists—Dwight Moody's *Prevailing Prayers* and *Great Sermons*, Harry Drummond's *Ideal Life*, Horace Bushnell's *The Character of Jesus*—along with the Protestant Bible.[22] They also distributed pamphlets on family and home, novels about successful American leaders, and poems celebrating American values such as individualism. Early New Mexico colporters traveled with horse and buggy or by train; later colporters traveled by automobile. They all served the same goals; they brought religious literature, visited residents, and preached the message of the Gospel. Through these means they persuaded people about the importance of religion by being available both as minister and counselor, by reinforcing the evangelical message, by organizing religious Sunday schools and fostering group study of the Bible, and by preaching the message of the Bible.[23]

One of New Mexico's successful colporters was Sherwood Young (S.Y.) Jackson, a Baptist. He worked as a colporter from 1900 to 1924. During this time he traveled thousands of miles, delivered hundreds of sermons, visited hundreds of families, and started several schools. He traveled throughout the state. His main work was in the South and East where he made frequent stops at Hyer, Las Cruces, Texico, Clovis, Melrose, Taiban, and Fort Sumner. He also worked in the northern sector of the state at Aztec, La Plata, Bloomfield, Flora Vista, and Farmington. His daughter Mae reflected on her father's work in this way: "They were brave and courageous people who settled this land.... Some of them had it terribly rough. Daddy tried to take hope to them.... They would gather in a home, in a saloon, in a store" and talk about Jesus and the Bible.[24]

Presbyterians, Methodists, Episcopalians, and Seventh-day Adventists also had their versions of the colporter. The Spanish-speaking lay and ordained evangelists, who traveled for the Presbyterian Home Missions until the 1920s, also distributed Bibles, visited families in remote areas, preached, and discussed the Bible. Some of this work was done by Presbyterians Juan Quintana and Nicholas Gurule.[25] Methodist circuit riders also were assigned to several locations within a region. They traveled long distances to preach, distribute tracts, conduct Sunday schools, and visit families.[26] Seventh-day Adventists made use of colporters on the Navajo reservation into the 1960s. Episcopalian Hunter Lewis took trains and buses throughout the state; he visited ranch houses, prayed with families, and established dozens of small missions.[27] In most areas, the need for colporters and circuit riders had been eliminated by the 1970s through the advent of modern transportation, the presence of support groups in organized churches, the availability of mass-produced books and tracts, and the prevalence of religious radio and television evangelistic programs.

Cowboy Camp Meetings

Evidence that the need for religious instruction in rural areas is not always met by contemporary mass media appears in the popularity of the cowboy camp meeting, an event that had its roots in the itinerant preaching of rural evangelists, colporters, and circuit riders but still takes place today. The yearly cowboy camp meeting now occurs in six states, but it began in New Mexico in 1940 and continues now as an annual summer event.

The idea of the cowboy camp meeting was inspired by the evangelical work of Ralph J. Hall and Roger Bennett Sherman. Hall recalled that during his early years he preached to newly arrived laborers flocking into southern New Mexico for jobs in the oil fields in the 1920s and 1930s. He remembered preaching in abandoned stores, among oil rigs, and in the open areas around the camp fire. He claimed that he often preached several sermons per day.[28]

Roger Bennett Sherman started as a cowboy evangelist in the Magdalena area of west-central New Mexico. He described his method of evangelism in this way:

One feature of my ministry is visiting the ranch homes, helping them occasionally with cattle, rounding them up, branding, bringing them into the shipping pens. In this way friendships are established. When they see you are willing to work, and that you can take the long rides, the heat, the cold, the wind, the hunger, along with the rest of them, then when you want to talk to them about spiritual things they are more willing to listen.[29]

The goals and format of cowboy camp meetings today resemble the tent services of revivalists during the Third Great Awakening. Yet the message differs from that of the early evangelists because it does not emphasize sin and evil, does not pressure participants to accept an altar call, and does not seek to convert those who are already members of a church.[30] Instead, the goal of the meeting is to bring Christianity to those without a church. For some participants, conversion may be the goal of the meeting, but for others the meeting deepens and enriches their existing faith. The evangelists hosting the meetings use a variety of persuasive means to reach their goals. They encourage several forms of religious expression—preaching, Bible study, prayer, music, common meals, and appreciation of an outdoor environment conducive to concentration. Generally the camp meeting tries to influence people toward an exemplary Christian life.

The entire four-day meeting is planned and financed by laypersons. As many as twelve hundred people attend a single camp meeting.[31] The format for the last forty-three years of the camp meeting was established at the first meeting at Nogal Mesa, located near Carizozo, New Mexico. The camp meeting usually runs from Thursday to Sunday evening on a scheduled weekend in the summer. The daily schedule is 6:30 A.M. for breakfast, family prayer at 8:30 A.M., preaching service at 11:00 A.M., lunch at 12:30 P.M., preaching service at 2:00 P.M., prayer service at 4:00 P.M., supper at 6:00 P.M., and campfire service at 7:00 P.M. The focus is nondenominational. Persons from Presbyterian, Methodist, Church of Christ, Baptist, Lutheran,

Assemblies of God, and Episcopal churches attend. Singing is an important part of the services. The favorite theme song is "Showers of Blessings," but other songs are common, such as "The Old Rugged Cross" and "Home on the Range." The meetings mix traditional secular songs with religious ones and Bible stories with cowboy and rural lore. On the final day of the camp meeting, preachers ask the unchurched and the backsliders to come forward and accept Jesus Christ as their Savior.[32] The camp meeting advocates traditional Protestant Bible instruction, nondenominational and upbeat religious values, and rural outdoor community experience.

The message is subtle and inspirational, emphasizing a kind, concerned, and available Jesus. This excerpt from one of Sherman's sermons at a camp meeting reflects the content of the evangelistic message of contemporary meetings:

> Man is powerless when he struggles alone. Oh yes, he may be able to amass great wealth, make a great name for himself, achieve renown in many fields of endeavor, but until a man is certain that there is help for him in times of testing, in the struggle of right with wrong, of evil with good—the case is hopeless. . . . Don't we see, don't we understand that the situation is hopeless without the Divine Presence; that we will go on being tempted, tried, and defeated without one standing by to whom all power is given in heaven and on earth.[33]

Ralph J. Hall emphasized the type of content he used in the final appeal for the unchurched to come forward, an appeal given at the campfire on the final night of the four-day meeting. He recalled these words as a typical altar call:

> You don't have to be in a big church building with big crowds of people, but you can give your heart and life to Christ right now. . . . Christ is here. I have heard the whispering of his voice in the beauty and glory of this precious place. . . . I know my Lord can and will help you if you will accept him as your Savior.[34]

Although both Hall and Sherman have passed away, they serve as models for preaching content that lives on in the contemporary cowboy camp meetings.

Prayer and music emphasize the theme of seeking God, sharing in the grace of His kingdom, and rugged individualism. The theme song of "Showers of Blessings" expresses the outcome organizers hope the meeting will have on participants, who sing the theme many times during the four-day meeting. Prayer rituals focus on a personal relationship to God. Men gather around a prayer tree, women gather at the tabernacle tent, and the youth gather at the cook's tent for prayer. The prayer time encourages participants to seek divine guidance and to share their religious needs with others. Camp meeting rituals and traditions emphasize the importance of personal salvation, a key feature of the evangelical spirit of New Mexico Protestantism.[35]

The response to the altar call at the end of the meeting is visual rather than verbal. The person who wishes to accept Jesus comes forward and stands at the front of the assembly next to the preacher. The conversion is personal and symbolic; it lacks the verbal detail and the public proclamations associated with early missionary evangelists and with some contemporary Pentecostal services.

Civic Goals

In addition to achieving evangelical goals, New Mexico Protestants showed their rhetorical skills in promoting civic goals by their advocacy in controversial legal trials. This advocacy emphasized the collective rights of the people to practice their religion freely without intrusions from the state. In one situation, the rhetorical advocacy of New Mexico Protestants supporting public schools placed them on the national stage from 1947 to 1951 in the famed "Dixon case." A discussion of the Dixon case background, its legal processes, and the religious consequences of the case illustrate this kind of Protestant advocacy.

Background

In 1881 New Mexico passed a public school law to combat the high rate of illiteracy among its citizens. This law gained force in 1910 with provisions "for the establishment and maintenance of a system of public schools which shall be open to the children of said state and free from sectarian control, and that said school shall always be conducted in English." The Constitution also claimed that "no person shall be required to attend any place of worship or support any religious sector or denomination" nor "shall preference be given to any religious denomination."[36]

To the dismay of Protestants, however, these provisions failed to make public education truly public. In 1915 Baptists lamented that bills were pending in the state legislature to support "Catholic institutions, schools, and hospitals.... [even when] it is clearly against the Constitution of the United States to appropriate public money for sectarian institutions."[37] By 1938, the extent of public subsidy of the sectarian schools nationwide was extensive: forty-two states, including New Mexico, gave direct aid to sectarian schools; eight states, including New Mexico, provided free transportation to students attending parochial schools; and three states, including New Mexico, provided textbooks to schools. This practice resulted in law suits in a number of states.[38]

New Mexico Protestants got involved in this controversy over church and state in 1947 in the small rural community of Dixon. For many years members of Catholic religious orders had taught public school in a Dixon church. In 1947, citizens raised enough money to build an independent public school. After the school was built, however, the local school board hired a nun as the school principal, and she staffed the school with several members of her religious order. This prompted the development of the Free Schools Committee. Originally it was composed of Reverend Portirio Romero, pastor of the Presbyterian church of Dixon; Miss Olive Bowen, sister of the superintendent of the Embudo hospital; Lydia Zellers, daughter of a former pastor and wife of the leading merchant in Dixon; Reverend Paul Stevens, pastor of the Presbyterian church in Taos; and Kenneth Kesler, pastor of the Presbyterian church in Santa Fe. Although the founders of the protest group were Presbyterians, 75 percent of the community were not Catholic. The non-Catholic citizens consisted of Pentecostals, Seventh-day Adventists, Mormons, and Presbyterians. Other Protestant groups from around New Mexico expressed support of the legal fight of the Free Schools Committee.[39]

The case had a long history. In 1947 citizens organized by the Free Schools Committee filed a complaint against the county school board. The complaint was not resolved at the local level but was referred to the State Board of Education, who then held closed hearings but failed to solve the dispute. The adverse public commentary about Catholic domination of public schools in all of the major newspapers in the state caused Archbishop Edwin Byrne to issue a statement to the 145 clergy teaching in New Mexico public schools forbidding them from teaching Catholic religion to their public school pupils. The bishop's action did not satisfy the Free Schools Committee.

The Legal Process

After the Board of Education failed to act to oppose Catholic domination of public schools, Protestants filed a civil suit on March 10, 1948, in the District Court in Santa Fe, under the title of *Zellers* (representing twenty-eight plaintiffs) v. *Raymond Huff* (representing 235 defendants). The two-week trial began in October 1948 in Santa Fe in the Court of Judge E. T. Hensley, Jr., Harry L. Bigbee represented the plaintiffs, and Joe L. Martinez, state attorney general, represented the defendants. The plaintiffs asked that all schools named in the complaint be declared parochial schools and ineligible to receive public funds; that all members of Catholic teaching orders be forever barred from teaching in New Mexico public schools; that salaries being paid teaching orders be declared illegal expenditure of public funds, that no New Mexico tax supported schools be conducted in church-owned property; that ... school boards [be barred] from ever hiring or paying any member of a Catholic teaching order as a teacher in a tax supported school.[40]

The motivation for the civil suit, according to the plaintiffs, stemmed from three problems. First, non-Catholic children had been forced for years by their Catholic clergy teachers to say Catholic prayers, go to confession, read Catholic books, go to Mass, attend Catholic religious instruction, and pay homage to Catholic saints. Second, the school board, state public school administrators, church leaders, and teachers conspired to violate the rights of non-Catholic children. These violations cost the state about one-half million dollars per year. Third, the state policy subsidized clergy, paid for religious learning materials, and in doing so, violated the principles of the U.S. Constitution and the New Mexico Constitution regarding separation of church and state.[41]

The trial proceeded tediously through the calling of dozens of the defendants to testify. By far the greatest amount of testimony came from the nuns of the religious orders serving in the twenty-six public schools subsidized by state funds. Each segment of testimony got the defendants to admit they wore religious garb, used Catholic instructional materials, and encouraged children to attend Catholic services. Additionally, witnesses for the clergy admitted that they owed their allegiance to their religious order and to religious authority, rather than to local school boards and state and local administrators.

The most interesting testimony in the case came from Protestant children. For example, Samuel Pachecho, a non-Catholic, testified about the use of Catholic prayers. He said, "In the morning when we first went in and then oh, in the evening, when we were dismissed, they knelt and prayed the Hail Mary and Our Father, and Act of Contrition." When attorney Bigbee asked him if he knelt or prayed with them, Pachecho answered, "Yes, I kneeled, I didn't pray."[42] The drama of the trial pitted the testimony of young Protestant children against their Catholic clergy teachers. The repetitious and dramatic testimony of the Protestant children showed they were the subjects of Catholic domination in the public schools.

The Protestants won a major victory for the separation of church and state on March 12, 1948, when Judge Hensley presented the decision of the court. He banned clergy from teaching in public schools; required that no public school would be held in church buildings; terminated free bus transportation for parochial students; prohibited the use of state-purchased textbooks for parochial students; barred the teaching of sectarian doctrines and the use of religious artifacts; and prohibited the use of state funds for sectarian instruction. Although the judge's decision supported the goals of the Protestant plaintiffs, they appealed the case by asking the New Mexico Supreme Court to disqualify all Catholic clergy from teaching in public schools. The plaintiffs won this appeal in 1951.

Effects

The Dixon case symbolized a midcentury transition, moving from a state where Roman Catholics dominated the religious and the political culture to one where Protestants had the Constitutional right to practice religion free from the Catholic domination that had affected them for the past hundred years.

Even after the victory in *Zellers* v. *Huff*, this case clearly did not entirely settle the question of separation of church and state. A different type of church–state issue surfaced in 1953 in Jemez, New Mexico. After securing an ordinance to hold services at Jemez Pueblo, Lee Roebuck performed Baptist services at the home of J. R. Toledo. The Indian Council protested: "The Pueblo is Catholic and we want no one winning the people away from their faith." Protestants were not allowed to advertise their church meeting, hold services, or bury their dead on the Jemez Pueblo. Several members of the pueblo protested this action and filed suit against Jemez Pueblo on August 3, 1953. This case eventually was thrown out on the grounds that it was subject to federal jurisdiction.[43]

In 1969, a bill was introduced in the state legislature for state-supported, unlimited indirect aid to parochial schools. After extensive lobbying by Baptist Dale Danielson and other Protestants from the Albuquerque branch of Americans United for Separation of Church and State, the legislation failed.[44] A proposal for offering state aid to parochial schools surfaced again and failed in 1981.

Despite some cracks in the wall between church and state, the Dixon case brought public attention to the need to separate religious culture from political policy. In doing so, the case echoed several national religious trends that affected American Protestantism. First, it demonstrated that the courts would not tolerate sectarian denomination of public institutions. Second, the case showed cooperation between Pentecostals, Mormons, Seventh-day Adventists, and Presbyterians—diverse denominations with a stake in protecting the religious rights of children.

The case also had implications for the voice of Protestants in New Mexico. First, the legal success of the Protestants showed their ability to challenge deeply embedded political practices favoring Catholics. Second, the case brought national attention to the rights of Protestants in New Mexico, showing they were no longer just a struggling cultural minority.[45] Third, the case renewed anti-Catholic sentiment among Protestants that was not publicly reconciled until the New Mexico Conference of Churches voted to allow Catholics to be members in 1967. Finally, the case demonstrated that religion, even when it is deeply embedded in culture, must be distinct from secular culture and institutions.

Today the church–state issues have moved far beyond the Dixon case. By the mid-1980s, Protestant and Catholic denominations under the leadership of the New Mexico Conference of Churches joined together to lobby for legislation supporting prison reform and health care for children and homeless adults. They also jointly fought against gambling and liberal alcohol use and distribution laws. Ironically, by the 1980s a task force of the New Mexico Conference of Churches had expanded its membership to include Jews and Christian Scientists and was advocating nonsectarian instruction about world religions in the public schools.[46]

Conclusion

Rhetoric, then, has been an important part of the life and mission of the Protestant churches of New Mexico, and how the particular historical circumstances in the state led Protestants to develop distinctive rhetorical strategies. Two areas especially stand out, one in evangelistic outreach and the other in legal advocacy.

With respect to evangelism, New Mexico Protestants created a special style appropriate to its frontier and multicultural environment. Conversion story techniques developed in the East as part of the Second and Third Great Awakenings were transformed in New Mexico into ways of bringing in converts from Roman Catholic and even Native American traditions. Similarly, New Mexico camp meetings took on a cowboy flavor. Circuit riders and colporteurs likewise adapted their methods to a state with greater distances and greater ethnic variety than had been otherwise common. Many of these distinctive ways of practicing evangelism continue today, even when they have been modified by the mass media and the new climate of ecumenical cooperation.

New Mexico Protestants have also made a definite contribution to civic goals by their rhetorical advocacy in legal contexts, as in the Dixon school case. In this situation, Protestants of diverse kinds, including some not usually allied in ecumenical circles, joined together to create a political climate for change and to make their legal case.

In these two ways, Protestants in New Mexico have used effective rhetorical strategies, at the same time as they were transforming these ways of persuasion to fit the special demographic and ethnic features of the state. The methods of the circuit rider and the colporter live today in the voice and face of the radio and television evangelists, even while the changing relationships among state ethnic groups and among the Protestant denominations themselves influence the message in subtle but significant ways.

Notes

1. William Packard, *Evangelism in America: From Tents to TV* (New York: Paragon Books, 1988), 1.

2. Jon Alexander, *American Personal Religious Accounts: 1600–1800* (New York: Edward Mellon Press, 1983), 3.

3. The success of these religious groups in training Navajo evangelists is explained in David Scates, *Why Navajo Churches Are Growing: The Cultural Dynamics of Navajo Religious Change* (Grand Junction, Colo.: Navajo Christian Churches, 1981). An example of a successful urban evangelical community is Calvary Chapel in Albuquerque.

4. One excellent source that explains the persuasiveness of mass media in contemporary religious culture is Quentin J. Schultze, *American Evangelicals and the Mass Media* (Grand Rapids, Mich.: Academie Books, 1990).

5. This period is discussed in William G. McLoughlin, *Modern Revivalism* (New York: Ronald Press, 1959), and *Revivals, Awakenings, and Reforms* (Chicago: University of Chicago Press, 1978); and Betty A. DeBerg, *Ungodly Women: Gender and the First Wave of American Fundamentalism* (Minneapolis: Fortress Press, 1990).

6. "Evangelism," *New Mexico Baptist* 2 (21 July 1909): 2.

7. These characteristics are adapted from Jerald C. Brauer, "Conversion: From Puritanism to Revivalism," *Journal of Religion* 58 (1978): 227–43.

8. "Evangelism of Brother Wyars," *Baptist New Mexican* 4 (15 September 1915): 2.

9. William H. Hodge, "Navajo Pentecostalism," *Anthropological Quarterly* 37 (July 1984): 88.

10. These conclusions are drawn by Mark T. Banker, "They Made Haste Slowly: Presbyterian Mission schools and Southwestern Pluralism, 1870–1920" (Ph.D. diss., University of New Mexico, 1987); Alice Blake, "Presbyterians of New Mexico," unpublished manuscript, Menaul Historical Library of the Southwest, Menaul School, Albuquerque, 1935; and Randi Jones Walker, *Protestantism in the Sangre de Cristos* (Albuquerque: University of New Mexico Press, 1991).

11. Interview with Sam Soleyn, Church of Christ pastor and local religious television host, conducted by the author, Albuquerque, N.Mex., 15 April 1993.

12. Gambino Rendon, *Hand on My Shoulder*, as told to Edith Agnew, rev. ed. (New York: Board of National Mission of the United Presbyterian Church of the U.S., 1953), 46.

13. Handwritten recollections appear in Gabino Rendon Papers, "As a Presbyterian Missionary," memoirs, n.d., Menaul Historical Library of the Southwest, Menaul School, Albuquerque.

14. "Revivalism," *Baptist New Mexican* 5 (10 September 1925): 1.

15. See John F. Freeman, "The Indian Convert: Theme and Variation," *Ethnohistory* 12 (Spring

1965): 113–28; Michael J. Warner, "Protestant Missionary Activity among the Navajos, 1890–1920," *New Mexico Historical Review* 45 (July 1970): 209–32.

16. "Christianity: The Only Hope of Indians," *La Aurora* 2 (21 Marzo 1902): 1.

17. "Home Mission Report of R. A. Pryor," *Baptist New Mexican* 2 (29 April 1937): 1–2.

18. Interview with Wendy Grayson conducted by author, Albuquerque, 4 November 1993.

19. Hodge, "Navajo Pentecostalism," 68.

20. Scates, *Why Navajo Churches Are Growing*, 84–85.

21. "Colporter's Report," *Baptist New Mexican* 2 (31 August 1914): 3.

22. E. P. Aldredge, "Tracts Recommended," *Baptist New Mexican* 1 (February-March 1912): 3.

23. Baptist colporter evangelism is discussed in Martin L. Massaglia, "Colporter Ministries," *Foundations* 24 (October-December 1981): 328–39. The use of Seventh-day Adventist colporters on the Navajo reservation is mentioned by Betty Stirling, *Mission to the Navajo* (Mountain View, Calif.: Pacific Press, 1961), 101–3.

24. My information about S. Y. Jackson comes from "S. Y. Jackson, King of the Colporters," an unpublished manuscript by Betty Danielson, found in her private collection of Baptist history in Albuquerque.

25. Numerous references appear in Alice Blake, "Presbyterians of New Mexico."

26. References to circuit riders and their work appear in Bryan Hall, *A Brief History of Methodist Churches* (Albuquerque: New Mexico Methodist Conference Archives, 1965). Hall identifies the following men as exemplary circuit riders: J. P. Terry, W. L. Self, J. D. Waggoner, T. A. Knight, and C. H. Hatsfield.

27. Rev. James M. Stoney, *Lighting the Candle: The Episcopal Church on the Upper Rio Grande* (Santa Fe, N.Mex.: Rydal Press, 1961).

28. See Ralph J. Hall, *The Main Trail* (San Antonio, Tex.: Naylor Publishing, 1971); "Memoirs of a Cowboy Preacher," *Presbyterian Life* 20 (15 November 1971): 17–19, 34–37; and "Ralph T. Hall Oral History," 1982, audiotape 35C, Menaul Historical Library of the Southwest, Menaul School, Albuquerque.

29. This recollection appears in Roger Bennett Sherman, "Christ's Great Promise," Sermon Collection, n.d., Menaul Historical Library of the Southwest, Menaul School, Albuquerque, 302.

30. See McLoughlin, *Revivals, Awakenings, and Reforms.*

31. Several testimonials emphasize this point in T. Wyatt, *Cowboy Camp Meetings* (Albuquerque: New Mexico Methodist Conference Archives, 1993). Other sources for this information are Paul Schubert, "Religion Hits the Road," *Saturday Evening Post* 229 (30 March 1957): 20–24; "Buelah Jackson Oral History," 1982, audiotape 34C, Menaul Historical Library of the Southwest, Menaul School, Albuquerque.

32. Wyatt, *Cowboy Camp Meet-*

ings; and Sherman, "Christ's Great Promise."

33. Sherman, "Christ's Great Promise," 304.

34. Hall, "Memoirs of a Cowboy Preacher," 18.

35. These features are affirmed in "Ralph T. Hall Oral History."

36. Constitution of the State of New Mexico, 1910 (Section 2, Articles l and 2).

37. "Public Taxes," *Baptist New Mexican* 3 (15 February 1915): 3.

38. Two sources explain the history of public subsidy of parochial schools: L. H. Lehmann, *The Catholic Church and Public Schools* (New York: Aurora Publications, 1947); and Leland Wayne Corbin, "The Educational Activities of the Evangelical United Brethren in New Mexico" (master's thesis, University of New Mexico, 1949).

39. This information appears in the Free Schools Committee Pamphlet, n.d., Dixon file, Menaul Historical Library of the Southwest, Menaul School, Albuquerque.

40. These charges appear in Free Schools Committee Pamphlet, n.d., Dixon file, Menaul Historical Library of the Southwest, Menaul School, Albuquerque. The charges also are part of the Trial Record, *Zellers v. Huff*, 1948, case number 5332 (Santa Fe: New Mexico Supreme Court Library), and *Zellers v. Huff*, 55 N.M. 501, 1951.

41. *Zellers v. Huff*, 1951.

42. Trial Record, *Zellers v. Huff*, 1427.

43. Betty Danielson, "The Struggle for Liberty in New Mexico" in Betty Danielson's private papers on Baptist history, n.d., Albuquerque.

44. "New Mexico's Agony," *Church and State* (November 1969): 3.

45. Stories about the case appeared nationwide in the Protestant and the secular press. See *Time Magazine,* 29 September 1947; Frank S. Mead, "Shadows Over the Public Schools," *Christian Herald,* February 1948; and Harold E. Fey, "They Stand for Free Schools," *Christian Century,* 2 July 1947; "Editorial Comment," *Christian Science Monitor,* 24–26 January 1948; and Lee O. Barber, "Supreme Court Defines Church–State Separation," *The Nation's Schools,* February 1952, 59.

46. See unpublished pamphlet entitled "Religious Studies and Public Education" n.d., New Mexico Conference of Churches, Albuquerque.

7

Boomer Dharma

The Evolution of Alternative Spiritual Communities in Modern New Mexico

Stephen Fox

IN 1993, TWENTY-FIVE YEARS AFTER THE INITIAL PEAK OF SPIRITUAL innovation by the countercultures of the late 1960s, a wide range of alternative religious groups in New Mexico continued evolving in form and content. As their twenty-fifth anniversaries approached, several of the most prominent reached developmental milestones. New Buffalo, the first and most famous 1960s commune in the state, once featured in the film *Easy Rider*, was reincarnated as an Arroyo Hondo bed and breakfast. Farther north, the Lama Foundation, scene of many retreats led by the Hindu initiate Ram Dass, formerly Richard Alpert of Harvard, celebrated a quarter-century as an ecumenical monastery. In Abiquiu, the Dar al-Islam Muslim community, with its adobe mosque designed by the world-renowned Egyptian architect Hasan Fathy, held the first-ever North American Muslim Powwow, although friction between Islamic sects had slowed Dar al-Islam's community growth. The enterprising, turban-wearing Sikhs of the Española Valley returned in 1993 to a quieter level of life, after health and lawsuit problems during the 1980s dimmed the vigor of their leader, Yogi Bhajan. The metaphysical and therapeutic group now known as Southwestern College, in Santa Fe, became a candidate for national accreditation to give master's degrees in counseling. And in 1993, Buddhist centers in Santa Fe Canyon, Jemez Springs, and Albuquerque were under the leadership of women, the most revolutionary innovation of American Buddhism.

Founded in New Mexico between 1963 and the 1980s, these groups cover a huge range of spiritual cultures and show distinct signs in 1993 of continuing adaptation to their American/New Mexican environment in five ways: (1) in the struggles of community and "center"-building; (2) in activist service vs. monastic self-study; (3) in clashes between Asian authority and American democracy; (4) in the emerging role of women; (5) and in a mass-cultural eclecticism making formerly secret teachings into a modern vernacular.

This essay will present an historical overview of alternative spiritual paths in the state, with some aspects of struggles toward community development. The emphasis is not on comparative analysis of world view and doctrine. The title reflects the fact that Baby Boomers and their collective counterculture have provided the membership for most of the "New Religions" in post-1950s America. The counterculture's free-floating spirituality is hard to pin down, but it has been fertile ground for the growth of old Asian traditions in America, as well as new eclecticisms.

Some Definitions

All the groups mentioned fit under a broad category called "the American alternative spiritual reality tradition."[1] This category embraces most spiritual phenomena that remain unwelcome in mainstream churches but are both widespread and persistent. It embraces historical eruptions of mysticism, like the followers of the eighteenth-century Swedish mystic Samuel Swedenborg, the American icon Johnny Appleseed,[2] and Henry David Thoreau, who wrote a friend in 1849: "Depend upon it that, rude and careless as I am, I would fain practice the yoga faithfully. To some extent, and at rare intervals, even I am a yogi."[3] This category also includes spiritualism and mental healing, like the nineteenth-century healers P. P. Quimby and Mary Baker Eddy, as well as the main Asian spiritual traditions that grew so rapidly in the United States after the 1950s. This essay will make little use of the term *cult* in its recent pejorative connotations. The term applies to the spiritual paths discussed only in its loosest sense, as "a group seeking ecstatic spiritual experience under a charismatic leader." Of course, Buddhism, Hinduism, and Sikhism only fall under this loose definition in their manifestations in America in relation to mainstream religions here.

Altered States

It is ecstatic or direct experience that distinguishes the alternative spiritual realities from the American mainstream. The experience may be a flood of contact with the divine, or the nontheistic realization that we are connected to everything. It may resonate in the heart or in the mind; it may come from dizzying Sufi whirling, silent Zen sitting, or Tibetan confrontation of emotional archetypes. Whatever its source or site of manifestation, the groups pursuing direct experience teach techniques for reaching it; they are spiritual technicians, mapping and stilling the mind, examining and merging with the body. These meditation and yoga practices are chief among the disciplines, techniques, methods, and active rituals characteristic of the alternative spiritual paths that have attracted so many thousands away from the mainstream religions that seemed, in the postwar years, to have forgotten their instrumentality.[4]

Another way of contrasting the alternative spiritual paths with the American mainstream is to distinguish between "transcendent" vs. "immanent" divinity, between a God outside us compared to a God within and part of anyone who seeks.[5] Yet another contrast refers to "exemplary" spiritual leaders vs. "emissary" leaders, the former embodying cosmic wonder as an enlightened example and the latter delivering a historical message, such as those conveyed by Christianity, Judaism, and Islam.[6]

Looking beyond the alternatives' exotic elements, like the mantras and prayer flags, it is easy to find several impulses common to the alternative spiritual realities that have also characterized the national religious life of the United States. These include a desire for restoration of former clarity and cohesiveness, millennialism and belief in the idea of a spiritual age, and efforts to create perfect communities.[7] Some or all of these ideas are obvious in the groups we will examine in detail in their New Mexico versions.

Intentional Community

This essay will use the term *community* to refer not to the "community of believers" common to all religious activity, but to collective efforts to establish cooperative living arrangements outside mainstream patterns. An American tradition from the Puritans' "city on a hill" through the nineteenth-century communities, like Amana and the Shakers, to the post–World War II hippie communes, the urge to perfect community has been broadened by the arrival of Buddhism in America, bringing a far older form of community, the *sangha* monastic order twenty-five hundred years old, perhaps the oldest continuously active human institution other than the family. The terms *centers* and *ashrams* will refer to what Buddhist historian Rick Fields views as "a peculiarly American form trying to integrate the intensity of monastic practice with an American community open to both men and women."[8]

This discussion does not encompass the myriad ideas of what has come to be called "New Age" culture, a vague, virtually undefinable collection of beliefs and practices focused on individual, rather than social, transformation. New Age entrepreneurs and enthusiasts use many terms and ideas taken from established spiritual paths, but very often the material is mixed in such a way—at the lowest common denominator of meaning—that it functions as alternative Muzak in the Spiritual Mall. The groups under consideration, though sometimes eclectic and syncretic, have taken specific coherent systems and combined them with more sustained effort and focus to create forms of intentional community.

"God is everywhere, but His address is in Española."
—Sikh leader Yogi Bhajan[9]

The presence of such a stunning array of spiritual communities in such a lightly populated state as New Mexico has often led to comment. Alternative religious leaders and participants usually cite New Mexico's beautiful light, mountains, and desert landscapes, but add allusions to cosmic energy, seeing the state as a zone of mysterious magnetism. This is a real, ongoing migration myth that serves to sanctify the settling of new traditions and participants. This myth is a new variant of the original tradition of sacred precincts central to the cosmology of the Pueblo tribes for over a thousand years, admired and borrowed by later comers, including Navajos, Apaches, Spanish, Mormons, artists, and tourists, and still vigorous among the Pueblo peoples today. Similarly, the state's well-remarked tolerance for cultural diversity, which has allowed the alternative spiritual groups to flourish here, has roots in the Pueblo resistance to Spanish colonizers and the Spanish settlers' ultimate accommodation with their Pueblo neighbors. Finally, it is worth noting that the alternative spiritual groups did not come directly to New Mexico, but discovered the state's beauty, slow pace, tolerant soul, and spiritual qualities after first establishing communities elsewhere, especially in California and New York.

And now to examine several key groups, centers, and communities more closely, starting with the first extant group to be established, Southwestern College in Santa Fe.

Southwestern College: From Cult to Vernacular

This small institute of higher education has evolved, since the 1950s, from a Detroit metaphysical group based on trance-channeling of spirit voices to a community in Alamogordo, then to a more eclectic college of transpersonal psychology and counseling. In 1963, Neva Dell Hunter, holder of a divinity degree, decided to move her metaphysical group from Detroit to Alamogordo. Dr. Hunter acted as a medium for the voice of a Dr. Ralph Gordon, a spirit who advised her and her followers on spiritual and practical matters throughout the late 1950s. Fearing the growing racial violence in Detroit, Hunter asked Dr. Gordon for advice in finding a new location. Dr. Gordon recommended White Sands, New Mexico, as a healing spot. After her assistants scouted the area, Hunter moved her large library, "aura balancing" business, and Sunday-service operation into two adjacent tract houses in Alamogordo, with couples and families locating in others nearby. The "aura-balancing" technique involved aligning a person's electromagnetic field, called the "aura," as he or she lay on a massage table and answered questions from a practitioner with intuitive powers. The belief in the aura's importance was taught by Dr. Gordon, who said he was passing on the knowledge from the spirit of P. P. Quimby, the historical founder of the nineteenth-century branch of psychosomatic healing called "Mind Cure."[10] Hunter named her Alamogordo community "Quimby Center."

Over the next decade, Hunter toured the country on the metaphysical circuit, attracted apprentices, and built Quimby Center into a spiritual-therapeutic school. She died in 1978; Robert Waterman, a protégé since the late 1960s, was her designated successor. With a doctorate in educational administration and advice from the California metaphysical leader John-Roger Hinkin (whose professional name is simply John-Roger), Waterman presided over the center's incorporation as the Southwestern College of Life Sciences and its move to Santa Fe in 1981.[11]

During the 1980s, as it attracted teaching associates and found its clientele, the Hunter/Quimby identity began to fade. Waterman and others participated in John-Roger's Movement for Spiritual Inner Awareness (MSIA), incorporated as a church in California. A former Mormon, John-Roger experienced psychic phenomena during a coma after a car accident. A basic tenet of the MSIA is that John-Roger is a member of the Mystical Traveler lineage that includes Sufi and Hindu masters, Socrates, Jesus, and St. Francis, and is empowered to recognize others in the lineage, such as Waterman.

Waterman's West Coast contacts led the Quimby people to adopt Asian influences. A major element in MSIA teachings is a yoga technique called Surat Shabda, one of a family of yogas teaching meditation on the "sound current" within, as the carrier of universal wisdom and love. The sound is said to arise from the actual physical processes and electromagnetic awareness of the body itself.[12] The MSIA and Southwestern College generally teach such techniques as aids in connecting people to their service roles in society via knowledge of their true selves.

In 1978 MSIA fostered Insight Training Seminars, offering five-day meditation and group interaction training sessions at centers in the United States,

England, Scotland, Australia, Canada, and Mexico. It is a classic human-potential course in "un-learning limitations," favored by counselors and therapists, and is a striking example of American pragmatic, mass application of Asian introspection techniques.[13]

In interviews, Waterman has explained that Southwestern College has progressed from the occult glamour of the sixties to a demystified, vernacular approach:

> Most of the people we get are looking for a deeper mystery, not just a belief or dogmatic explanation. They want the mystery, so we have tools to explore the mystery. It's not hard to go down a list of western psychologies and eastern yoga practices and see which are talking about the same things. I try to divest the glamour around these psychic phenomena. When things become vernacular instead of esoteric, I don't think it changes their depth.
>
> We avoid attachments to teachers here; although we know we do learn by reflection, and we like to have teachers who are on a path themselves, we avoid "religious" teaching. We don't convert people; we try to turn them into themselves.
>
> At the school, we're very much identified with Americana, American spiritual development. We're in a sense, academically, students of the American spiritual experience. So there's a strong Christ theme—not Christian—and a lot of service in our programs.[14]

The college bulletin board details another aspect of modern Americana seen everywhere on such boards: glossy brochures and fliers with tastefully symbolic logos advertising the availability in Santa Fe of every combination of dance, meditation, energy channeling, and therapy for past, present, and future lives, including the "Ashtar Command Ascension Center" and "Electronic Shaman."

Southwestern College has fifteen core and four adjunct faculty, most with degrees in psychology or counseling fields. The college has been advanced to candidacy for accreditation by the North Central Association of Colleges and Schools.[15]

A kindred institution combining Western esoteric traditions with therapeutic practice, also with roots predating the counterculture, is Dr. Jay Victor Scherer's Massage Academy. Scherer was born around 1905 and raised in Idaho. His mother was an herbalist and graduate of the Rudolph Steiner School in Germany.[16] Scherer combined Naturopathy and the I Am mystical Christian sect with Steinerism. He opened the Niagra [sic] Health Center in Santa Fe in 1953, treating many Hispanics who valued massage and herbs. Scherer, who died in 1991, estimated his graduates at fifteen hundred, some of whom have founded four other therapeutic academies in Santa Fe and Albuquerque. These schools drew many students to the state, contributing to the spiritual network and business activity of the two cities.[17]

The Religious Aspect of New Mexico Communes

New Mexico became a Mecca for hippies and seekers of alternative lifestyles in 1967, as the first Baby Boomers reached the age of twenty-one and the counterculture flowered on both coasts. These flamboyant counterculturalists were building on Bohemian and Beat traces laid down in northern New Mexico during the 1920s and 1940-50s by artists, writers, and reformers like Mabel Dodge Luhan in the twenties and Jenny and Craig Vincent in the sixties. It was an apocalyptic time, with official repression of Vietnam War protests and student Free Speech Movements, the beatings and deaths of civil-rights marchers, and the hallucinogenic drug LSD dissolving many boundaries formerly observed in music, graphic arts, and social behavior. Two important New Mexico communal enterprises were founded in 1967 with money and inspiration from outside the state—New Buffalo and Lama Foundation—and in 1969, West Coast bohemians brought a third spiritual community to the state, the Sikhs of Yogi Bhajan.

Participants and observers alike have commented on the elusive but central role of spirituality in the counterculture in general and communes in particular. Although popular press accounts of communes often emphasized drugs and naïvete, the feelings that careful observers perceived were essentially religious. As Terry Klein, wife of the founder of New Buffalo, noted, "There was really a religious movement going on here, but it's hard to put your finger on what to call it."[18] Paul Goodman, one of the most perceptive analysts of sixties youth, saw in 1969:

> I had imagined that the worldwide student protest had to do with changing political and moral institutions, to which I was sympathetic, but I now saw that we had to do with a religious crisis of the magnitude of the Reformation in the 1500s, when not only all institutions but all learning had been corrupted by the Whore of Babylon. . . . Religiously, the young have been inventive . . . they keep pouring out a kind of metaphysical vitality. . . . it is religion that constitutes the strength of this generation.[19]

In a sense communes served as improvised American monastery-retreats. People moved in and out of them and often left spiritually renewed. One observer of New Mexico communes characterized their intentions as "a life composed of community, hard work, family, and religion . . . what they want is . . . only a real life."[20] A *Look* magazine bureau chief toured the New Mexico communes in 1970 and saw interaction between communitas and individualism:

> In linking up with others here they experience what is, perhaps, their first exposure to a sense of "us-ness." . . . Most importantly, these new communitarians discover, in time, that the placing of themselves into this sort of austere alternative setting makes them more clearly defined to themselves. On reaching this discovery, most then feel prepared at last to jog on off toward even more benign horizons.[21]

However, some Hispanic residents failed to see the spirituality. Articles in the press and letters to editors expressed disgust at the influx of "especially offensive Anglos," and a group of Taos educators issued a plea for authorities to "crush this cancerous epidemic for all time."[22]

New Buffalo's most definable religious activity was the creation of several sites in the Arroyo Hondo area, twelve miles north of Taos, where mixed groups—mostly Anglo, with some Chicanos and a few Native Americans—held the all-night peyote meetings of the Native American Church. Those meetings, as they are called, were mentored by three Taos pueblo elders, and continued into the 1980s, perhaps to the present. Because it is the only widespread spiritual group whose sacrament is considered by most to be an illegal drug, members have always sought privacy. Nothing has been published about these Anglo converts and they are not inclined to give interviews. The New Buffalo commune gradually declined in the late 1970s and only one family lived there by the mid-1980s.[23]

Lama: Ecumenical Monastery

> "We try to awaken consciousness on the physical, mental, and emotional levels—my idea of what a spiritual person should be."
> —Steve Durkee, Lama founder[24]

Beginning as a collective somewhat similar to New Buffalo, Lama Foundation quickly moved in the direction of a monastery and then became a retreat center. Lama's founders included well-off partners interested in the Asian religious paths then being investigated by the hip, and important influences came from New York and California. In 1966, Stewart Brand, frequent camper in New Mexico and founder of the Whole Earth Catalog and later Coevolution Quarterly, leading countercultural publications based in the San Francisco area, convinced friends Stephen and Barbara Durkee to move to New Mexico. The Durkees had created the first multimedia light show in New York in 1966, "Why America Needs Indians." Brand introduced the Durkees to Herman Rednick, a sixty-four-year-old Taos painter who had studied metaphysics and Asian religions since the 1930s.[25] Rednick had a vision one day that led to the Durkees finding land for sale on Lama Mountain, the third-highest New Mexico peak, overlooking the Rio Grande Gorge. (Despite the coincidence, the place name *Lama* is not related to Tibetan monks, called *lamas*.)[26] Durkee and friends incorporated Lama Foundation in 1968.[27] A crew of Taos Indians taught them adobe skills. When Stewart Brand mentioned the project in the Whole Earth Catalog, five hundred people came during the next two years to volunteer a week's labor, "constantly probing, like some organized troupe of Thoreaus," an observer noted, "to affirm the ancient validity of their existence on this land."[28]

Another figure from the East Coast played the most important continuing role in Lama's visibility for twenty-four years. Richard Alpert arrived in New Mexico in 1966, after being fired at Harvard by regents who disapproved of his use of undergraduates in LSD experiments. Alpert and his partner Timothy Leary had been known as drug-and-mysticism propagandists, as well as scientists, since 1960.[29] Leary played the role of drug showman/shaman, getting LSD passed out free at events like the Human Be-In in San Francisco's Golden Gate Park in 1967 and urging people to "Tune in, turn on, and drop out." Alpert chose to go to India. He secured a grant from Santa Fe's Museum of International Folk Art to collect Hindu musical instruments, and according to his account, trekking by Land Rover into the interior, Alpert and friends found a tall, bearded twenty-three-year-old American longhair named Hari Dass Baba who appeared to have become a yogi. He agreed to take Alpert to see his guru in the mountains. Alpert got disoriented and dependent; villagers greeted Hari with joy and tears as they neared the guru. Hari kept admonishing the anxious and intellectualizing Alpert, "Be here now." The guru, Neem Karoli Baba, shattered Alpert's rational understanding by telling him in detail, the first time he saw him, the dream Alpert had had the previous night about his dead mother. Apparently no more than a provincial village holy man to the Indians, Neem Karoli converted Alpert to yogic studies by the force of his beaming clairvoyance and uncanny loving focus. He renamed Alpert "Baba Ram Dass," meaning "servant of God," and sent him back to the United States to "continue to make many people laugh." Ram Dass tells this affecting conversion narrative in the book, *Be Here Now*,[30] which he wrote upon returning to Lama Foundation in 1969. The book was handprinted, assembled loose in a box, and distributed free at first. It caught on and still sells steadily, inspiring pilgrimages to India and Lama, with 770,400 copies in thirty-two printings having been sold by 1991. This trickle of income allowed Lama to support staff over the winters and mount annual summer retreat programs featuring Ram Dass and masters from many traditions, and soon its reputation became national.

Neem Karoli and Ram Dass are in the Hindu tradition of semiautonomous holy men. Hinduism became probably the most visible Asian spiritual tradition in the United States, with the robed Hare Krishnas and the Beatles' sojourn with Maharishi Mahesh Yogi. This tradition couldn't have contrasted more with Protestantism, with its "sensuous and surreal gods and goddesses as brilliant and dreamlike and bizarre as tropical flowers," as religious scholar Robert Ellwood put it. He explains,

> It is India's willingness to explore and exploit the full magic of mankind's psychosomatic nature that has appealed to many westerners.... If Christianity ... is a religion for those not religious, Hinduism is a religion for the naturally religious—those who take sheer delight in religion's color, festivities, devotional fervor, ... in the grim romance of asceticism, and in the deep waters of meditation.[31]

Santa Fe scholar David Frawley puts the old term *Hindu* into perspective:

> More simply it is just called "Dharma," a Sanskrit term meaning the law or truth of one's own nature ... It is not so much a religion in particular as a compendium of religious and spiritual teachings. It has no one messiah, one prophet, savior or great teacher or bible.... It says that whatever way we approach the divine will not work until we recognize the deity within ourselves. Hence, we could say it is the religion of individualism.... The least organized of all religions, ... border[ing] on anarchism, it is ... most in harmony with the individual who wishes to go beyond organized belief. In this respect it is the most global of religions because it can be adapted to any individual of any time or place, any religious or nonreligious background, without any violation of their nature.[32]

Such a structure makes Dharma an obvious vehicle for the individualist American seeker who may be "naturally religious."

In 1979, Ram Dass went to India and commissioned a marble statue of Hanuman, the monkey god symbolizing service, revered by over 100 million Hindus. This lovely pink statue, with a seductively serene human-ape face in stylized makeup, is now the chief icon at Neem Karoli Baba Ashram, a half-mile west of Taos plaza, where it sits in a converted adobe milk barn. The ashram has Sunday services and can feed nine hundred at their twice-yearly festivals. Ram Dass is not a resident or leader at Lama or Neem Karoli. There is widespread respect for the fact that Lama has survived twenty-five years without a guru, relying on a skillful blend of long-term and short-term residents, although none reside permanently. Interestingly, many Lama participants have been Jewish; one participant observer puts the average at "six of ten," and other alternative spiritual groups note a strong Jewish presence. Perhaps Jewish background gives people a tradition of religion's strong role in daily life; perhaps familiarity with a sense of differentness gives easier access to alternative traditions. In any case, for all the groups discussed in this essay, members came almost exclusively from middle-class and professional-class whites, and trust funds, inheritances, and philanthropy bought the property. As Pico Iyer observed in a similar context, "only those with money can afford not to think about money."[33]

Lama Spawns a Second Community

In 1976, having gone to Jerusalem and studied Islam, Lama founder Steve Durkee, his first name changed to Nurideen, asked if he and twenty followers could take over Lama. Voted down, he left and returned to Saudi Arabia to study in Mecca. Returning to build a center in the United States, and finding that New Mexico land was ten times cheaper than anywhere else, Durkee found, in 1980, three hundred acres on the Chama River at Abiquiu at the same latitude as Islamic homelands in the Middle East. King Khaled of Arabia gave 1.4 million dollars, Taos Indians were hired on as adobe crew again, the Eight Northern Pueblos association supplied the bricks, and the Islamic center Dar al-Islam was born.[34] Egyptian architect Hassan Fathy, called the foremost adobe architect in the world, designed a mosque with barrel vaults and domes, all done with unreinforced adobe.[35] A detail shows scientific updating of Islamic tradition: the prayer door faces north instead of east; builders explain that the polar route is the shortest way to Mecca from Abiquiu.

By 1985, 139 Muslims, many ethnic Pakistanis and Afghanis, lived in the Abiquiu–Española area, hoping Dar al-Islam would become a community with schools, craft shops, an Islamic studies institute, and a clinic. However, in 1992 the project's board, dominated by the Saudi Sunni sect, discovered that key people at Dar al-Islam were closet Sufis, firing them and cutting funding. Nurideen Durkee left; the community development is on hold.

In June 1993, Dar al-Islam hosted the first North American Muslim Powwow. Three hundred of the estimated four to six million U.S. Muslims attended. Anas Coburn, a spokesman who has lived in Abiquiu for six years, said, "In different countries, different flavors of Islam have surfaced. We don't think the American flavor has yet emerged. It's still being defined, and what this is about is tasting it."[36]

Sikhs

Besides New Buffalo, Lama, and Dar al-Islam, there is another spiritual community whose presence in New Mexico can be traced to the late-sixties counterculture. The Sikhs, usually dressed in turbans and white clothes, have an ashram and extended community in Sombrillo/La Mesita, on the southern edge of Española. Their Indian-born leader, Yogi Bhajan, changed Sikh traditions to fit American culture when he came to the United States in 1967, and he has built the Sikhs into one of the most financially successful sects in the United States, with dynamic businesses and political contacts in the New Mexico Democratic Party. The Sikhs have experienced particularly intense controversy over master–student relations and group orientation to the outside world.

Sikhism has often been called a sect of Hinduism, a sect of Islam, or a blend of the two, but it appears to be a distinct religion.[37] Sikhs trace their tradition to Guru Nanak (1469–1539) and a succession of nine other gurus over the next two hundred years who fought for Sikh rights. The ninth guru is revered for sacrificing his life to Muslim invaders on behalf of the rights of the Hindus, whose religion had been banned. The tenth guru established a spiritual order, the Khalsa, who would follow the "five Ks": Kesh (uncut hair and beard); Kanga (comb symbolizing cleanliness); Katchera (cotton underwear, modesty); Kara (steel bangle, truth); and Kirpan (sword, defend the weak). All New Mexico Sikhs have Khalsa as part of their names, which are given by Yogi Bhajan. In his last days, the tenth guru conferred the guruship on a book that compiled the Sikh writings.[38]

It is a tribute to the serendipity and opportunism of the California counterculture that the Sikhs, one of the most disciplined and ritually formal New Mexico communities, became established in the United States through the help of one of the loosest hippie groups, the Jook Savages. The Jooks were "a little psychedelic family of our own," a founder noted, four or five couples connected to the music scene in Los Angeles.[39] They included an actress on the Smothers Brothers Show and the road manager for Peter, Paul, and Mary. When Yogi Bhajan immigrated to Los Angeles in 1968 (having first tried Toronto), the Jook Savages discovered him teaching

Kundalini yoga at the East–West Center, with about ten older women attending his classes.[40] They brought a hundred more longhairs to Bhajan's classes, all enthused at the idea of "getting high without drugs!" They arranged for a friend to donate his furniture store on Melrose Street for the yogi's first ashram.

According to Lisa and Tom Law, core members of the Jooks, it was Lisa who spontaneously suggested to Bhajan the advantages of a dress code for his followers. One day, as a group was preparing to go from the ashram to a Renaissance Fair, Lisa suggested that Bhajan exchange his customary slacks and short sleeve shirt for his Sunday dress whites: "They'll think we're a religious group and let us in cheaper!" It indeed happened, and that was the start of the American Sikhs' "Asian" look.[41]

The Jook Savages couldn't pay for Bhajan's yoga classes, so he asked them to found ashrams wherever they went to teach others his Karma and Kundalini yoga. The Savages, with Tom Law's promotion and managerial background, became the "front people" for an even looser group, the Hog Farm, who were minding an L.A.-area hog farm in exchange for camping privileges. The Hog Farm was organized around Hugh Romney's inspired clowning. Romney became "Wavy Gravy," a savvy, improvisational figure grinning through powwows, happenings, and "acid tests" (public events making LSD available to everyone) with Ken Kesey, the Merry Pranksters, and the Grateful Dead. Tom Law, Reno Myerson, and Richard Moon urged the whole tribe to go on the road to the Southwest. Lisa Law was pregnant and wanted to do natural childbirth; hearing from a friend that Santa Fe's Catholic Maternal Services was the only place doing natural births, she insisted they go there. "We felt like frontier people," she recalls.[42]

The Savages and Hog Farmers barnstormed around northern New Mexico in their psychedelic school buses in 1967 and 1968, holding a Summer Solstice Celebration in Aspen Meadows on Tesuque Pueblo land in 1968 and 1969. They invited Yogi Bhajan to teach yoga at the event in 1969, and then the Woodstock organizers came to New Mexico to ask the Hog Farmers and Savages to provide food, security, and "bad trip" care at Woodstock. Tom Law recalls: "I taught kundalini from the stage at Woodstock and there was this huge surge in interest. A scene of it got into the movie of Woodstock. I sort of became Yogi's main man without planning it; I know that sounds pompous, but I can hear him now, when he came to my place in Truchas wanting me to go on the road and teach for him, saying, 'Hoondred tousand dollars a yeeer, Tom!' That was when we began to bow out."[43]

By 1970, followers were operating an ashram on West Alameda in Santa Fe and a restaurant in town. In 1971, a group of eleven called Bhajan in Los

Angeles to ask for advice on finding a new place. "I'm very hesitant to say I had a vision," Bhajan says, "but there's no other way to describe it."[44] He told them the next day would be cloudy and that they should drive until the sun broke through and shone on a house. They did this, it happened, and the house it shone on in Sombrillo was for sale. The house became Hacienda Guru Ram Das (one "s," named after the builder of the Sikh's Golden Temple in India), and the start of the Sikh Dharma community that would grow to seventy families and nineteen acres. In another uncanny prediction, Bhajan urged followers to look for mountain-retreat land down a road everyone knew went only into National Forest. There was a single inholding, and it was for sale. It became the 150-acre camp where the Sikhs hold summer meditation intensives, an annual ecumenical Peace Prayer Day, and a women's yoga camp.[45]

Bhajan bought a ranch near the Sikh center, and Sombrillo became his summer home and summer headquarters for North American Sikh operations. Bhajan continued molding the Sikh tradition to his image: he taught vegetarianism, though Indian Sikhs eat meat; he made women's turbans daily wear instead of for special occasions, and had them add a white shawl; he pronounced himself chief religious authority for the Sikhs in the West, though Sikh priests in India are elected.[46] Many who joined had money and middle-class backgrounds; there was one African American and no Hispanics. The businesses flourished; by 1986, Akal Security had contracts for White Sands Missile Range, the New Mexico State Fair, and others in three states, billing 2.4 million dollars in 1986.

However, beginning in 1984, charges of abuse of power became public against Yogi Bhajan. Between December 1983 and February 1984, twenty-two adults, including the ashram's former director and his wife and several leaders of the group's eight operating divisions, left the sect, taking their ten children. Eighteen more followed during 1984, citing their growing sense that the turbans and white clothes were creating community resentment against their elitism. They also said Bhajan told them that the money they had invested created a collectively owned compound, but they found out that he personally held the deed.[47]

Allegations of sexual misconduct followed. In 1986 two women who had been with the sect seventeen and eleven years, respectively, charged Bhajan with holding them captive for sexual abuse. Three male guards from Bhajan's personal security force spoke in support of the women's allegations. Bhajan's attorney argued that the yogi could not come to New Mexico to give depositions due to recent heart surgery. The suits were settled out of court in 1988.[48] Commenting on the general problem of sex between masters and followers, a New Mexico woman responsible for a Buddhist center pointed out that students' maturity may be involved; unless total passivity by students is postulated, the students' intentions must be evaluated along with the leader's "abuse."

A case in 1989 brought the Sikhs into high-level political circles. A former Sikh, Mark Baker of Santa Fe, got a seventy-five hundred dollar settlement from the New Mexico State Police because, on suddenly reversed testimony from Sikhs who had once recommended him, he was dismissed from State Police Academy as "unfit and a threat to Yogi Bhajan." Baker claimed the Sikhs destroyed his police career to hide Sikh money laundering. In 1991, Gurujot Singh Khalsa of Great Falls, Virginia, and Española was indicted by the San Francisco Grand Jury for smuggling thousands of pounds of marijuana into the United States.[49] There was no allegation that Bhajan was involved.

After this rocky decade, the Sikh community stepped up its public relations efforts, inviting former governor Toney Anaya and the current governor Bruce King to Sikh events. Those attending Yogi Bhajan's birthday party at Sombrillo in August 1991 included Governor and Mrs. King, Attorney General Tom Udall, State Personnel Director Judy Basham, the state tourism director, Democratic National committeemen, Supreme Court Justice Gene Franchini, former Interior Secretary Stewart Udall, and other Democratic Party figures.[50] Yogi Bhajan's wife, Indirjit Kaur, has been inducted into the state Democratic Party Hall of Fame for her party work.

Since the Sikhs strongly emphasize family units, it is useful to consider the testimony of children who grew up as Sikhs. A number of Sikh children have been quite successful attending New Mexico Military Institute, reflecting their sect's familiarity with guns and discipline.[51] Systematic interviewing of many children was beyond the scope of my research, but one young man, now nineteen, who was born to American Sikh converts, recalled a constructive life as a young Sikh. His parents quit the Sikh religion when he was eight, and even though he was stung by the taunting of public school classmates and now has no intention of joining such a group, he recalls his Sikh childhood positively: "I only feel a little different from everybody else now; it must have made me independent. I remember I had a lot of adult friends I loved to hang out with. It was such happiness—white light happiness!"[52]

The Growing Pains of American Buddhism

In 1887, from a cabin above Santa Cruz, California, a man calling himself Philangi Dasa took a vow to publish *The Buddhist Ray*, the first Buddhist periodical in America, for seven years. Mocking the pretensions of society types (like Theosophical Society mavens), he disparaged his skin as "too light" and his reputation as having "no mahatmic credentials from the Himalayas, a serious obstacle indeed." He quietly "extinguished" the *Ray* when his seven years had passed.[53] In 1991, a publishing company called Buddhist Ray, Inc., began publishing *Tricycle: The Buddhist Review*, reflecting in its writers, pictures, and articles the rich diversity and sophisticated perspectives of the path in America, now "one of the most vital Buddhist countries in the world."[54]

Born in the person of Shakyamuni in northern India around 500 B.C.E., Buddhism has evolved in all the great lands of Asia, which have given it the forms that we find in the United States and in New Mexico. Rick Fields of Boulder, Tibetan practitioner and author of the narrative history of Buddhism in America, *How the Swans Came to the Lake*, characterizes Buddhism as "a radical critique of wishful thinking and the myriad tactics of escapism—political utopianism, psychological therapeutics, simple hedonism, or (and it is this that primarily distinguishes Buddhism from most of the world's religions) the theistic salvation of mysticism."[55]

There are many sects of Buddhism in Asia and much sectarian disagreement, but for the purposes of this short essay we could divide the Buddhist world into three broad sources: the baroque and emotionally bold Tibetans, with four main schools and lineages; the Theravadan schools of Southeast Asia's ascetic "forest monks"; and the austere formalism of the Chinese Ch'an (Japanese "Zen") schools. All are based on cross-legged sitting meditation practice as a way of life conducive to developing the habit of mindful action at all times, which, if all goes well, should lead to the falling away of attachments and realization of the interconnectedness of all things, or enlightenment. The meditative quiet of their practices gives no hint that they, like the Muslims and Sikhs, are struggling with volatile issues of authority, sex, and doctrinal direction.

From the Himalayas to the Sangre de Cristos

The Chinese annexation of Tibet in 1959 propelled representatives of that isolated plateau into exile in the West. The Tibetans feel that their Indo-European language has preserved more faithfully than Chinese or Japanese the early spirit of Buddhism (Sanskrit scholars took refuge in Tibet when Buddhism was suppressed in India seven hundred years ago.) The 1959 escape added desperate courage to Buddhism's legends: for example, nineteen-year-old Chogyam Trungpa, Rinpoche, led three hundred followers out, marching at night and eating boiled leather. "Trungpa" is a reincarnating identity, a line of teachers; "Rinpoche" means jewel, a perfected teacher.

Tibet was not the "Lost Horizon" of James Hilton's travel romance, but the crossroads of the Buddhist world, and Tibetans developed four schools of Buddhism rich in the scholarship of Indian and Chinese texts and in lay leadership.[56] Heirs of two of the schools have founded centers in Santa Fe. The first was the Khang Tzag stupa (reliquary monument) on Cerro Gordo Road in 1973, designed by Dudjom Rinpoche of the Nyingmapa school ("ancient ones," "treasure finders" of cached manuscripts). This center is no longer Tibetan; in the mid-1980s it was run by an American heir of the Japanese Roshi (Zen master) Shunryu Suzuki, Richard Baker. Baker-roshi inherited Suzuki's leadership of the San Francisco Zen Center and Tassajara, the first American mountain monastery, in 1971.[57] Baker was forced to leave the Bay Area in 1984 because of an extravagant lifestyle and sexual improprieties with female students. He took over the Cerro Gordo zendo and one in Crestone, Colorado, in 1985. He relinquished the Santa Fe zendo in 1992; it is now called Maha Bodhi, is ecumenical, and a lay priest in the Vietnamese tradition, Joan Halifax, is in charge. It will become a center for the service-oriented sect of Thich Naht Hanh, a Vietnamese monk once nominated by Martin Luther King, Jr., for the Nobel Peace Prize, who now lives in France.

The second Tibetan center in Santa Fe was founded by The Venerable Kalu Rinpoche, a saintly yogi in his seventies, in 1975. Kalu Rinpoche then, in 1981, sent Lama Dorje, a monk, to visit various centers in Europe, New York, Los Angeles, and Seattle. In 1980, His Holiness, the Sixteenth Karmapa, head of the Kagyu school, took the vows of five hundred Santa Fe followers. At the request of the Santa Fe followers, Lama Dorje came to live in Santa Fe and establish a large stupa, the first in the United States that worshipers could enter. Painted stunningly inside, serene white outside, it stands on a narrow lot on Airport Road, sandwiched between a bronze-casting business and the Shalom Trailer Court. Lama Dorje has also built a small stupa in Taos.

A Tibetan lineage gave American Buddhism its most dire shock in the late 1980s: Osel Tensing (Thomas Rich), made the dharma heir of Chogyam Trungpa, Rinpoche, and leader of Trungpa's Colorado sanghas, had sex with male and female followers even though he knew he had AIDS. He was forced into retreat and died in California in 1991. The devastated community has struggled to recover.[58]

The Zen Path

"To take this posture is itself to have the right state of mind."
—Shunryu Suzuki-roshi.[59]

The first Japanese Zen master arrived in the United States over one hundred years ago for the World Parliament of Religions in Chicago, and several others followed over the next few decades. Then, after World War II, a new wave of masters came, and their eldest American students have become our first native-born lineage holders. The largest two schools of Chinese-derived Zen in Japan are Soto, focused on sitting, and the somewhat smaller Rinzai, featuring the verbal riddles called *koans*. There is one prominent Japanese form of Buddhism, Nichiren Shoshu, an ancient sect that became bonded to a civic organization, and now is the fourth largest party in the Japanese parliament. Nichiren Shoshu of America (NSA) vigorously proselytized, teaching members to chant "Namu Myoho Ringe Kyo" to obtain whatever they wanted. The NSA's 140,000 American members were excommunicated en masse in 1991 by the Japanese head temple, and NSA is now Soka Gokkai International. It is the only Asian sect in the United States with substantial African-American membership, estimated at 20 percent, including singer Tina Turner.

The first Zen monastery in New Mexico was established in 1974 by Michelle Martin, a student of Joshu Sasaki-roshi at his Mount Baldy mountain retreat near Los Angeles, renowned for its tough seven-day intensive sessions. Sasaki-roshi, eighty-six, is a strict Rinzai master and abbot of one of the two Los Angeles Zen centers. Martin found her land in the Jemez Mountains when the Catholic priest treatment center, The Servants of the Paraclete, moved to larger quarters. Now known as Bodhi-Manda, the Jemez Zen center is run by a female abbess, and its women call themselves monks, not nuns. Bodhi-Manda is home to Sasaki-roshi's Summer Seminars, a program cosponsored by the University of New Mexico Philosophy Department. The Jemez center spun off an Albuquerque Zen center, on Madeira Southeast, in 1989. During the summer of 1993 a female monk was in charge there.[60]

Also in Santa Fe is the Mountain Cloud Zen Center on Old Pecos Trail, founded in 1981 by students of Philip Kapleau's Rochester (New York) Zen Center. Kapleau, who was the chief court reporter for the War Crimes Tribunal at Nuremburg and Tokyo, wrote *Three Pillars of Zen* (1965), which had an enormous influence on a new generation of Americans. Now eighty-one, Kapleau is semi-retired in Florida.

The struggles to adapt Asian traditions of devotion, study, and authority in the West are clearly seen in American Buddhism in the 1990s. In Asia, emphasis has always been on "the enlightened one"; in America it is on building communities in which one can manifest enlightened life. Poet Gary Snyder, who studied eight years in Japan, observes that "the single most revolutionary aspect of Buddhist practice in the U.S. is that everywhere, fully 50% of students are women. What that is going to do to these inherited teaching methods and attitudes is going to be quite interesting."[61] One of the women with leadership responsibility in a New Mexico Zen center points out that the rash of master–student trouble in the 1980s is traceable to the lack of structure surrounding the centers:

> People get very open psychologically when doing spiritual practice, and Americans need support structures to handle upheavals that arise. Americans also want democracy, and Zen isn't democratic. Exercise of authority is not ipso-facto abuse of power. Even sexual contact is at least partly the student's responsibility too. Masters set few limits, trying to get us to set them.

American Buddhist Philip Whalen declares: "The worst-case scenario [is] that Buddhism in America will simply become coopted like everything else, ... just what you do on Sunday. It's getting more and more watered down."[62]

Conclusion

Like the counterculture that had so much to do with their growth, these alternative spiritual groups have left lasting traces on the cultural fabric of New Mexico. Their chief innovation has been in broadening the public's knowledge of spiritual practices, that is, physical and mental disciplines that lead to awareness and more integrated living. The groups have also extended the reach and diversity of ideas that were already old in American culture—indeed, thought of as characteristically American—before the counterculture arose as a mass phenomenon in the middle 1960s. These new bottles for older wine include an emphasis on spirituality and simplicity as opposed to technocracy and consumerism, commitment to community building as resistance to individualism, advocacy of environmental preservation, and expansion of New Mexico's tradition of desert retreat centers.

Their techniques for reaching enlightenment, serenity, or spiritual ecstasy comprise the common thread running through these groups, and they enrich mainstream traditions by sharing these techniques. As mentioned earlier, the mainstream religions so routinized and abstracted their messages that they had all but abandoned practices and disciplines. Most of the state's teachers of meditation developed their knowledge while practicing in one of the alternative traditions. Members of the Bodhi Manda Zen Center in Jemez Springs, for example, have taught meditation to Catholic laity at church retreat centers in Albuquerque's South Valley. Popularly imagined as cultlike esoterica, the meditation techniques Buddhists teach aim to permeate and transform everyday life. "The ultimate purpose of Zen," a Roshi (master) told writer Pico Iyer, "is not in the going away from the world but in the coming back. Zen is not just a matter of gaining enlightenment; it's a matter of acting in a world of love and compassion."[63]

The various techniques of meditation, whether sitting, walking, or archery, designed to empty the mind or control the body's energies, belong to a family of practices devoted to exploring the integration of body, mind, emotions, and spirit, subjects of great interest to citizens of a fragmented and fragmenting society like that in the United States. The emerging paradigm of holism in the field of medicine illustrates the applicability of these body–mind integration practices in a field long known for its conservatism and positivist-scientific ethos. The schools of nursing and medicine at the University of New Mexico have, for the last two decades, been innovators in health-science curriculum design, incorporating concepts of healing touch and the psychosocial components of disease long pioneered by the alternative spiritual groups. Many practitioners of massage, acupuncture, and dietary reform credit the spread of these ideas to the "New Age" movement, that vast and vague collection of ideas considered outside mainstream culture. Whatever its limitations may be, the New Age movement is a tidewater zone where systems of thought mingle and exchange, bringing a stream of the curious to the established Asian and minority traditions while sending ideas, symbols, and disciplines back with visitors to their mainstream denominations. Food may be among the longest-lasting and most far-reaching innovations brought by adherents of Asian spirituality; brown rice, tofu, yogurt, and oriental seasonings are now staples of the American supermarket, probably spread as much by the do-it-yourself counterculture via food co-ops and health-food stores as by Oriental restaurants.

In addition to the new ideas the spiritual groups have brought to the larger society, they have also served to renew older American values. Like the Puritans, Shakers, Oneidans, and Mormons before them, these groups argue that the primacy of spirit over unfettered materialism depends on careful community building. Their exotic architecture, iconography, or personal habits focus attention on their efforts in conscious social control and serve to expand the range of spirituality available to the community. Community building is, of course, another old American idea renewed by these groups. "Communities of believers" like all religious groups, they are also communities of practitioners whose endeavors to renew their ways of living make notable additions to the state's landscape. As communities apart, they advertise focus amid sprawl and impersonality, embody cohesion amid fragmentation, and speak for tradition over drift. The New Mexico–based Hog Farm's influence at the 1969 Woodstock Festival of Music and Culture, as recounted in the Sikh section of this essay, was the nucleus of the counterculture's "call to community."[64]

In the New Mexico context, the communitarian efforts of the new spiritual groups expanded a state tradition of desert or mountain retreat centers. There is a long line of retreat centers drawn by the excellent climate, clean air, sparse population, oases-like river and mountain habitat zones, and the Pueblo Indian and Spanish village tradition of sacred sites and shrines. The lists of retreats includes the tuberculosis sanitaria that proliferated between 1880 and 1940, religious retreats like Glorieta Baptist Retreat Center, the Catholic Servants of the Paraclete in the Jemez Mountains, the Benedictine Christ in the Desert Monastery near Abiquiu, and the Philmont Scout Ranch near Cimarron. The newest type of healing resort is the Vallecitos Mountain Retreat Center northwest of Abiquiu, run by American advocates of the Vipassana (Southeast Asian) Buddhist tradition as a meditative center for environmental activists fighting burnout and seeking renewal. Like the sanitaria before them, which brought the families of future U.S. senators, business tycoons, and cultural innovators to the Southwest, the newer retreat centers bring people with money and motivation who may impact the state's economy and culture in many ways.

One such significant impact on New Mexico is the environmental preservation values taught by the contemplative traditions. The Buddhist and Hindu beliefs in compassion for all beings and the oneness of life are closer to the attitudes of Native American traditions in the state than to the mainstream. One example of this affinity is the ten-year leadership of Ike Eastvold in the protection of the Indian petroglyph districts on Albuquerque's west-side escarpment, which lie directly in the path of suburban development. Eastvold, whose life has been threatened by prodevelopment figures and whose story is told in a 1995 *National Geographic* feature, has made analogies between the Zen Buddhist regard for life taught him by Joshu Sasaki-roshi of the Los Angeles and Jemez Bodhi Manda zen centers and the meaning of the petroglyph districts as articulated by Sandia Pueblo elders. Another connection between these traditions and political activism is the work of Greg Mello, a Zen practitioner who brought American dharma-heir Philip

Kapleau-roshi's group from Rochester, New York, to Santa Fe in 1980. Mello later cofounded the Los Alamos Study Groups in Santa Fe, whose watchdog scrutiny of the national laboratory's environmental record has had significant impact on the Hazel O'Leary reform era in the Department of Energy. The Study Group organized the Los Alamos Coalition of towns, villages, and Indian Pueblos studying the lab's past and future environmental impacts on the region, bringing collective strength to isolated protestors. Mello's rise from obscure critic to invited consultant in the Washington debate over the Los Alamos National Laboratory's future in northern New Mexico parallels the development of the alternative spiritual groups themselves over a quarter-century, from tentative steps to maturing institutions.

Notes

1. Robert S. Ellwood Jr., *Religious and Spiritual Groups in Modern America* (Englewood Cliffs, N.J.: Prentice-Hall, 1973), chaps. 1, 2.

2. Ibid, 66, 73.

3. Letter to H. G. O. Blake, quoted in Rick Fields, *How the Swans Came to the Lake: A Narrative History of Buddhism in America* (Boulder, Colo.: Shambhala Publications, 1981), 64.

4. Jacob Needleman, *The New Religions* (Garden City, N.Y.: Doubleday, 1970), 17–18.

5. Bishop John A. T. Robinson of Woolwich, England, made this distinction a hallmark of the "New Theology" with his 1963 book, *Honest to God*. But Buddhists believe a deity is superfluous to the realization of the unity of all.

6. Ellwood, *Religious and Spiritual Groups*, xii–xiii.

7. Dewey Wallace, "Sects, Cults and Mainstream Religion: A Cultural Interpretation of New Religious Movements in America," *American Studies* 26 (Fall 1985): 8–9.

8. Fields, *How the Swans Came to the Lake*, 45.

9. Demetria Martínez, "New Mexico's Hills Cradle Ashrams, Stupas," *Albuquerque Journal*, *Impact Magazine*, 3 December 1985; Joseph Dispenza, "Hallowed Ground," *New Mexico Magazine* 65 (March 1987): 48.

10. Ferenc M. Szasz, "'New Thought' and the American West," *Journal of the West* 23 (January 1984): 83–90.

11. William Price, "The Quimby Center: A Case of Shamanism in Contemporary America" (Ph.D. diss., Washington State University, 1982).

12. David Frawley, *From the River of Heaven; Hindu and Vedic Knowledge for the Modern Age* (Salt Lake City: Passage Press, 1990), 133. Sound current meditation is generally associated with the lineage of Sikh gurus in the fifteenth and sixteenth centuries in Punjab province of India. Also using a similar type of meditation are Paul Twitchell's American Eckankar group and the American Sikhs. "Eckankar" is phonetically the first three syllables of the main mantra (chanted phrase believed to convey power) taught by the Yogi Bhajan Sikhs.

13. Author interviews with Robert Waterman, 14 May 1983 and 13 July 1993; John-Roger, *The Path to Mastership* (Los Angeles: The Church of the Movement of Spiritual Inner Awareness, 1983); *Insight Training Seminars: Inside Insight* magazine, March/April 1983. All notes of interviews in author's possession.

14. Author interview with Robert Waterman, 13 July 1993.

15. *1993–94 Catalog*, Southwestern College, 66–70.

16. Steiner (1861–1925) was chosen to edit Goethe's papers at the age of twenty-three. He worked as literary editor for the Theosophical Society, founded in the United States in 1875 by Helena Petrovna

Blavatsky (1831–1891), a magus from Europe, and the American attorney Col. Henry Steele Olcott. Kicked out of Theosophy for refusing to recognize Krishnamurti as an avatar, Steiner founded Anthroposophy in 1913, with its headquarters in Switzerland. Lecturing in all basic fields, he described the human essence as having physical, etheric, astral, and soul (or "I") bodies.

17. Steve Fox, "Healing, Imagination, and New Mexico," *New Mexico Historical Review* 58 (July 1983). Also, see Dispenza, "Hallowed Ground," 46.

18. Author interview, 30 July 1993; see also Lisa Law, *Flashing on the Sixties* (San Francisco: Chronicle Books, 1987), 77.

19. Paul Goodman, "The New Reformation," *New York Times Magazine*, 14 September 1969, 32–33, 142–47, 150, 154–55.

20. Gorken [sole name], "Notes from New Mexico," *Rag*, 10 July 1969, quoted in Timothy Miller, *The Hippies and American Values* (Knoxville: University of Tennessee Press, 1991), 90.

21. William Hedgepeth and Dennis Stock, *The Alternative: Communal Life in New America* (New York: Collier Books, 1970), 156.

22. Hedgepeth and Stock, *Alternative*, 72.

23. Leslie Linthicum, "New Buffalo, Shuffling into the '90s," *Albuquerque Journal*, 28 February 1993, A-1, 10.

24. Hedgepeth and Stock, *Alternative*, 162.

25. Herman Rednick, *The Earth Journey: From Birth to Fulfillment* (New York: Vantage, 1980), Introduction.

26. Robert H. Julyan's *The Place Names of New Mexico* (Albuquerque: University of New Mexico Press, 1996) says that the local Hispanics with roots in the village of Lama for generations told him they don't know where the name comes from.

27. Martínez, "New Mexico's Hills Cradle Ashrams, Stupas," 4.

28. Hedgepeth and Stock, *Alternative*, 163.

29. William O'Neill, *Coming Apart; An Informal History of America in the 1960's* (New York: Quadrangle Books, 1971), 238.

30. Ram Dass, *Be Here Now* (Berkeley, Calif.: Hanuman Foundation, 1969).

31. Ellwood, *Religious and Spiritual Groups*, 215, 218, 250. The term *Hindu* does not appear in any of the classical texts; it is merely Greek transliteration for the name the Persians gave to those they encountered on the Indus River. Never limited to India, the spiritual tradition was prevalent a few centuries ago in Indochina, Indonesia, Cambodia, and Afghanistan, and Bali is still Hindu. "The correct name for what we call Hinduism," according to David Frawley, one of the few Westerners recognized in India as an expert, "is 'Sanatana Dharma', which means literally 'the eternal teaching'" (Frawley, *From the River of Heaven*, 26).

32. Frawley, *From the River of Heaven*, 27–28.

33. Pico Iyer, *Video Night in Kathmandu and Other Reports from the Not-so-far East* (New York: Vintage, 1989), 94.
34. Martínez, "New Mexico's Hills Cradle Ashrams, Stupas," 5.
35. Jean Dethier and Centre Georges Pompidou, *Down to Earth: An Old Idea, A New Future* (New York: Facts on File, 1982, 1983).
36. "300 Muslims to Converge for First-Ever Powwow," *Albuquerque Journal*, 19 June 1993, D1.
37. Arvind Sharma, "The Sikh Crisis in India: A Question of Identity," in *The Politics of Religion and Social Change: Religion and the Political Order*, ed. Anson Shupe and Jeffrey K. Hadden, (New York: Paragon House, 1988), 2: 190–203.
38. "Sikh Dharma" (Los Angeles: Sikh Dharma International Headquarters, n.d.).
39. Author interview with Tom Law, 31 July 1993.
40. *Time*, 5 September 1977, quotes Judith Tyberg, "respected founder of Los Angeles's East–West Center," to the effect that she fired Bhajan after three months for reasons she will not divulge. Kundalini yoga aims to channel sexual energy from lower centers up the spine to higher uses.
41. Author interviews with Lisa Law, 12 July 1993, and Tom Law, 31 July 1993.
42. Law, *Flashing on the Sixties*, 74.
43. Author interview with Tom Law, 31 July 1993.
44. Martínez, "New Mexico's Hills Cradle Ashrams, Stupas," 5.
45. Author interview with Lisa Law, 12 July 1993; interview with Shanti Kaur Khalsa, Sikh Dharma spokesperson, 14 July 1993.
46. "Yogi Bhajan's Synthetic Sikhism," *Time*, 5 September 1977, 70–71, quoting High Priest Guruchuran Singh Tohra, president of the management committee for northern India's Sikh temples.
47. "Former Sikhs Tell Why They Left New Mexico Religious Community," *Albuquerque Journal North*, 9 February 1984, D1; "Ex-Sikhs' Reverence Becomes Revulsion," *Santa Fe New Mexican*, 10 July 1989, A1, 2.
48. "Two Sikh Women Say Sikh Yogi Held Them as Captives," *Albuquerque Journal*, 19 July 1986, B1; "Lawsuits against Sikhs Settle Quietly," *Rio Grande Sun* (Española), 6 October 1988, A1, 14.
49. "Former Sikh Gets Settlement from State Police," *Rio Grande Sun*, 20 July 1989, A1, 14.
50. "Growing Role for the Sikhs," *Santa Fe Reporter*, 5–11 February 1992, 1, 17.
51. Lisa Kaplowitz and Ginger John Williams, "The Sikh Dharma in New Mexico: Religion as Process" unpublished manuscript, University of New Mexico Anthropology Department research paper, Fall 1991.
52. Author interview with David Mattes, 21 July 1993.
53. Fields, *How the Swans Came to the Lake*, 132.
54. Ibid., 358.
55. Ibid., 7.
56. Ibid., 283.
57. Ibid., 259, 265.
58. Rick Fields, "The Changing of

the Guard: Western Buddhism in the Eighties," *Tricycle: A Buddhist Review* 1 (Winter 1991): 43–49.

59. Fields, *How the Swans Came to the Lake*, 229.

60. "A History of Rinzai-ji," parts 1 and 2, *Albuquerque Zen Center Newsletter*, April, May 1993.

61. The point about community was made by Maezumi-roshi of the Los Angeles Zen Center; it and the Snyder quote are from Fields, *How the Swans Came to the Lake*, 363.

62. "Buddhist Journal Beat," *Tricycle: A Buddhist Review* 2 (Winter 1992): 83.

63. Pico Iyer, "The Lady and the Monk," *Tricycle: A Buddhist Review* 2 (Summer 1993): 63.

64. Miller, *Hippies and American Values*, 89.

8

The United States and New Mexico
A Twentieth-Century Comparative Religious History

Ferenc M. Szasz

Introduction

ORGANIZED RELIGION HAS BEEN MUCH IN THE NEWS IN THE LAST two decades but seldom for reasons that would please the theologians. The dilemmas seem endless: steadily declining membership in most of the mainline denominations; the rise of bizarre sects that have targeted America's youth; forged Mormon historical documents that led to murder; Protestant television evangelists who laced their messages with greed and hypocrisy; and a relentless stream of sexual impropriety cases that shocked the powerful Roman Catholic church to its foundations. Mere mention of the names of the Rajneesh, Rev. Jim Jones, and David Koresh brings forth bewildered shakes of the head. Where will it all end? Nobody is very optimistic.

If any private corporation had displayed such a record, it would have collapsed long ago. By any "rational criteria," organized religion should have followed the path of Amalgamated Buggy Whip, the Edsel, or Bon Vivant vichyssoise soup.

But it did not. In spite of predictions to the contrary, organized religion has not disappeared from American life. In fact, a 1993 survey found that 90 percent of the nation believed in God, and 35 percent felt "very close" to God—a higher percentage than in any other industrialized country. Perhaps religion is a human perennial. Perhaps, as sociologist Emil Durkheim has suggested, organized religion reflects society at large. Or perhaps, as theologian Paul Tillich once observed, a people's culture is simply the manifestation of its most deeply held faith.

If religion in America has not "disappeared," however, it surely has changed over the last century. The purpose of this essay is to chart those changes on both national and state levels and to explore the interactions between the two. Since this goal has to be accomplished in about thirty pages, it will call for some rather broad historical strokes.

Periodization in religious history is always challenging, for everywhere religion intersects with culture, and religious changes seldom coincide with the more frequently used political divisions. For purposes of discussion, however, let me divide the religious history of the twentieth century into four overlapping eras:

(a) the 1890s to the 1920s,
(b) the 1920s to the 1940s,
(c) the late 1930s to the 1960s,
(d) the 1960s to the present.

1. The Turn of the Century

On a national level, the first period, from ca. 1893 to ca. 1922, might be termed the era of "Protestant cultural hegemony." Although the Roman Catholic church had long been the nation's largest single denomination, the combined Protestant church memberships gave them the statistical nod. Graduates of the Chicago Divinity School, New York's Union Theological Seminary, the Episcopal Theological School (New York), the Yale Divinity School, Rochester Divinity School, and others were not seriously challenged by those from Bible institutes or from the numerous institutions that trained rabbis or Roman Catholic priests. The most popular news magazine, *Outlook*, was edited by Congregational minister Lyman Abbott, who mixed solid stories with extensive coverage of the religious world. The scholarly *American Journal of Theology* confidently predicted in 1902 that Christian [Protestant] theology again would be "the queen of sciences" by the close of the century. Republican politician Theodore Roosevelt once observed that he preferred to address a Methodist audience because the Methodists represented the great middle class and, hence, the heart of the American people.

Except for select urban and ethnic areas, America in these years witnessed a "voluntary religious establishment." The upper class spokesmen for this elite often looked down upon non-Protestant immigrants, while they, in turn, viewed the establishment with a mixture of envy and resentment. Thanks to America's famed separation of church and state, however, this "cultural hegemony" proved rather mild, as much "moral" as it was doctrinal. The world of Chautauqua and the prevalence of biblical rhetoric during this period will help to illustrate this theme.

Born in the 1870s as an institution to train Methodist Sunday School teachers, the Chautauqua made its permanent home in western New York State and its temporary home in thousands of American small towns across the land. Utilizing a well-managed program of traveling speakers and entertainers, Chautauqua lecturers discussed such themes as women's rights, world peace, the single tax, and slum reform, whereas other performers gave dramatic readings or acted snippets from Shakespeare's plays. One observer called the traveling Chautauqua "the most American thing in America." No Chautauqua presentation ever approached the risqué, and management yanked a performer at the slightest suggestion of a double entendre. The best firsthand memoir of this life is entitled (appropriately enough) *Morally We Roll Along*.

This Victorian "moral" outlook on the world relied on a biblical framework that was reflected in the speeches of the foremost political/social figures of the era. Democratic hopeful William Jennings Bryan achieved lasting rhetorical fame for his 1896 peroration: "You shall not press down upon mankind this crown of thorns; you shall not crucify mankind upon a cross of gold." Woodrow Wilson, son of a Southern Presbyterian minister, often drew upon similar cultural assumptions for his messages. When Roosevelt founded the Progressive party, he gave his followers a "confession of faith," and the theme song for the party in the election of 1912 was "Onward Christian Soldiers."

Ironically, the radical social critics of the time drew upon the same biblical imagery. American freethinkers spoke of the "new trinity" of "reason, science, and observation" and of "science the redeemer." Socialist lecturers denounced the country for "crucifying" mankind through an unjust economic system. Many of the most rousing IWW lyrics were sung to old Methodist hymn tunes. Clearly a broad use of Scripture provided a lingua franca for the turn-of-the-century years.

The pre–World War I era also found the nation's clerics at the height of their influence. Monday newspapers regularly printed Sunday sermons, and common concern over "the social question" offered a wide arena for both cooperation and public social statements. Pope Pius's encyclical *Rerum Novarum* (1891) laid the basis for Catholic social concern. The books by Baptist theologian Walter Rauschenbusch, especially *A Theology for the Social Gospel* (1918), did the same for Protestants. Organized Judaism had long expressed similar social interests. Thus, conservative evangelists could work alongside various liberals to help end prostitution, "clean up the slums," save the children, and reform corrupt government; all sides hoped to usher in their own version of an ideal social order: the Kingdom of God. As Lyman Abbott once phrased it, "My Roman Catholic brother, and my Jewish brother, and my agnostic brother, and I, an evangelical minister, have started in various quarters, and are going in different directions, but we are all aiming for the same place."

Figures of respect in virtually every community, the American clerics were listened to on a variety of issues. The most prominent city priest or minister virtually always helped create the first organized charity. In 1900, Congregational clergyman Charles Sheldon actually ran the Topeka *Daily Capitol* for a week, printing only what he considered "moral" news. And everywhere, the nation's clerics were expected to provide the "proper atmosphere" for resolution of perplexing social issues.

But this broad-based Protestant "cultural hegemony" could not last. Steady streams of Catholic, Jewish, Orthodox, and other non-Protestant immigration began to shift the demographics of the population. From the 1890s forward, other faiths began to claim their rightful share of the nation's much-respected "freedom of religion."

Perhaps the best manifestation of this increasing religious pluralism came with the World's Parliament of Religions, held in conjunction with the 1893 Chicago World's Fair. A British rabbi's phrase—"Have we not all one father? Hath not one God created us?"—served as the official motto for the conference, but it was the *pluribus* rather than the *unum* that struck most contemporaries. Spokespeople for the Baha'is, the Brahmins, Christian Scientists, and adherents of Islam, plus a wide variety of smaller sects, received considerable publicity. The Hindu philosopher Swami Vivekananda remained in the country for an extended lecture tour that catered mainly to upper-class women. Thus, by the turn of the new century, the nation's religious pluralism was steadily widening, the results of which would clearly be seen in the aftermath of the First World War.

2. The 1920s to the 1940s

The second era proved far less harmonious than the first. Indeed, during much of the interwar period the nation's religious forces dealt with one another in anger or at arm's length. The religious conflict of the 1920s had two chief dimensions: the liberal vs. conservative Protestant clash over theology, and the extremist Protestant alliance with the Ku Klux Klan against the nation's Catholics, Blacks, and Jews.

The intramural Protestant conflict has been termed the "fundamentalist-- modernist controversy," and it divided American Protestantism into two warring camps that even today remain suspicious of one another. Northern Presbyterians, Northern Baptists, Disciples of Christ, Northern Methodists, and Episcopalians were the denominations most affected, but the quarrel brushed up against all organized Protestant groups.

The issues varied from denomination to denomination, but they revolved around these main items: (a) a literal vs. a metaphorical reading of Scripture; (b) the necessity for a conversion experience; (c) pre- vs. postmillennialism, and (d) which group would control the resources of the denomination.

The fundamentalist–modernist controversy began as a dispute over theological doctrines and biblical interpretation, but did not stay there. Within a short time, this controversy had moved from denominational assemblies into the public realm, and the issue that took it there was Charles Darwin's theory of evolution. As Baptist fundamentalist William B. Riley noted in 1927, "When the Fundamentals Movement was originally founded, it was supposed that our particular foe was the so-called 'higher criticism'; but, in the onward going affairs, we discovered that basal to the many forms of modern infidelity is the philosophy of evolution." And here we must turn to the career of William Jennings Bryan.

Searching for an explanation for the causes of World War I, Bryan concluded that the Darwinian theory of "might makes right" was the "false philosophy" that had led to "German militarism." He also blamed the theory for America's postwar labor troubles. Bryan argued that a "survival of the fittest" philosophy countered the universal code of morality that he found in Scripture. If that code of ethics were not applied to nations as well as individuals, he said, there was no moral code that could regulate human affairs. For Bryan, as for many of his generation, evolution had become "the totality of error." Such concern culminated in the Scopes trial in Dayton, Tennessee, in July 1925.

The incredible publicity surrounding this controversy points to the increasingly important role that the media would play in forging twentieth-century American religious history. Journalists discovered that religious events make the best copy when things are going badly. Which story would sell more newspapers: "Rev. John Doe and parishioners enjoy picnic," or "Rev. John Doe and parishioners decapitated by ax murderer?" After World War I, the emphasis on religious coverage began to shift from reprinting Sunday sermons to lurid stories of catastrophe. Thus, many religious groups concluded that they needed to utilize the media on their own. (Ironically, religious conservatives saw the potential of the newest mass medium—radio—long before the liberals.)

No national religious figure realized the potential of media coverage better than Los Angeles Pentecostal minister Aimee Semple McPherson. In 1918, "Sister Aimee" arrived in Los Angeles and later founded her Four Square Gospel Church, which had been revealed to her in a dream. Drawing on radio (KFSG—Kall Four Square Gospel) and, especially on the dramatic aura of nearby Hollywood, Sister Aimee created, costumed, and staged "religious performances" that made her into the nation's first religious "superstar." There would be more to come.

The most extreme aspect of the postwar religious/cultural clash came with the right-wing Protestant alliance with the newly revived Ku Klux Klan, which proceeded to denounce immigrants, Roman Catholics, Jews, and Blacks as "un-American." The first KKK had its roots in the American South, but the revived version proved strong in western states, including Oregon, Colorado, and Texas. A parallel form of revived religious intolerance may be seen in Bureau of Indian Affairs' directives against Native American faiths. All told, the interwar years produced a series of "cultural wars" that soured Protestant–Catholic–Jewish relationships for over a decade. It also forever ended the Protestant "cultural hegemony" in the United States.

3. The Late 1930s to the 1960s

The third period, from ca. the 1930s to ca. the 1960s proved far more irenic for mainline American religion. Given the severity of the Great Depression, one might have expected a nationwide religious revival, but no such revival occurred. Instead, as historian Robert C. Handy has noted, America suffered from a "spiritual depression" that both antedated and paralleled the economic one. It was not until the outbreak of the Second World War that the national religious forces began to revive, as virtually all major faiths joined in the battle against Fascism. This renewed cooperation was dramatically highlighted in 1944 when four chaplains on the troop transport *Dorchester*—two Protestants, a rabbi, and a Catholic priest—gave up their life jackets to the evacuating troops. The four were last glimpsed, arms linked in prayer, as the ship went under. The army awarded them each a posthumous Distinguished Service Cross, and the incident was later immortalized in a stamp.

Two penetrating social analyses reflected this new outlook. In 1960, Jesuit John Courtney Murray penned his *We Hold These Truths*, subtitled "Catholic reflections on the American proposition." In it, he argued that Catholic doctrine regarding the state was crucial to comprehending contemporary religious pluralism. Civil society is a fundamental need of human nature, he argued, but its ideals are expressed in legends that go beyond facts and its existence is sustained by loyalties that are not logical. Yet he postulated a body of truths that all people of sound reason could attest to; recognition of this fact lay at the base of civility. What is a civil society? Murray's reply: "Civilization is formed by men locked together in argument."Five years earlier, sociologist Will Herberg had written his classic account, *Protestant-Catholic-Jew*. The thesis lay in the title, as Herberg argued that the three great historic faiths provided three equal ways of achieving an "American Identity." The United States Army of the postwar period allegedly asked recruits, "Are you Protestant, Catholic, or Jewish?" If one said he or she was an unbeliever, the army put them down as "Protestant."

The gradual realization of the horrors of the Holocaust produced a wave of sympathy toward American Judaism, and ecumenical activities grew in number. Many civic occasions in this era had a rabbi, priest, and minister to preside over ribbon cuttings. Restaurants in the 1950s began to place placards on their tables suggesting grace before meals and providing representative Protestant, Catholic, and Jewish graces. These prayers were often indistinguishable from one another, as were the writings of three national spokesmen: Catholic priest Fulton J. Sheen's *Peace of Soul*, Rabbi Joshua Liebman's *Peace of Mind*, Rev. Norman Vincent Peale's *The Power of Positive Thinking*. Clearly, by the 1950s the "ghetto mentality" that had played so great a part in the immigrant Catholic and Jewish experience had all but disappeared. The three historic faiths now shared in the nation's "cultural hegemony."

On the media front, the prestigious National Council of Churches controlled the free air time that each denomination received, thus forcing the fundamentalists and evangelicals (who were excluded) to *purchase* their radio and television space. Along with "The Lutheran Hour," the most popular religious program was the TV show led by Fulton J. Sheen, whose urbane manner charmed a number of non-Catholics and resulted in several prominent conversions. In the world of print, William Randolph Hearst allegedly told his Los Angeles editors in 1949 to "puff Graham," a directive that thrust William Franklin (Billy) Graham into the national spotlight, from which he would never depart.

Political analysts of the era also gave the works of theologian Reinhold Niebuhr considerable coverage. A severe critic of both fundamentalists and liberals, Niebuhr argued that the biblical insight into the nature of humankind was universally valid so long as the species walked the earth. His classic *Moral Man and Immoral Society* reflected his belief that although individuals could approach morality, all relationships between collectives (church, state, classes, nations) had to be based on power. Given the Cold War atmosphere and Niebuhr's hard critique of the Soviet Union, his writings were deemed essential reading for a generation of intellectuals. As a rabbi once quipped, "Thou shall love thy Niebuhr as thyself."

Finally, the Age of Consensus proved to be a "brick and mortar" period for most national religious groups. Both church and synagogue attendance rose steadily and new buildings followed suit. "Attend the church or synagogue of your choice" was a popular motto. During the 1950s, "social respectability" and "organized religion" overlapped to a considerable degree. But this, too, was about to change.

4. The 1960s to the Present Day

Writing in 1972, Yale historian Sydney Ahlstrom termed the decade of the 1960s "the end of Puritan America." He probably meant "Victorian America," with its reluctance to discuss sexuality and other items deemed "improper," but little has happened since to challenge Ahlstrom's observation. In fact, one might expand the term to "the end of Christian America" or the "end of Judeo-Christian America" as well.

From the 1960s forward, even the central terminology has changed meaning. In the early years of the century, *Christian* often meant (depending, of course, on the speaker and the circumstances) *Judeo-Christian*, that is, the whole heritage of Western civilization, including the Enlightenment and the onset of the scientific revolution. Certainly, the terms *Christian civilization* or *Christian gentleman* implied this, as did Roosevelt's choice of his party's theme song. From about 1970 forward, however, the term *Christian* began to take on far more narrow connotations. When one reads today of a Christian bookstore, Christian private school, Christian country music, Christian radio station, or Christian youth camp, the implication is no longer "the Western cultural tradition." Rather, it now implies "conservative evangelical Protestantism." As one southern coach recently remarked, he hoped to field a Christian football team that would be as strong as Notre Dame's. Those who advocate a Christian "Kingdom of God" today appeal to a far different audience from those who used the phrase in the 1910s.

Thanks to increasingly sophisticated polling techniques, we have much more information on the current demographic changes among the churches. Since the early 1970s, the mainline Protestants, Catholics, and Reform Jewish groups have all been steadily losing ground. In a single year, for example, 174,000 people left the Methodists, 104,000 the Presbyterians, and 70,000 the three leading Lutheran bodies. Among Catholics, weekly attendance at Mass fell 30 percent from 1977 to 1989, and recently the nation's Catholic bishops publicly complained about the Pentecostal attempts to "steal their sheep." By the mid-1980s, about one in three Americans had left the denomination into which they had been born. Recently the Episcopal church celebrated that they had *stopped* declining and were now holding their own. As writer Garry Wills observed about his Catholic church, no sooner had it succeeded in American life than it proceeded to commit hari-kari. Although the Vatican II reforms of the 1960s liberalized church doctrine, they virtually institutionalized dissent on a number of issues: priestly celibacy, birth control, divorce, and women priests. The church has shifted from a "devotional Catholicism" to a "selective Catholicism" as young Catholics strive to combine the heart of Catholic traditions with the post–Vatican II call to revitalize both church and society. The rise of feminist theology has also brought into question a number of traditional assumptions.

Even though sociologists agree that the exodus from organized religion has produced a growing body of "nothingarians" (the exact boundaries of which are impossible to discern), the groups that have gained from this realignment have generally been conservative ones. Within Judaism, this gain has meant growth in the Orthodox or Conservative branches; within Catholicism, it has meant a growth of the traditionalists and others who oppose the reforms of Vatican II. But in terms of publicity and raw numbers, it meant the rise of a wide variety of conservative evangelical Protestant denominations: the Evangelical Free Church, Church of the Nazarene, the Pentecostals, countless independent groups, and (especially) the Southern Baptists. With a firm emphasis on family values, the Latter-day Saints also grew steadily during this period. Clearly a powerful new force has emerged on the national religious scene. With a goal of "spreading the Gospel" by any means, these conservative groups dominate the airwaves and the nation's rear bumpers. Sociologists estimate that conservative evangelicals may be between 15–20 percent of the population.

But a number of other groups, often very nontraditional, have also arisen to claim a share of the nation's religious heritage. A variety of Asian immigrants brought the Buddhist faith to the country during the 1960s, and the popularity of books on Zen helped spread it to nonimmigrants as well. Disillusioned by the slow pace of civil rights, many Black Americans were attracted to some form of Islam. Today there are about 5.2 million Muslims in America, 42 percent African-American converts. This makes Islam the second largest non-Christian faith in the nation. In 1993, the streets of the nation's major cities bear a remarkable resemblance to the Chicago Parliament of Religions. There are over five hundred American denominations.

Simultaneously, in a rather abrupt reversal of earlier trends, the growing positivist faith in science has suddenly given way to a celebration of (at worst) the irrational or (at best) several new varieties of spirituality. "Organized religion" may have declined, but "religion" has certainly continued in a myriad of forms. Here we meet the "New Age" movement, one seen on special racks in virtually every bookstore. An umbrella phrase, the "New

Age" draws from a variety of belief systems—including Eastern faiths, Native American spirituality, and Theosophy—to encourage each person to create his or her own "reality."

Cartoonist Doug Marlette had his character Rev. Will B. Dunne read the Twenty-third Psalm to spoof these new trends:

> The Lord is my therapist,
> I shall not experience negative
>   feedback.
>
> He maketh me to mellow out
> In green pastures. He leadeth
> Me beside Perrier waters.
>
> He gives me permission to
> Get in touch with my
>   feelings.
>
> He leadeth me in the
> Paths of positive
>   Self-image.
>
> Yea, though I walk
> Through the valley of bad vibes
> I won't get uptight.

Dunne then concludes, "I hate these new translations."

In 1978, Congress also passed the American Indian Religious Freedom Act to protect Indian sacred sites. Although controversies over Indian religious liberties tend to be local rather than national (compare the return of Mount Adams to the Yakima Nation or the return of Blue Lake to Taos pueblo), they often create intense regional controversy. Native peoples do not restrict "the sacred" to a single book, church, or graveyard; rather, for them "the sacred" may encompass a river, bluff, lake, mountain, or even an entire region. In 1987, a group of prominent liberal church spokespeople in Seattle issued a "formal apology" to the First Nations of the region for their churches' historic assault upon Native faiths. They urged joining hands in a united battle, concluding, "May the God of Abraham and Sarah, and the Spirit who lives in both the Cedar and Salmon People, be honored and celebrated." Never have Native American faiths been given a more respectful hearing than at present.

There is also a legal aspect to the shifts in contemporary religious history. In the 1780s founder James Madison argued that a person's loyalty to the Creator superseded all loyalty to the state. Thus, he helped construct the First Amendment—"Congress shall make no law respecting an establishment of religion, or prohibiting the free exercise thereof"—to prevent the *federal* government from intruding upon religion. Prior to World War II, the Supreme Court dealt with relatively few church–state cases. Not until 1947 did the Supreme Court interpret this in a way that outlawed *any* level of government—national, state, or local—from so interfering. As a result, the Court has had to rule on a variety of recent cases: aid to parochial schools, busing, textbooks, plus, of course, abortion in *Roe vs. Wade* (1973). The Court's decisions in this area are perhaps less important than the fact that Americans have agreed to allow the justices to make these decisions. It's a game, historian Sidney E. Mead once remarked, a game that Americans have agreed to play for the high stakes of freedom.

As the nation's religious forces realigned, the issues involved naturally spilled over into politics. The catch phrase has become "national values," but there is little agreement as to what those are.

Over the years, politicians have generally constructed the civic arenas so as not to offend any specific religious group. Thus, the state has become increasingly "secular." In the words of Catholic priest Richard John Neuhaus, America has created a "naked public square."

Whose values will fill this square? This is, perhaps, the most crucial socioreligious question of the day. In the Progressive era, the nation seemed to share a broad consensus on biblical rhetoric and social values; but ever since the 1960s this "consensus" has been conspicuous by its absence.

What are "national values"? Where do they come from? The home? Tradition? The extended community? And who is responsible for passing them on to the next generation? These are not easy questions to answer.

From the 1960s forward, however, a number of observers have suggested that the nation's values are being dominated by (if not actually created by) an agency far removed from public control, the media: radio, the wire services, television, the music industry, video, and, of course, film.

The optimists have pointed to the media's great ability to spread the best of Judeo-Christian principles. Scholars have found theological messages and an African-American "secular spirituality" in many Black popular songs. Others have discovered biblical insights in cartoonist Charles Schultz's comic strip *Peanuts* or in the lyrics of songwriters Bob Dylan, John Lennon, and Cliff Richard. Catholic priest Andrew Greeley has argued that Bruce Springsteen songs such as "Reason to Believe" and superstar Madonna's "Like a Virgin" reflect the Catholic values of their youth. But this, it must be admitted, is the minority opinion.

For many observers, "the media" have assumed the role "evolution" played during the 1920s: they have become the source of all evil. But perhaps the attack has been misdirected. If Rutgers media critic Neil Postman is correct, the problem does not lie with the 270 on-screen murders that Arnold Schwarzenegger in his film personae has personally perpetrated; nor with the 8,000 on-screen murders and 100,000 on-screen violent acts that the average seventh grader will have observed; nor with the 14,000 sexual encounters that he or she will have seen by age fourteen; nor with the stereotypical roles assigned to nonmainstream cultures; nor with the use of crudity to sell every product imaginable; nor with the "forcing" of visual images upon a viewer in a way that no book could ever do; nor with the decay of language, especially in the music industry. Instead, Postman argues, the chief result of media dominance of American life has been to trivialize "the sacred." Within a generation, the electronic media have reduced every aspect of life to a single level: entertainment. And what is the goal of entertainment but to amuse and to make money? And as conservationist John Muir once wryly noted, "nothing dollarable is safe."

That is why, sociologists argue, we are living in the midst of a genuine "culture war." As sociologists Robert Wuthnow and James Davison Hunter have shown, the nation's religious forces have begun to realign drastically. Now liberal Protestants and Catholics and Jews team on one side versus conservative Protestants, Catholics, and Jews on the other. The dynamic questions today usually involve sexuality, especially the issues of abortion and homosexual legislation. In the spring of 1993, for example, the Catholic bishops of New York aligned themselves with Baptist Rev. Pat Robertson of Virginia to oppose the proposed New York school curriculum with its liberal stance on homosexuality.

The battle is heated. What is at stake, proponents argue, is the ethical, moral, and religious content of the "naked public square." Unlike the theory of evolution, which faded from public view during the 1930s and has not really returned, the issues regarding sexuality are likely to have far more staying power.

While this noisy, bitter battle is raging on the national scene, a parallel, more quiet revolution is going on as well. The baby boomer generation (1946–1965) gained fame for its rejection of hierarchies and organizations (especially organized religion). But as it now raises its own children, there has been a drift back to the churches and synagogues, but often on their own terms. As sociologist Robert Bellah has noted, many Americans seem to be forging their own faiths, a concept he labeled "Sheilaism," after Sheila, an interviewee, who had cobbled together her own sincere but very individualistic religious faith. Indeed, Bellah has suggested that this "individualized faith" may well be the most common faith perspective in the nation today.

If this is so, then the fate of organized religion will continue to shape *individual* lives but will probably fail to shape the *social order*, except, perhaps, in isolated subregions. Rather than serving as a broad, necessarily vague ultimate social goal, religion will become the core of an increasingly restrictive "tribal" identity, varying drastically from "tribe" to "tribe." Only in one respect will it share a universality. It will be the faith of a variety of "outsiders," that is, people who do not feel comfortable with mainstream, secular culture. In short, if trends continue, the "mainstream" of American religious history simply will not be "mainstream" anymore.

Just where does New Mexican religious history fit into this tale? The answer varies with the period under discussion.

1. The Turn of the Century

From 1890 to 1920, the Roman Catholic church in New Mexico assumed roughly the same role for the state as the eastern Protestant establishment played for the nation at large. The state's largely French and Italian clerics presided over what might be termed a "New Mexican Catholic Cultural hegemony." (In 1906, for example, there were 122,000 Catholics and only 13,000 Protestants in the state.)

In general, the hierarchy was not pleased with the steady influx of non-Catholics into New Mexico. The Jesuits used the pages of *Revista Católica* (which was published in New Mexico until 1917) to counter the Protestant position, and when the bishop of Tucson, Henry Granjon, visited the Mesilla Valley in 1902, he had little good to say about the immigrant Anglos. (In turn, the immigrants also had little good to say about the Catholic church.)

But, again like the national situation, the Catholic "cultural hegemony" proved relatively mild and basically tolerant. New Mexico's Catholic–Jewish relations generally remained cordial. The Hebrew inscription over the entrance of Bishop Lamy's cathedral in Santa Fe and the political role of the Seligman family attest to that. Similarly, Catholic–Protestant tensions remained confined to editorials, diaries, and harsh words. In truth, New Mexican Catholicism showed remarkable flexibility toward the faiths of the newcomers.

There are several reasons for this situation. To begin with, New Mexico boasted not one but three overlapping "Catholicisms." First was the European-oriented strand, represented by the Belgian, German, Italian, French, and Irish priests. (In 1912, the state had but one Hispanic cleric.) The architectural monument to this aspect of New Mexico's history is Bishop Lamy's French Romanesque cathedral in Santa Fe. Second was the persuasive Hispanic folk Catholicism of the Rio Grande borderlands, once described by historian Arnoldo De León as "an attitude consonant more with life experience than theology." Hispanic Catholics in New Mexico celebrated a variety of religious holidays that had only dim echoes east of the Mississippi: January 17, the Feast of San Antonio, a day for blessing the animals; June 24, San Juan's Day, linked with the first fruits and vegetables of the season; and Los Pastores, a Spanish medieval miracle play. The healing skills of the *curanderas*, about which Rudolfo Anaya writes so well, the solemn public processions during holy week, and the "healing mud" of the chapel at Chimayo—the "American Lourdes"—also were distinctive to the region. The symbolic representation of this theme would be the Penitentes, a lay brotherhood of northern New Mexico that astounded the Protestants and perplexed the European Catholics until New Mexico's archbishop finally granted the group official church recognition in 1935.

The third unique aspect of Catholic New Mexico lay with the syncretization and accommodation that the Native American groups had made with the prevailing power structure. The Jicarilla and Mescalero Apaches, the Navajos, the Rio Grande Pueblos, and Zuni pueblo have all retained their native traditions under a Christian overlay. The Pueblo dances may bear the names of saints, but they reflect ceremonies that antedate European contact by centuries. Isleta leader Pablo Abeita (1871–1940) probably served as the most distinguished Pueblo spokesman of his generation. While a Catholic priest intoned a brief funeral service for him, he was buried primarily with tribal, not Christian, rites.

New Mexico's Catholics and Protestants each engaged in parallel efforts, from 1900 to 1920, to create the state's "Social Gospel." Lacking urban areas or industrial poverty, New Mexicans had little need for institutional churches or Social Gospel theologians. In fact, the frontier churches had almost always seen social issues as a central part of their mission. But the emerging concerns over health and education in the early years of the century called forth a new commitment from all churches.

During the first decades of the twentieth century, tuberculosis (TB) ranked as perhaps the state's major industry. In 1900, the "white plague" loomed as the nation's number one killer, far ahead of cancer or heart disease, claiming over 150,000 people a year. No cure existed save rest, high altitude, and (perhaps) a dry climate. Thus, thousands of "lungers" made their way to the state to try to regain their health. Photos of Albuquerque's Central Avenue show a predominance of sanitoria, and by 1920 perhaps 10 percent of the state population consisted of health seekers.

The state's churches responded to this need. In 1902, the Sisters of St. Joseph began their hospital in Albuquerque. Two years later, the American

Baptists sent a trained nurse to aid the city in public health; the Northern Methodists also established a TB sanitorium in the Manzano Mountains. In 1906, Presbyterian minister Hugh A. Cooper (who had TB himself) began what would become Presbyterian Hospital. The city of Albuquerque is unique even today in that its two major hospitals are church-related, rather than civic, institutions.

The other arena that brought forth parallel church effort concerned the region's schools. The fledgling University of New Mexico (founded 1889) had no secondary school system to support it. Thus, both Protestants and Catholics viewed parochial schooling as the key to the future. The Catholics worried that the public schools would be essentially Protestant, whereas the Protestants worried that the teachers might be largely nuns and priests. But territorial and state coffers were so limited that a viable system was never put in place until the advent of paved roads and school buses made long-distance transportation feasible. This change did not occur until the 1930s. Thus, the Methodists (Harwood Schools), the Presbyterians (over fifty schools headed by Allison James School in Santa Fe and the Menaul School in Albuquerque), the Christian Brothers (several schools in Taos and Mora plus the College of Santa Fe), and the Jesuits (several Albuquerque schools) all established educational institutions. Parallel parochial school systems became the order of the day.

From the 1890s forward, much of the religious history of New Mexico has flowed *outside* the boundaries of the prevailing "religio-cultural establishment." The saga of Francis Schlatter, the "mysterious healer" and prophet, certainly fits this category. During the 1890s, Schlatter spent a winter with Agnes Morley Cleaveland on the plains of San Augustin and when he departed predicted a war between classes and the establishment of a New Jerusalem in Datil, New Mexico.

The saga of the Land of Shalam (1884–c.1908) in the Mesilla Valley also fits into this tradition. Born from the fertile mind of Dr. John Ballou Newbrough, Shalam was based on the "automatic writing" from spirits who used Newbrough as a medium to produce the *Oahspe Bible*. Less well known than the *Book of Mormon*, the *Oahspe Bible* is America's second indigenous scripture. It also formed the basis for the utopian experiment, the Land of Shalam, near Las Cruces, with its motto: "Let not these come, the lawyer, doctor, preacher, or politician or others who desire to live by their wits." The Faithist community took in orphans and practiced communal farming, but could not convince the next generation that their rules were the key to life's happiness. Historian Lee Priestly once termed the colony "heroic even in failure."

2. New Mexico, 1920–1940

The fundamentalist–modernist controversy of the 1920s and the activities of the Klan had little impact on New Mexico. In fact, several refugees from Colorado and Texas harassment sought employment in the state. The collapse of Protestant hegemony could hardly affect a region where the Protestants had never been "hegemonic" in the first place. In 1927, writer Erna Fergusson wrote an essay for the *New Republic* arguing that Santa Fe was the only American city that did *not* want a Chautauqua.

The national evolution controversy had only moderate impact on New Mexico. The Albuquerque *Morning Journal* covered the Scopes trial on the front page, but it devoted equal attention to the Mary Pickford trial and the persistent drought of that year. In the editorial column, the paper ridiculed Bryan as "a political quack" and dismissed the quarrel as largely a "prejudice against the monkey tribe." Significantly, it mentioned no state concern over evolution.

In California, former Massachusetts Yankee Charles Fletcher Lummis successfully convinced a number of midwestern Protestant arrivals that Spanish missions and iconography should become part of their new western self-image. He argued that the Franciscan missions of California resembled the Puritan churches of New England and that one need not hold to the Catholic faith to appreciate their symbolic power. The 1920s promotion of tourism in New Mexico argued along similar lines, but never quite as convincingly. Although the Santa Fe Railroad and Fred Harvey hotels enticed thousands of visitors to the Land of Enchantment, tours of the state's Franciscan mission churches never approached the popularity of the California "mission tours" or visits to Tucson's San Xavier del Bac (both restored in the early years of the century).

The area where New Mexico did share national concerns during the interwar period lay with church expansion and institution building. As the east side of the state—"Little Texas"—was homesteaded, the settlers brought their denominational preferences with them. As the *Southwestern Baptist* put it in 1907, "The Lord is simply filling this country with Baptists." The interdenominational Bloys Camp Meeting in Marfa, Texas, also drew many supporters from southeastern New Mexico, and the three-day singing festivals of the region's Pentecostal churches found their way into the WPA state guidebook. But so, too, did the Catholic church expand, founding the College of St. Joseph (later the University of Albuquerque) and establishing a steady stream of primary and secondary schools. Simultaneously, the Protestants began to close their parochial school systems, leaving the field to a (presumably secular) public school system and a parallel Catholic parochial system.

For years, however, the two systems overlapped in New Mexico. In fact, as late as 1948 about 150 Roman Catholic nuns and brothers were teaching in the state public school system. Many of them wore their clerical garb in the classroom, a situation probably not duplicated in any other region of the nation.

Eventually this was challenged in a complex legal case, *Zellers et al. v. Huff et al.* (usually known as the "Dixon case"), and finally decided by the state supreme court in 1951. As lawyer and historian Janelle Haught has noted, a group of Protestants in tiny Dixon, New Mexico, brought suit regarding the separation of church and state. The case had a bitter dimension to it as the Protestants wanted all teachers who had taught Catholic doctrine in the schools forever banned from teaching in the state. (The gym teacher eventually was acquitted after denying that she had taught Catholic P.E.) Protestant governor Thomas Mabry defended the Catholics, praising them for providing education in out-of-the-way places that could not have offered it without them. Archbishop Edwin V. Byrne eventually withdrew the religious teachers from the public schools just before the case reached the court, thus making it essentially moot and obviating any adverse national publicity. Although the decision favoring the plaintiffs may have solved the issue on a legal basis, it had disastrous local consequences. The popular Sisters left the community for their mother house in St. Louis, never to return. Because of low enrollment the Dixon High school was eventually closed, and the students had to be bused over fifteen miles each way to Española. Had Byrne not removed his religious teachers, however, the Dixon case had the potential to become a national Supreme Court pathbreaker; as it happened, however, it simply became a local issue.

3. The Late 1930s to the 1960s

As with the nation at large, church membership in New Mexico experienced considerable growth during this time period. For the Catholics, this continued to be very much a "brick and mortar" time. Archbishop Edwin Byrne (1943–1963) ably oversaw an enormous church-building program. In addition to parish expansion, this included a Trappist monastery in the Pecos Mountains north of Santa Fe and a Benedictine monastery, Christ in the Desert, near Abiquiu, with a striking chapel designed by famed architect George Nakashima. In 1947, Father Gerald Fitzgerald used seed money from Cardinal Francis Spellman to fund the monastery Via Coeli, in Jemez Springs, to rehabilitate parish priests with psychological problems. In 1966, the Servants of the Paraclete established its first program there to rehabilitate clerical alcoholics (not pedophiles, whom Fitzgerald wanted sent to an island retreat off the coast of California). In a move that would later have serious long-term consequences, this program reported directly to Rome, not to the archbishop of Santa Fe.

The Protestants were similarly active. Church growth followed the expansion of the cities, especially Albuquerque, Hobbs, Las Cruces, and Santa Fe. And the two largest denominations built major conference centers for the region. Led by Rev. Harry Stagg, the Southern Baptists created the Glorieta Assembly between Santa Fe and Las Vegas; similarly, the Presbyterians utilized land donated by rancher Arthur N. Park to build their Ghost Ranch Conference Center near Abiquiu. Both would become nationally known.

In 1951, Irish-born Brother Mathias Barrett moved to Albuquerque to found a new order, The Little Brothers of the Good Shepherd. A charismatic and forceful personality, Brother Mathias borrowed used coffee grounds from restaurants and badgered wealthy Catholic parishioners for funds to serve the homeless of the city. From these beginnings the order grew to become international. In 1970, the Conservative congregation B'nai Israel completed its impressive temple near I-40 in Albuquerque. Even though the Catholic "cultural hegemony" remained in many rural sections of the state, in the urban areas, especially, the church shared its "cultural dominance" with the other mainline groups.

4. The 1960s–1990s

From 1960 to the present, New Mexico began to emerge as a "spiritual magnet" for the rest of the nation. In a number of areas, the state paralleled national trends. Beginning in the late 1940s, the Southern Baptists began to grow rapidly so that by 1993 they were larger than all the other state's Protestant denominations combined. Unlike those in many other areas, however, New Mexico Southern Baptists have retained a Social Gospel emphasis. For years, the First Baptist Church of Albuquerque, for example, has run an extensive free lunch program, funded largely by philanthropist Calvin Horn. Other conservative evangelical groups, such as Victory Love and Calvary Chapel, have also flourished.

Similarly, the liberal Protestant groups have suffered steady attrition. First Congregational Church of Albuquerque has seen an annual loss of three to four members for almost two decades. An Albuquerque Presbyterian church has gone from two thousand to less than four hundred in the same period.

The Catholic church, too, has suffered from a number of embarrassing losses. Probably the most telling attacks on the authority of the New Mexico Catholic church came with the numerous charges of sexual impropriety in the late 1980s and early 1990s, with many stemming from inadequate supervision of former residents of Jemez Springs Via Coeli. Some of these accusations forced the resignation of popular Archbishop Robert Sanchez, a most painful time for all involved.

As the Catholic "hegemony" began to subside, New Mexico became home to a wide variety of both traditional and nontraditional faiths. By the mid-1970s, a Sikh community had become a prominent part of both the Española Valley and Santa Fe life. In 1976, their community had become the group's national headquarters. The 1980s also witnessed the rise and decline of an Islamic community near Abiquiu. Their mosque, Dar-al-Islam, remains as one of New Mexico's many architectural wonders. Nearby Santa Fe also boasts a number of Zen centers.

The study of religion on the university level has also grown. Eastern New Mexico University in Portales has long had a unique relationship with the faiths of the region, whereas the College of the Southwest in Hobbs has a Baptist connection. At the University of New Mexico, philosopher Andrew Burgess heads a popular Religious Studies major. The Anthropology Department boasts such experts as Alfonso Ortiz and the Sociology Department houses Patrick McNamara, former head of the national Association for the Sociology of Religion. Various compromise programs allow state university students to earn credit from denominationally taught classes. In addition, the research of historian Stanley Hordes of Santa Fe has created a good deal of popular interest in New Mexico's "crypto-Jewish" heritage.

All these movements reflect national trends, but in a number of areas New Mexico may be emerging as a potential leader for the religious history of the twenty-first century. This can be seen in three areas.

First, although the major Protestant–Catholic–Jewish faiths may be realigning, they are all still very active in New Mexico. Indeed, they perform a myriad of functions, for their congregations and for the community. Thus, much of the state's religious energies still flow through the traditional institutional forms.

Simultaneously, these historic faiths have begun to accommodate the increased growth of more "personalized faiths." Nowhere is this "Sheilaism" more evident than in Santa Fe. Only the Pacific Northwest, Sedona, Arizona, Boulder, Colorado, and perhaps Los Angeles can rival "the city different" in its variety of religious offerings, traditional and nontraditional. From spiritual healing to ghost writing, from Protestantism, Catholicism, Judaism, and Mormonism to denominations that consist of a handful of people, Santa Fe has it all.

Third is the increasing interest in Native faiths. As ecology has begun to emerge as (perhaps) the most ecumenical issue of the late twentieth century, non-Native people are looking to Indian perspectives on life to enlarge their understanding. New Mexico's Navajos, with their emphasis on "balance and harmony"—as seen in Nizhoni Days—and the thousand-year-old ceremonials of the Pueblos are attracting larger audiences. As writer Peggy Pond Church once observed, when the Pueblo Indians dance, they dance for us all.

The historic tolerance of the Catholic establishment, the easy accommodation of the Jews, the rise of conservative evangelicals, the growth of new faiths, and the cultural and physical landscape, especially the landscape, have combined to bring an almost endless variety of religious groups to New Mexico.

Although each group steadfastly hews to its particular emphasis, all (or almost all) have contributed to the growth of common good, available to believer and nonbeliever alike. The vitality of organized religion in New Mexico reminds us that the church and synagogue are first and foremost institutions. It is as *organized bodies of the faithful* that they have had their greatest historic impact. The focus on Native American (and New Age) concern over the land echoes a comment by an elderly apple rancher that "all civilization boils down to one word—dirt." And the evangelical emphasis on the Bible reminds us that, even in an electronic age, some words are more important than others. In short, the future of religious America will probably revolve around a spirituality that flows *within* and *outside* denominational structures. But in New Mexico, at least, that has been the case for over five hundred years.

For Further Reading

1. The Nation

The literature on religion in twentieth-century America is enormous. One should start with the two best bibliographies, Nelson R. Burr et al., *A Critical Bibliography of Religion in America*, 2 vols. (Princeton, N.J.: Princeton University Press, 1961), and John F. Wilson, ed., *Church and State in America: A Bibliographical Guide*, Vol. 2, *The Civil War to the Present Day* (Westport, Conn.: Greenwood Press, 1987).

Edwin S. Gaustad's *Historical Atlas of Religion in America*, rev. ed. (New York: Harper and Row, 1976); and Roger Finke and Rodney Stark, *The Churching of America, 1776–1990* (New Brunswick, N.J.: Rutgers University Press, 1992), are essential for statistical information.

Overviews by Herbert Wallace Schneider, *Religion in Twentieth Century America* (New York: Atheneum, 1969); William R. Miller, ed., *Contemporary American Protestant Thought: 1900–1970* (Indianapolis: Bobbs-Merrill, 1973); and even the magisterial Sydney E. Ahlstrom, *A Religious History of the American People* (New Haven: Yale University Press, 1972), sound a bit dated, so rapidly is the religious scene changing.

Martin E. Marty has begun a four-volume history of religion in the twentieth century under the overall title, *Modern American Religion*, which promises to be definitive. At this time, three have been published: *Volume 1: The Irony of It All, 1893–1919, Volume 2: The Noise of Conflict, 1919–1941*, and *Volume 3: Under God, Indivisible, 1941–1960* (all Chicago: University of Chicago Press, 1986, 1991, and 1996, respectively). See also the readings collected in Patrick McNamara, ed., *Religion American Style* (Belmont, Calif.: Wadsworth, 1984); and the shrewd analysis by Garry Wills in *Under God: Religion and American Politics* (New York: Simon and Schuster, 1990).

The increasing role of women in modern religion may be found in Rosemary Radford Reuther and Rosemary Skinner Keller, eds., *Women and Religion in America*, Vol. 3, 1900–1968 (San Francisco: Harper and Row, 1986). See also the numerous works by Catholic gadfly Mary Daly, especially *The Church and the Second Sex* (New York: Harper and Row, 1975), and *Beyond God the Father: Toward a Philosophy of Women's Liberation* (Boston: Beacon Press, 1973). The role of women in the various contemporary witchcraft and goddess movements is covered in Margot Adler, *Drawing Down the Moon* (Boston: Beacon Press, 1986).

A good overview of the groups not considered "mainstream" is R. Laurence Moore, *Religious Outsiders and the Making of Americans* (New York: Oxford University Press, 1986). The secularist view may be found in

Howard B. Radest, *The Devil and Secular Humanism: The Children of the Enlightenment* (New York: Praeger, 1990).

Probably the two best single volumes on the Catholic experience are John Tracy Ellis, *American Catholicism*, 2d ed. (Chicago: University of Chicago Press, 1969); and Jay P. Dolan, *American Catholic Experience: A History from Colonial Times to the Present* (Garden City, N.Y.: Doubleday and Company, 1985). See also the more specific coverage by David O'Brien in *American Catholics and Social Reform: The New Deal Years* (New York: Oxford University Press, 1968), and the insightful essays by John Courtney Murray, S.J., *We Hold These Truths: Catholic Reflections on the American Proposition* (Kansas City: Sheed and Ward, 1960, 1988). The documents of Vatican II have been collected in J. L. Gonzalez and the Daughters of St. Paul, *The Sixteen Documents of Vatican II* (Boston: The Daughters of St. Paul, 1967). The works by Andrew Greeley, especially *The Catholic Myth: The Behavior and Beliefs of American Catholics* (New York: Charles Scribner's Sons, 1990) and his autobiography *Confessions of a Parish Priest* (New York: Pocket Books, 1987), are always insightful.

For American Judaism in the twentieth century, see Irving Howe, *World of Our Fathers* (New York: Harcourt, Brace, Jovanovich, 1976); Joseph L. Blau, *Judaism in America: From Curiosity to Third Faith* (Chicago: University of Chicago Press, 1976); and Charles E. Silberman, *A Certain People: American Jews and Their Lives Today* (New York: Simon and Schuster, 1985).

Perhaps the best twentieth-century studies of the Latter-day Saints are Thomas G. Alexander, *Mormonism in Transition: A History of the Latter-day Saints, 1890–1930* (Urbana: University of Illinois, 1986); Klaus J. Hansen, *Mormonism and the American Experience* (Chicago: University of Chicago Press, 1981); and Leonard Arrington and Davis Bitton, *The Mormon Experience: A History of the Latter-day Saints* (New York: Alfred A. Knopf, 1979). Jan Shipps, author of *Mormonism: The Story of a New Religious Tradition* (1985), has just completed a study of twentieth-century Mormonism.

The evolution controversy may be followed in Ferenc Morton Szasz, *The Divided Mind of Protestant America, 1880–1930* (University: University of Alabama Press, 1982); George M. Marsden, *Fundamentalism and American Culture: The Shaping of Twentieth-Century Evangelicalism: 1870–1925* (New York: Oxford University Press, 1980); and Edward J. Larson, *Trial and Error: The American Controversy over Creation and Evolution* (New York: Oxford University Press, 1989). In *The Creationists: The Evolution of Scientific Creationism* (New York: Alfred A. Knopf, 1992), Ronald L. Numbers takes the story up to the present day.

A number of scholars have tried to assess the current state of religious affairs. Representative interviews with modern Americans with strong faith perspectives may be found in Ralph Carnes and Valerie Carnes, *The Road to Damascus: A Journey into the New American Religious Consciousness* (New York: St. Martin's Press, 1986); Phillip L. Berman, *The Search for Meaning: Americans Talk about What They Believe and Why* (New York: Ballantine Books, 1990); and Randall Balmer, *Mine Eyes Have Seen the Glory: A Journey into the Evangelical Subculture in America* (New York: Oxford University Press, 1989).

The collapse of the mainline churches was first documented by Dean M. Kelley, *Why Conservative Churches Are Growing* (New York: Harper's, 1972). With the assistance of R. Scott Appleby, Martin E. Marty has edited several books of essays that explore fundamentalism in a worldwide context: *Fundamentalisms and the State* and *Fundamentalisms and Society* (both Chicago: University of Chicago Press, 1993).

Historians such as Ronald B. Flowers, *Religion in Strange Times: The 1960s and 1970s* (Macon, Ga.: Mercer University Press, 1984), and Erling Jorstad, *Holding Fast/Pressing On: Religion in America in the 1980s* (New York: Praeger, 1990), provide a narrative account of events during these tumultuous decades, but for analysis one turns chiefly to sociologists.

The books by James Davison Hunter, *Culture Wars: The Struggle to Define America* (New York: Basic Books, 1991), and Robert Wuthnow, *The Restructuring of American Religion* (Princeton, N.J.: Princeton University Press, 1988), ably set forth the main poles of the current realignment. Sociologists Jeffrey K. Hadden and Anson Shupe have explored the media in *Televangelism: Power and Politics on God's Frontier* (New York: Henry Holt and Co., 1986), while Steve Bruce has analyzed the politics of American right-wing religion in *The Rise and Fall of the New Christian Right: Conservative Protestant Politics in America, 1978–1988* (Oxford: Clarendon Press, 1990). Also, Peter W. Williams provides an overview in *Popular Religion in America: Symbolic Change and the Modernization Process in Historical Perspective* (Urbana: University of Illinois Press, 1989). Perhaps the most insightful study of all is Robert Bellah et al., *Habits of the Heart: Individualism and Commitment in American Life* (Berkeley: University of California Press, 1985).

The New Age movement has so far defied easy analysis. One should begin with the classic account by Charles S. Braden, *Spirits in Rebellion: The Rise and Development of New Thought* (Dallas: Southern Methodist University Press, 1963). A good presentation of their point of view is Marilyn Ferguson, *The Aquarian Conspiracy: Personal and Social Transformation in the 1980s* (Los Angeles: J. P. Tarcher, 1980). See also Catherine L. Albanese,

Nature Religion in America: From the Algonkian Indians to the New Age (Chicago: University of Chicago Press, 1991).

2. New Mexico

Any study of religion in modern New Mexico must begin with Richard W. Etulain, comp., *Religion in the Twentieth-Century American West: A Bibliography* (Albuquerque: Center for the American West, 1991). As Etulain shows, one must glean a good deal of New Mexico's modern religious history from regional studies.

Historians have hitherto devoted most of their attention to the colonial period and early nineteenth century. Consequently, much of twentieth-century New Mexico's religious history remains to be told. For example, we still lack a modern history of the New Mexico Roman Catholic church. At the moment, one must turn to the regional coverage by Carol Jensen, in Jay P. Dolan, ed., *The American Catholic Parish: A History from 1850 to the Present*, Vol. 2, *Pacific States, Intermountain West, Midwest* (New York: Paulist Press, 1987); and various local or parish studies, such as Joe L. Montoya, *Isleta Pueblo and the Church of St. Augustine* (Isleta: St. Augustine Parish, 1986); Octavia Fellin, *Yahweh, The Voice that Beautifies the Land: A Brief Historical View of the Diocese of Gallup, New Mexico . . .* (Gallup: Diocese of Gallup, 1976); Henry Heitz, *Historical Notes on St. Vincent de Paul's Parish* (Silver City, N.M.: n.p., 1924), and *The Lord and New Mexico* (Santa Fe: The Archdiocese, 1975). Marta Weigle, *Brothers of Light, Brothers of Blood: The Penitentes of the Southwest* (Albuquerque: University of New Mexico Press, 1976), remains the definitive work on the Penitentes, as does Carol N. Lovato on Brother Mathias: *Brother Mathias: Founder of The Little Brothers of the Good Shepherd* (Huntington, Ind.: Our Sunday Visitor, 1987). Patrick H. McNamara, *Conscience First, Tradition Second: A Study of Young American Catholics* (Albany: State University of New York Press, 1992), draws on two thousand questionnaires from students at "St. Martin's" (actually Albuquerque's St. Pius High School).

There are virtually no twentieth-century Catholic memoirs or autobiographies. The historian needs additional firsthand accounts, such as found in Michael Romero Taylor, ed., *Along the Rio Grande: A Pastoral Visit to Southwest New Mexico in 1902* [by] Monsignor Henry Granjon, Bishop of Tucson (Albuquerque: University of New Mexico Press, 1986).

Only recently have photographers, architectural specialists, and art historians begun to give the historic New Mexican churches the attention they deserve. See Christopher Wilson, *A Survey of Historic Churches of Northwest New Mexico, 1988–89* (Santa Fe: The New Mexico Community Foundation, 1989); Michael Miller, *Monuments of Adobe: The Religious Architecture and Traditions of New Mexico* (Dallas, Tex.: Taylor Publishing Company, 1991); and the photographic coverage by Robert Brewer in *The Persistence of Memory: New Mexico's Churches* (Santa Fe: Museum of New Mexico Press, 1990).

The state's Presbyterians also lack a denominational history, but Randi Jones Walker, *Protestantism in the Sangre de Cristos, 1850–1920* (Albuquerque: University of New Mexico Press, 1991), and Mark T. Banker, *Presbyterian Missions and Cultural Interaction in the Far Southwest, 1850–1950* (Urbana: University of Illinois Press, 1993), provide solid analyses of the early twentieth century. See also Carolyn Atkins's two studies: *Los Tres Campos: The Three Fields: A History of Protestant Evangelists and Presbyterians in Chimayo, Cordova and Truches, New Mexico* (Albuquerque: Menaul Historical Library, 1978), and "Menaul School, 1881–1930 . . . Not Leaders, Merely but Christian Leaders," *Journal of Presbyterian History* 50 (Winter 1980): 279–94. The story of regional Hispanic Presbyterianism may be found in R. Douglas Brackenridge and Francisco O. García-Treto, *Iglesia Presbiteriana: A History of Presbyterians and Mexican Americans in the Southwest* (San Antonio: Trinity University Press, 1974).

The twentieth-century Methodist story has yet to be told. Thomas Harwood touches on the period in his *History of New Mexico Spanish and English Missions of the Methodist Episcopal Church from 1850 to 1910*, Vol. 2, 1886–1910 (Albuquerque: El Abogado Press, 1910). Otherwise, the chief source is John W. Hood, *Methodism in Albuquerque, 1879–1939* (Albuquerque: University of New Mexico Press, 1947). For the Congregationalists, see Margaret Connell Szasz, *First Congregational Church of Albuquerque, New Mexico: A Centennial History, 1880–1980* (Albuquerque: First Congregational Church, 1980). For the Episcopalians, see James M. Stoney, *Lighting the Candle: The Episcopal Church on the Upper Rio Grande* (Santa Fe: Rydal Press, 1961).

Of all the Protestant denominations, the New Mexico Baptists have received the most historical treatment: David H. Stratton, *The First Century of Baptists in New Mexico, 1849–1950* (Albuquerque: Woman's Missionary Union of New Mexico, 1954); and Lewis A. Myers, *A History of New Mexico Baptists* (Albuquerque: Baptist Convention of New Mexico, 1965). Their most prominent minister, Rev. Harry Stagg, is the subject of a biography by Bonnie Ball O'Brien, *Harry P. Stagg, Christian Statesman* (Nashville: Broadman Press, 1976). One should also mention the series of brief biographical sketches by Betty Danielson in the *Baptist New Mexican*.

For the Faithist community near Las Cruces, see Lee Priestley, "Shalam, Land of Children," *La Crónica* (November 1978). Their scripture, *Oahspe:*

A New Bible in the Words of Jehovih . . . (London: Kosman Press, 1882; 1929), may still be found in used bookstores around the state.

Modern New Mexico Jewish history has also been slighted. Abraham I. Shindling has written *History of the Los Alamos Jewish Center, Los Alamos, New Mexico, 1944 to 1957* (Albuquerque: Valliant Printing, 1958). El Paso Rabbi Floyd S. Fierman wrote several studies on the Jews of the Southwest, but he usually concentrated on the nineteenth century. An example of his work is *Guts and Ruts: The Jewish Pioneer on the Trail in the American Southwest* (New York: KTAV Publishing House, 1985). Gary Herz and Stanley M. Hordes have penned *Stones of Remembrance: The Historic Jewish Cemetery in Las Vegas, New Mexico* (Santa Fe: New Mexico Jewish Historical Society, 1990). There is also a *New Mexico Jewish Historical Society Newsletter*. The major work, however, remains the study by Henry J. Tobias, *A History of the Jews of New Mexico* (Albuquerque: University of New Mexico Press, 1990).

The theme of Native American religion has been analyzed more by anthropologists than historians. Elsie Clews Parsons's controversial *Pueblo Indian Religion*, 2 vols. (Chicago: University of Chicago Press, 1939), should be supplemented by Alfonso Ortiz, *The Tewa World: Space, Time, Being and Becoming in a Pueblo Society* (Chicago: University of Chicago Press, 1969). Pueblo Indians are very private about such matters and remain decidedly uncomfortable with scholarly analysis of their faith. For the Navajo, see David M. Brugge and Charlotte J. Frisbie, eds., *Navajo Religion and Culture: Selected Views* (Santa Fe: Museum of New Mexico Press, 1982), and Nancy J. Parezo, *Navajo Sandpainting: From Religious Act to Commercial Art* (Albuquerque: University of New Mexico Press, 1993).

For Further Reading
An Annotated Bibliography

Daniel R. Carnett and John J. Griffin

THIS LISTING OF SUGGESTED FURTHER READINGS SUPPLEMENTS SOURCES cited in the notes of the preceding essays. Our brief summary and evaluative annotations are intended to help general and specialist readers interested in locating additional information on the religious cultures of modern New Mexico. After the initial section on General Studies, subsequent sections deal with the topics covered in this volume.

General Studies

Ahlstrom, Sydney. *A Religious History of the American People*. New Haven: Yale University Press, 1972. The author maintains that in the "post-Puritan" era that followed the 1960s, the church was unable to provide an acceptable alternative to "Americanism" and hence had nothing singular to offer a spiritually hungry nation.

Handy, Robert T. *A Christian America: Protestant Hopes and Historical Realities*. New York: Oxford University Press, 1972. A general history tracing Protestantism from the seventeenth through the twentieth centuries. The author emphasizes the church's loss of leadership and power and its captivity within general sociocultural norms.

Herberg, Will. *Protestant, Catholic, Jew*. Garden City, N.Y.: Doubleday, 1955. Herberg views the increase in religious affiliation during the fifties as a search for meaning and identity, not as a return to the concept of the Judeo-Christian God. His "secularization" thesis argues that the American way of life, not Christianity, has become the real religion of the nation.

McNamara, Patrick, ed. *Religion American Style*. Belmont, Calif.: Wadsworth, 1984. A valuable collection of primary and secondary sources that helps place religion in America in a sociological perspective.

Malone, Michael P., and Richard W. Etulain. *The American West: A Twentieth-Century History*. Lincoln: University of Nebraska Press, 1989. Includes sections on religious development and its impact on the West. During the first half of the twentieth century, the issues and controversies in religion in the West closely paralleled those in the rest of the nation; but after World War II, those parallels began to disintegrate.

Marty, Martin. *A Nation of Behavers*. Chicago: University of Chicago Press, 1976. Records a shift in American religious behavior in which people embrace a faith that promises them the most personal success. People often use religion to confirm what they are, rather than to inspire them to become something more.

Szasz, Ferenc Morton. "The Clergy and the Myth of the West." *Church History* 59 (December 1990): 497–506. Pursues overarching themes of religion in the West. The author seeks to answer the question of why the clergy never produced a comparable mythical image like the trapper, outlaw, scout, cowboy, and rancher.

———. *The Protestant Clergy in the Great Plains and Mountain West, 1865–1915*. Albuquerque: University of New Mexico Press, 1988. A regional religious history that depicts ministers as "purveyors of culture." Illustrates this author's clear standing as the leading authority on religion in the American West.

Szasz, Ferenc Morton, ed. *Religion in the West*. Manhattan, Kans.: Sunflower University Press, 1984. A collection of essays that documents the impact of the major religious groups on the development of the West. The overriding contention is that the Judeo-Christian tradition, along with democracy, became the basis of pioneer thought patterns.

Wuthnow, Robert. *The Restructuring of American Religion: Society and Faith since World War II*. Princeton, N.J.: Princeton University Press, 1988. Wuthnow asserts that the consensus civil religion of Herberg began to break down in the sixties. Special-interest groups representing more narrow religious content have increased in significance as the mainline denominations have declined. The nation has experienced a "restructuring" into liberal and conservative camps over societal issues such as abortion, with a subsequent breakdown in communication between the two sides.

Roman Catholics

Dolan, Jay P. *The American Catholic Experience: A History from Colonial Times to the Present.* Garden City, N.Y.: Doubleday, 1985. The author emphasizes Catholic experiences from the bottom up, those of parishioners rather than those of the clergy. Sections four and five deal with the twentieth century and stress the impact of Vatican II on American Catholics.

Hennesey, James. *American Catholics: A History of the Roman Catholic Community in the United States.* New York: Oxford University Press, 1981. The author avoids religious and theological issues. Instead, he casts his work in a political narrative with emphasis on relations with Rome, the U.S. government, and internal ethnic pressures.

Jensen, Carol. "Deserts, Diversity, and Self-Determination: A History of the Catholic Parish in the Intermountain West." In *The American Catholic Parish: A History from 1850 to the Present*, ed. Jay P. Dolan, Vol. 2, 137–276. New York: Paulist Press, 1987. This extensive article pulls together a variety of related facts concerning Catholics in the mountain states of the West. In the process, the author discovers areas of commonality in a region of great geographical, cultural, and religious diversity. Jensen's research demonstrates that in response to Vatican II, intermountain Catholics became involved in more self-determined religious practices.

Lovato, Carol M. *Brother Mathias: Founder of the Little Brothers of the Good Shepherd.* Huntington, Ind.: Our Sunday Visitor Publishing Division, 1987. A chronological narrative of the growth and service of this order and the man who founded it.

Nash, Edward T. "New Faces of Isleta Catholics." Ph.D. dissertation, University of New Mexico, 1981. An examination of the validity of the "compartmentalization thesis" that Pueblo Indians put on a Catholic veneer to maintain their own faith and to keep the two spheres separate. The author found that although elements of compartmentalization were still operative, individual experience with a secular Anglo culture has often caused a syncretization of the two religious systems.

Owens, Lillian P. "The History of the Sisters of Loretto in the Trans-Mississippi West, 1812–1935." Ph.D. dissertation, St. Louis University, 1935. An extensive study of the pioneering educational efforts of the Sisters of Loretto in the West.

Rapagnani, Phyllis Burch. "A Tradition of Service: Roman Catholic Sisters in New Mexico, 1852–1927." Master's thesis, University of New Mexico, 1988. Rapagnani found that nuns in New Mexico functioned as they did elsewhere, but because of unique conditions in the state they made two notable alterations in their service—teaching in the public schools and countering the proselytizing efforts of Protestants.

Mainline Protestants

Atkins, Carolyn. "Menaul School: 1881–1930 . . . not leaders, merely, but Christian leaders." *Journal of Presbyterian History* 58 (Winter 1980): 279–98. Provides an overview of Presbyterians in New Mexico. Of particular value is information concerning the denomination's change from Indian to Hispanic education.

Banker, Mark T. *Presbyterian Missions and Cultural Interaction in the Far Southwest, 1850–1950.* Urbana: University of Illinois Press, 1993. Banker challenges the traditional view of Native cultures of the Southwest passively falling before Anglo-Protestant imperialism. He argues, instead, that indigenous peoples selectively adopted and rejected certain aspects of the invading cultures. He adds that through interactive ethnocultural mission schools, many Presbyterians embraced religious and cultural pluralism.

Brackenridge, R. Douglas, and Francisco D. García-Treto. *Iglesia Presbiteriana: A History of Presbyterians and Mexican-Americans in the Southwest.* San Antonio: Trinity University Press, 1974. Emphasizes the major impact of the Mexican Revolution of 1910 on the course of Presbyterian work in the Southwest. The authors demonstrate that the influx of immigrants from the revolution caused the church to alter its emphasis from conversion to "Americanization."

Connell Szasz, Margaret. "Albuquerque Congregationalists and Southwestern Social Reform: 1900–1917." *New Mexico Historical Review* 55 (July 1980): 231–52. Connell Szasz maintains that the rural nature of the Southwest restricted Social Gospel reform activities to prohibition and education. The coming of the railroad allowed for the expansion of schools to rural areas, where the Congregationalists had their greatest impact.

Myers, Lewis A. *A History of New Mexico Baptists.* Albuquerque: Baptist Convention of New Mexico, 1965. A collection of data loosely organized around a chronological context. The author assembled a vast quantity of statistical information, cameos of leaders, and useful insights on Baptist participation in New Mexico.

O'Brien, Bonnie Ball. *Harry P. Stagg: Christian Statesman.* Nashville: Broadman Press, 1976. A collection of anecdotes and interesting stories of her subject's life, arranged chronologically around important events in Baptist development.

Stoney, James M. *Lighting the Candle: The Episcopal Church on the Upper Rio Grande.* Santa Fe: Rydal Press, 1961. The only modern study that treats the impact of this influential, upper middle-class denomination on New Mexico.

Stratton, David H. *The First Century of Baptists in New Mexico, 1849–1950.* Albuquerque: Women's Missionary Union of New Mexico, 1954. A chronological narrative of Baptist efforts in the state. Stratton argues that the denomination's success lay in its approach to New Mexico as a "foreign country," planting churches and building colleges.

Walker, Randi Jones. *Protestantism in the Sangre de Cristos: 1850–1920.* Albuquerque: University of New Mexico Press, 1991. Deals with Presbyterian, Methodist, Baptist, Congregational, and United Brethren efforts in northern New Mexico and southern Colorado. The author argues that Protestant churches declined in that area because the school and health-care services used there did not integrate Protestant religious ideas into their programs.

Yohn, Susan Mitchell. "Religion, Pluralism, and the Limits of Progressive Reform: Presbyterian Women Home Missionaries in New Mexico, 1870–1930." Ph.D. dissertation, New York University, 1987. Sees women's home missionary work as an attempt to build strong citizens by inculcating Protestant beliefs; later there was a shift to social-reform efforts in an attempt to "Americanize" those whom they served. Yohn asserts that Presbyterians made a major shift in their approach to build strong citizens when church resources proved to be insufficient to carry out their efforts. Forced to turn to the government for support, they embraced a halfhearted acceptance of cultural and religious pluralism.

Jews

Fierman, Floyd S. "The Impact of the Frontier on a Jewish Family: The Bibos." *American Jewish Historical Quarterly* 59 (June 1970): 460–522. An elaborate study of New Mexico's Bibo family. Illustrations and correspondence add to Fierman's comments about this notable mercantile family and their dealings.

Freedman, Morris. "The Jews of Albuquerque." *Commentary* 28 (July 1959): 55–62. A look at 1959 Albuquerque emphasizing the city's Jewish community. A respectful assessment of the constructive religious environments of Santa Fe and Albuquerque.

Goldstein, Brigitte Katz. "Jewish Identification among the Jews of Albuquerque, New Mexico: The Maintenance of Jewishness and Judaism in the Integrated Residential Setting of a Sunbelt City." Ph.D. dissertation, University of New Mexico, 1988. A valuable source celebrating the Albuquerque Jews' determination to maintain their identity and Jewishness. Comparisons are drawn between Albuquerque's Jewish population and those of larger cities.

Meketa, Jacqueline Dorgan. *Louis Felsenthal: Citizen-Soldier of Territorial New Mexico.* Albuquerque: University of New Mexico Press, 1982. Although largely a biography of Felsenthal, Meketa's book also highlights key aspects of New Mexico's social and cultural history.

Rochlin, Harriet, and Fred Rochlin. *Pioneer Jews: A New Life in the Far West.* Boston: Houghton Mifflin Company, 1984. Focus is on Jewish westward migration. Numerous illustrations add much to this regionalized social and occupational history.

Rollins, Sandra Lea. "Jewish Indian Chief." *Western States Jewish Historical Quarterly* 1 (July 1969): 151–63. An engaging study of Solomon Bibo that touches on Bibo's involvement with New Mexico's Acoma pueblo. In addition, Rollins furnishes an interesting look at New Mexico's economic development.

Rosenfeld, Albert. "In Santa Fe, The City Different: Old Jewish Settlers and New." *Commentary* 17 (May 1954): 456–60. An illuminating commentary on religious diversity in Santa Fe. Emphasis is on mutual involvement of Catholics, Baptists, Episcopalians, Christian Scientists, and Jews in this capital city's daily regimen.

Rothenberg, Gunther, and Israel C. Carmel. *Congregation Albert, 1897-1972.* Albuquerque: n.p., 1972. Rothenberg and Carmel place this brief history of a local congregation in the context of the Jewish move westward. Emphasis is on Congregation Albert's beginning and subsequent development.

Sharfman, Harold. *Jews on the Frontier.* Chicago: Henry Regnery Company, 1977. Scharfman emphasizes Jewish population growth and its subsequent influence on the prosperity of a land different from any the immigrants had ever known. An excellent treatment of people in transition.

Shinedling, Abraham I. *History of the Los Alamos Jewish Center, Los Alamos, New Mexico, 1944–1957.* Albuquerque: New Mexico Valliant Printing Company, 1958. Shinedling offers insight into the workings of a devoted group of worshipers in Los Alamos surrounded by the atomic research machine on "the Hill." An interesting look at religious devotion in a progressive social environment.

Tobias, Henry J. *History of the Jews in New Mexico.* Albuquerque: University of New Mexico Press, 1990. A valuable, detailed history of Jewish contributions to the history of New Mexico. The outstanding source on this topic.

Mormons

Alexander, Thomas G. *Mormonism in Transition: A History of the Latter-day Saints, 1890–1930.* Urbana: University of Illinois Press, 1986. Focus is on Mormon church's political structure and the forty years of change that its members have experienced. Additional insights on the roles of notable leaders and on church mission work.

Allen, James B., and Glen M. Leonard. *The Story of the Latter-day Saints.* Salt Lake City: Deseret Book Company, 1976. A concise, readable history of the Mormon church from conception to the late 1970s. Authors comment on contemporary concerns and the church's transformation since the early nineteenth century. Special emphasis is on Mormonism in American politics and culture. Also includes observations on Mormon missionary efforts.

Arrington, Leonard J., and Davis Bitton. *Mormon Experience: A History of the Latter-day Saints.* 2d ed. Urbana: University of Illinois Press, 1992. A thorough treatment of Mormon history. This volume cites the difficulties Mormons encountered during their early years as a society and traces their migration westward to Utah and then around the world.

Gottlieb, Robert, and Peter Wiley. *America's Saints: The Rise of Mormon Power.* New York: G. P. Putnam's Sons, 1984. An interesting look at contemporary Mormonism that emphasizes the practical elements of the faith. Paying particular attention to Mormon financial status and their rise in popularity and political influence, the authors provide a journalistic document.

Gunn, Rodger S. *Mormonism: Challenge and Defense.* Salt Lake City: Hawkes Publications, 1973. An open-minded approach to the theology and history of Mormonism, with a thorough discussion of doctrinal positions regarding issues like repentance and baptism. Moreover, the author boldly discusses seeming contradictions in Mormon Holy Writ and Joseph Smith's role as leader and prophet.

Hansen, Klaus J. *Mormonism and the American Experience.* Chicago: University of Chicago Press, 1981. Key focus is the impact of Mormonism on American culture. In addition, the church's views on minorities, sexuality, and marriage are emphasized. Especially interesting are comments on the ways in which Mormonism and American culture tolerate each other.

Larsen, Dean L. *You and the Destiny of the Indian.* Salt Lake City: Bookcraft, 1966. An intriguing history of the "Lamanites" and the Mormon church's efforts to evangelize them. The book is at once a history of the Native Americans from a Mormon perspective and a statement of church policy regarding missions to the Native Americans.

Leone, Mark P. *Roots of Modern Mormonism.* Cambridge, Mass.: Harvard University Press, 1979. A reliable study of Mormon mission efforts to the Native Americans, particularly to the Navajos and the Apaches. The author touches on the history and polity of Mormonism in the twentieth century.

McKiernan, F. Mark, Alma R. Blair, and Paul M. Edwards, eds. *The Restoration Movements: Essays in Mormon History.* Lawrence, Kans: Coronado Press, 1973. An overview of nineteenth- and early twentieth-century progress in the Reorganized Church of Jesus Christ of Latter Day Saints. Leonard Arrington and D. Michael Quinn offer an insightful assessment of Mormon efforts with Native Americans in New Mexico.

Mauss, Armand Lind. *Mormonism and Minorities.* Ph.D. dissertation, University of California, Berkeley, 1970; Ann Arbor: University Microfilms, 1970. Focuses on Mormon attitudes toward Jews, African Americans, and Native Americans from the perspective of Mormon theology. An engaging study.

Meinig, D. W. "The Mormon Culture Region: Strategies and Patterns in the Geography of the American West, 1847–1964." *Annals of the Association of American Geographers* 55 (June 1965): 191–220. Emphasis is on the regional evolution of Mormondom in Utah and its impact on surrounding areas. Fascinating, too, are Meinig's conclusions regarding the complex relationships between a religious subculture and its central core of power.

Shipps, Jan. *Mormonism: The Story of a New Religious Tradition.* Urbana: University of Illinois Press, 1985. Another strong study of the Mormons. Shipps's provocative comparison of evangelical Christianity with Mormonism clarifies differences between the two groups.

Evangelicals

Bassett, Paul M. "A Study in the Theology of the Early Holiness Movement." *Methodist History* 13 (April 1975): 61–84. An aid in understanding Holiness teachings and a dynamic phase of recent American religious history. Complements other texts regarding Holiness denominations' mission efforts toward Native Americans in the Southwest.

Belknap, Helen O. *Church on the Changing Frontier: A Study of the Homesteader and His Church.* New York: George H. Doran, 1922. The author offers a glimpse into the church's role in the transformation of four counties in Montana, Wyoming, South Dakota, and New Mexico. Belknap writes about the economic and religious strains each area experienced when changing from cattle raising to an agriculture-based society.

Etulain, Richard W., and Raymond M. Cooke, eds. *Religion and Culture.* Albuquerque: Far West Books, 1991. Of interest is Etulain's helpful article "Regionalizing Religion: Evangelicals in the American West, 1940–1990," which concentrates largely on celebrity-status clergy and their respective denominations. The essay encourages further study of evangelicalism's effect on twentieth-century western history.

Guarneri, Carl, and David Alvarez, eds. *Religion and Society in the American West: Historical Essays.* Lanham, Md.: University Press of America, 1987. This collection includes several key essays regarding New Mexico's religious history. Overall, a valuable place to begin a study of the role of evangelicalism in the modern American West.

Hamilton, Robert. *The Gospel among the Red Men: The History of Southern Baptist Indian Missions.* Nashville: Sunday School Board of the Southern Baptist Convention, 1930. Intriguing account of Baptist missions to the New Mexican Navajo and Pueblo Indians. Notes the dedication required to fulfill mission goals in the early twenties.

Nash, Ronald H. *Evangelicals in America: Who They Are, What They Believe.* Nashville: Abingdon Press, 1987. Intended as a primer for those desiring additional information regarding evangelicalism. Provides thorough discussion of characteristic evangelical doctrine and compares it with that of other prominent Protestant religious movements.

Paloma, Margaret M. *The Assemblies of God at the Crossroads: Charisma and Institutional Dilemmas.* Knoxville: University of Tennessee Press, 1989. An overview of Assembly of God history and a prophetic look at future trends in this growing denomination. Includes an assessment of the social dimensions of the faith.

Pearson, G. H. *The Transformed Red Man.* Kansas City: Beacon Hill Press, 1956. An excellent discussion of the Church of the Nazarene's work in Native American missions. Clearly, a layman's perspective on Native American religion and evangelical efforts to offer an alternative belief system.

Smith, Timothy L. *Called unto Holiness: The Story of the Nazarenes: The Formative Years.* Kansas City: Nazarene Publishing House, 1962. This book offers an insightful look at the denomination's genesis from several groups. In addition, Smith discusses the Holiness movement in the United States.

Templin, J. Alton, Allen D. Breck, and Martin Rist. *Methodists, Evangelicals, and United Brethren Churches in the Rockies, 1850–1976.* Denver: Rocky Mountain Conference of the United Methodist Church, 1977. Focuses primarily on specific denominations in Colorado. The book proves helpful, however, in understanding these same groups in New Mexico. Recommended reading for its extensive scholarship and its references to further needed research.

Topping, Gary. "Religion in the West." *Journal of American Culture* 3 (Summer 1980): 330–50. Offers key commentary focusing on church influence in the West from the seventeenth to the twentieth centuries. Proves indispensable as a source for further research in the history of religion in the West.

Wells, David F., and John D. Woodridge, eds. *The Evangelicals: What They Believe, Who They Are, Where They Are Changing.* Nashville: Abingdon Press, 1975. A commendable collection of essays presenting various approaches to the subject of evangelicalism. Especially appealing is the diversity of perspectives on the theme.

Alternative Religions

Cox, Harvey. *Turning East: The Promise and Peril of the New Orientalism.* New York: Simon and Schuster, 1977. Examines the effect of American culture on Eastern religion. Interestingly, Cox suggests that this turn to the East may lead to a rediscovery of the spiritual heritage of the West.

Ellwood, Robert S. *Alternative Altars: Unconventional and Eastern Spirituality in America.* Chicago: University of Chicago Press, 1979. This groundbreaking study examines in depth three movements: Spiritualism, Theosophy, and American Zen. The author also shows how these groups, seen as one emergent spiritual core, have begun to compete with Christianity as a center for national consensus.

Etulain, Richard W., comp. *Religion in the Twentieth Century American West: A Bibliography.* Occasional Papers, No. 4. Albuquerque: Center for the American West, University of New Mexico, 1991. A valuable source for studies pertaining to New Mexico and the Southwest, including groups that lie outside the Judeo-Christian tradition.

Ferguson, Marilyn. *The Aquarian Conspiracy: Personal and Social Transformation in Our Time.* Los Angeles: J. P. Tarcher, 1980. Charts individualistic trends in religious beliefs. The author maintains that people are turning inward for spiritual nourishment, which will produce societal change through personal transformation.

Fox, Stephen D. "Healing, Imagination, and New Mexico." *New Mexico Historical Review* 58 (July 1983): 213–37. Study of health seekers who came to New Mexico around the turn of the century. Fox points to the search for alternative methods of healing as the origin of several new religions.

Groothuis, Douglas R. *Unmasking the New Age*. Downers Grove, Ill.: Inter-Varsity Press, 1986. The author asserts that the counterculture of the 1960s entered the political and social mainstream of the 1970s. Rather than revolutionary change from without, evolutionary change from within has become the preferred path to social change.

Simundson, Daniel Nathan. "John Ballou Newbrough and the Oahspe Bible." Ph.D. dissertation, University of New Mexico, 1972. An examination of the community of Shalam (near present-day Las Cruces), which sought to separate itself from the outside world instead of providing an example for it. Ghost writing, used today in some New Age circles, figured prominently in their beliefs.

Native Americans

Bowden, Henry Warner. *American Indians and Christian Missions*. Chicago: University of Chicago Press, 1981. Excellent discussion of twentieth-century bureaucratic developments influencing Native American religious history. Helps in understanding the complex relationship between Native American beliefs and Christianity, not to mention the complicating role of the Bureau of Indian Affairs.

Fergusson, Erna. *Dancing Gods*. Albuquerque: University of New Mexico Press, 1931. Considers the close relationship between ritual and belief among the southwestern Native Americans. The author offers a comprehensive discussion of Navajo religion.

Gill, Sam D. *Native American Religions: An Introduction*. Belmont, Calif.: Wadsworth Publishing Company, 1982. Illuminates Native American mythology and rites and includes an informative discussion of the Rio Grande pueblos of New Mexico. Gill also treats the influences of Anglo-American Christianity on Indians.

Hirschfelder, Arlene, and Paulette Molin. *The Encyclopedia of Native American Religions: An Introduction*. New York: Facts on File, 1992. A sweeping compendium of subjects and persons involved in historical and contemporary Native American religions. Particularly helpful on twentieth-century New Mexico religious cultures and the state's Native American faiths.

Hultkrantz, Åke. *Native Religions of North America: The Power of Visions and Fertility*. San Francisco: Harper Collins Publishers, 1987. Offers a thorough explanation of the complexity of the Zuni religion. The author's comments pertaining to Native American religions are helpful, too, especially the discussions of the dramatic impact of the white man's religion on Native American cultures.

La Barre, Weston. *The Peyote Cult*. New Haven: Yale University Press, 1938. The most thorough overview of the Peyote religion. Concentrates on the biological, psychological, and spiritual elements of the plant and practice, including the effect on the user's body and mind. Worthwhile reading for this facet of Native American religion.

Quam, Alvina, trans. *The Zunis: Self-Portrayals by the Zuni People*. Albuquerque: University of New Mexico Press, 1972. A helpful look at Zuni cosmology and the ritual meaning of particular dances in the words of the religion's practitioners and observers. Particularly important to studies of ancient Native American religious symbolism.

Reichard, Gladys A. *Navajo Religion: A Study of Symbolism*. Princeton, N.J.: Princeton University Press, 1963. An enormously informative book focusing on Navajo dogma, symbolism, and ritual. Reichard defines the significance of ideas and their equivalent symbolic representations.

Starkloff, Carl F. *The People of the Center: American Indian Religion and Christianity*. New York: Seabury Press, 1974. An attempt to synthesize Native American ritual and beliefs with notable Christian concepts. Asks what will happen to Christianity as it mixes with Native American perspectives on issues such as the deity and creation. Interesting comparisons throughout between Native American and Christian thinking on these notions.

Steltenkamp, Michael F. *The Sacred Vision: Native American Religion and Its Practice Today*. New York: Paulist Press, 1982. Highly informative discussion of the Native American Church and peyotism. A worthwhile general discussion of Native American beliefs and practices.

Tyler, Hamilton A. *Pueblo Gods and Myths*. Norman: University of Oklahoma Press, 1964. Focuses on discussions of Pueblo deities and what the author calls "lesser supernaturals." Pays particular attention to Acoma, Hopi, and Zuni deities and accompanying symbolic elements. A thorough discussion of the thriving Pueblo belief systems.

Underhill, Ruth M. *Red Man's Religion: Beliefs and Practices of the Indians North of Mexico*. Chicago: University of Chicago Press, 1965. A comprehensive source for Native American religious systems and practices throughout the United States. Gives attention to the impact of established faiths on cultures tied to centuries-old belief systems. Examines religious movements that evolved from these contacts, for example, the Native American Church.

Vecsey, Christopher, ed. *The Study of American Indian Religions*. New York: Crossroad Publishing Company, 1983. This book contains six of Åke Hultkrantz's essays that proffer an ambitious discussion of scholarly approaches to the study of Native American religions. Illustrates well Hultkrantz's expertise in Native American religious history and practices.

Waters, Frank. *Masked Gods: Navaho and Pueblo Ceremonialism*. Albuquerque: University of New Mexico Press, 1950. Focuses on the Navajos, Rio Grande Pueblos, and the Zunis. A clear account of the significance of their faiths as earnest attempts to relate to the immediate world and beyond. Waters addresses specific rituals and ceremonials integral to southwestern cultural history.

Waugh, Earle H., and K. Dad Prithipaul, eds. *Native American Traditions*. Edmonton: Corporation Canadienne des Sciences Religieuses/ Canadian Corporation for Studies in Religion, 1979. A fine anthology of essays addressing the religious rituals of several tribes. See especially Karl W. Luckert's discussion of Navajo mythology. Elucidates purely Native American belief systems and practices without discussing missionary influences.

Index

Boldface numbers indicate extended treatment of a subject

Abbott, Lyman, 172, 173
Abeita, Pablo, 184
Acoma pueblo, 90–91, 104
African-American Baptists, 37, 50–51
African Americans, 27, 50–51, 174, 179
Ahlstrom, Sydney, 178
Albuquerque Zen Center, 162
Allison James School (Santa Fe), 185
Alpert, Richard. *See* Dass, Ram
Altered Landscapes: Christianity in America, 1935–1985 (Marty, Introduction), 28–29
Alternative spiritual communities, **145–70**, 206–7
American Buddhism, 145, 147–48, 159–63, 179
American Indian Religious Freedom Act (1978), 5, 85, 91, 92, 96
Americans United for Separation of Church and State, 138
Anaya, Toney, 159
Anderson, Clinton P., 71, 88
Annual Prayer Pilgrimage for Peace, 18–19

Apache New Testament, 94
Apaches, 81, 86. *See also* Jicarilla Apaches; Mescalero Apaches; White Mountain Apaches
Archaeological Resource Protection Act (1979), 92.
Arrington, Leonard J., **101–23**
Ashkenazic Jews. *See* Germanic Jews
Ashtar Command Ascension Center, 150
Asians, 27
Assemblies of God Church, 33, 126, 134
Assimilation, 82–85

Baby Boomers, 146, 151
Baha'is, 174
Baptists, 127, 128, 133–34. *See also* African American Baptists; Colporters; Southern Baptists
Barrett, Brother Mathias, 188
Beatles, The, 154
Be Here Now (Dass), 153
Bellah, Robert, 182
Blacks. *See* African Americans
Blue Lake Controversy, 87–90, 180
"Blue laws," 43

B'nai B'rith, 68
Bodhi Manda Zen Center, 162, 164
"Boomer Dharma: The Evolution of Alternative Spiritual Communities in Modern New Mexico" (Fox), **145–70**
Brahmins, 174
Bryan, William Jennings, 173, 175
Buddhist Ray, The, 159–60
Bureau of Indian Affairs, 84
Bureau of Land Management, 90–91
Burgess, Andrew, 189
Burke, Charles, 84–85, 88
Byrne, Edwin V., 187

Calvary Chapel, 188
Carnett, Daniel R., ix, **197–209**
Carson National Forest, 87
Catholicism. *See* Roman Catholicism
Chamberlain, Kathleen Egan, **81–99**
Charbonneau, Jean Baptiste, 102–3
Charismatic Renewal, 18
Chautauqua, 172–73, 186
Chavez, Martin, 90
Christian Scientists, 174
Church, Peggy Pond, 190
Church of Jesus Christ of the Latter-day Saints. *See* Mormons
Church of the Nazarene, 179
Churches of Christ, 33, 133–34
Circuit riders, 131–32
Circular 1665, 84–85
Cold War, 48
College of St. Joseph, 186
College of the Southwest, 189
Collier, John, 85, 93
Colporters, 131–32
Colson, Charles, 130–31
Columbus quincentennial, 4
Comparative religious history, **171–96**

"Competition for the Native American Soul: The Search for Religious Freedom in Twentieth-Century New Mexico" (Chamberlain), **81–99**
Congregation Albert, 68
Congregation B'nai Israel, 71–72
Congregation Montefiore, 69
Congregationalists, 37
Conversion narratives, 126–31; and anti-Catholicism, 128–29
Cooke, Phillip St. George, 102–4
Cowboy camp meetings, 132–35
Cox, Harvey, 48
Cruz, Margarita, 43–44

Dar al-Islam Muslim community, 145, 155–56, 189
Dark Wind (Hillerman/Redford), 91–92
Darwin, Charles, 175
Dass, Ram (Richard Alpert), 145, 153–55
Death of God: The Culture of Our Post-Christian Era, The (Vahanian), 48
Del Norte Baptist Church, 55
Disciples of Christ, 37
Dixon case, 16, 135–39, 187
Dorchester, 176
Dunne, Rev. Will B., 180
Durkee, Barbara, 152–53
Durkee, Stephen, 152–53, 155
Durkheim, Emil, 171
Dylan, Bob, 181

Eareckson, Joni, 130–31
Eastern New Mexico University, 189
Easy Rider, 145
Eddy, Mary Baker, 146
Edgerton, Faye, 94
Electronic Shaman, 150
Episcopalians, 132, 134

Index

Etulain, Richard W., vii–ix
Evangelical Free Church, 179
Evangelical Lutheran Church in America, 37
Evangelical United Brethren, 37
Evangelicals, 204–6

Fergusson, Erna, 186
Fields, Rick, 160
First Amendment, 81, 85
First Baptist Church of Albuquerque, 188
"For Further Reading: An Annotated Bibliography" (Carnett and Griffin), **197–209**
Four Square Gospel Church, 175–76
Fox, Stephen, **145–70**
Free Schools Committee, 136–38
Fundamentalist-Modernist controversy, 174–76

Germanic Jews, 64–69
Ghost Ranch Conference Center, 188
Goldwater, Barry, 89
Gordon, Ralph, 149
Goulesque, Florence, ix
Graham, William Franklin (Billy), 177
Grant Chapel African Methodist Episcopal Church, 50
Grant's "peace policy," 83–84
Greeley, Andrew, 181
Griffin, John J., ix, **197–209**
Gurule, Nicholas, 132

Hacienda Guru Ram Das, 158
Hall, Ralph J., 133, 134
Handy, Robert C., 176
Harwood, Emily, 43
Haught, Janelle, 187
Hearst, William Randolph, 177
Herberg, Will, 176–77

Hillerman, Tony, 91–92
Hillside Community Church, 55
Hinduism, 154
Hinkin, John-Roger, 149
Hispanics, 49–51, 113–14, 126, 152
Hodge, William H., 128
Hoffmantown Baptist Church, 55–56
Hog Farm, 157, 165
Hopis, 84–85, 91–92, 95, 111; and arts and crafts, 117–18
Horn, Calvin, 188
How the Swans Came to the Lake (Fields), 160
Howard, Jill, ix
Hukill, Traci, ix
Hunter, James Davison, 182
Hunter, Neva Dell, 148–49
Hutton, Paul Andrew, 154

Indian Civil Rights Act of 1968, 85
Indian Claims Commission, 88
Indians. *See* Native Americans
Industrial Workers of the World (IWW), 173
Insight Training Seminars, 149–50
Islam, 174, 179
Isleta pueblo, 104, 105–6

Jackson, Sherwood Young (S. Y.), 132
Jemez pueblo, 3, 138
Jensen, Carol, **1–26**
Jews, **63–79**, 155, **171–96**, 201–2; and intermarriage, 66, 75; and the creation of Israel, 74–75; and Zionism, 72. *See also* Germanic Jews; Reform Judaism; Sephardic Jews
Jicarilla Apaches, 118, 184
Jones, Rev. Jim, 171
Jook Savages, 156–57
Judaism. *See* Jews

Kachinas, 91, 95
Kalu Rinpoche, The Venerable, 162
Kaplan, Rabbi J. H., 70–71
Kapleau, Philip, 162, 165–66
Khang Tzag stupa, 161
King, Bruce, 159
Koresh, David, 171
Krohn, Rabbi A.L., 71
Ku Klux Klan, 174, 176

Laguna pueblo, 104, 105–6, 118
Lama Foundation, 145, 151–55
Lamy, Jean Baptiste, 7, 16, 70, 183
Land of Shalam, 185
Latter-day Saints, Church of Jesus Christ. *See* Mormons
Law, Lisa, 157
Law, Tom, 157
Lee, George P. (Navajo), 116
Lennon, John, 181
Liebman, Joshua, 177
Little Brothers of the Good Shepherd, The, 188
Lummis, Charles Fletcher, 186
"Lungers," 184–85
Lutheran Hour, The, 177
Lutherans, 133–34

Mabry, Thomas, 187
McNamara, Patrick, 189
McPherson, Aimee Semple ("Sister Aimee"), 175–76
Madonna, 181
Maharishi Mahesh. *See* Yogi Maharishi Mahesh
Marlette, Doug, 180
Marty, Martin, 28–29
Mead, Sidney, E., 181
Menaul School, 185
Mescalero Apaches, 83, 184
Methodists, 127, 132, 133–34, 172. *See also* Circuit riders
Mexican Mission, 104–5
Moral Man and Immoral Society (Niebuhr), 177
Morally We Roll Along, 173
Moravians, 83
Mormon Battalion, 101–4
Mormons, 33, 37, 39, **101–23**, 83, 93, 136, 138, 179, 203–4; and Indian arts and crafts, 117–19; and Native Americans, 111–13, 116; and women, 108–9, 115
"Mormons in Twentieth-Century New Mexico" (Arrington), **101–23**
Mount Adams, 180
Mount Olive Baptist Church, 50–51
Mount Zion Baptist Church, 50–51
Mountain Cloud Zen Center, 162
Movement for Spiritual Inner Awareness, 149
Murray, John Courtney, 176
Muslims. *See* Dar al-Muslim community

"Naked Public Square," 181
National Council of Churches, 177
Native American Church, 93, 152
Native American Graves Protection and Repatriation Act of 1990, 92
Native American Religious Arts and Crafts, 91–92
Native American Self-Determination Act (1975), 5
Native Americans, **1–6**, 50–51, **81–99**, 126, 184, 190, 207–9; and Mormons, 111–13; and polygamy, 41–42; and religious arts and crafts, 117–19; and Roman Catholics, 1–6. *See also names of individual tribes*
Navajo Community College, 96
Navajo New Testament, 94
Navajos, 81, 84, 85–86, 95, 129, 184; and arts and crafts, 117, 118–19; and conversion narratives, 128–30; and Mormons, 104, 116. *See also* Ramah Navajo

Nephites, 105–6
Neuhaus, Richard John, 181
"New Age" culture, 147–48, 164
New Agers, 92, 179–80, 190
Newbrough, John Ballou, 185
New Buffalo, 151–52
"New Mexico Catholic Cultural hegemony," 183–89
New Mexico Council of Churches, 52, 89
New Western Historians, vii
"New Western History," 119–20
Niebuhr, Reinhold, 177
Nixon, Richard, 89
Niza, Fray Marcos de, 3
Nizhoni Days, 190
Nogal Mesa, New Mexico, 133
North American Muslim Powwow, 145, 155–56

Oahspe Bible, 185
Oñate, Juan de, 2
Ortiz, Alfonso, 82, 189
Outlook, 172

Peace of Mind (Liebman), 177
Peace of Soul (Sheen), 177
Peace Prayer Day, 158
Peale, Norman Vincent, 177
Peanuts (Schultz), 181
Pelotte, Donald E., 5
Penitentes, 21
Pentecostals, 126, 127, 136, 138, 179; and conversion narratives, 130
Petroglyphs, 90–91, 96, 165
Peyote, 93, 152
Pinchot, Gifford, 87
Polygamy, 41–42, 105
Pope John Paul II, 2
Pope Pius, 173
Postman, Neil, 181–82
Power of Positive of Thinking, The (Peale), 177

Prayer Pilgrimage for Peace, 18–19, 53
Presbyterian Hospital, 185
Presbyterians, 37, 132, 133–34, 136, 138
Protestant-Catholic-Jew (Herberg), 177
"Protestant cultural hegemony," 172–77
Protestant evangelism, **125–43**. See also Evangelicals
Protestantism, **27–62, 171–96**, 200–201; and racial prejudice, 48–49; and women, 43–44, 54–55. See also *names of individual denominations*
"Protestantism in Modern New Mexico," **27–62**
Pueblo Revolt of 1680, 3, 96
Pueblos (Indians), 81, 84–85, 86, 184, 190

Quimby Center, 149
Quimby, P. P., 146, 149
Quintana, Juan, 132

Rajneesh, 171
Ramah. *See* Savoia
Ramah Navajo, 90–91
Rauschenbusch, Walter, 173
Redford, Robert, 91–92
Reform Judaism, 65, 69–70, 76–77. *See also* Jews
"Religious Culture of the Jews in Modern New Mexico, The" (Tobias), **63–79**
Rendon, Gabino, 128–29
Rendón, Petrita, 43–44
Rerum Novarum (1891), 173
Revista Católica, 183
"Rhetorical Approach to Protestant Evangelism in Twentieth-Century New Mexico, A" (Schuetz), **125–43**

Richard, Cliff, 181
Riley, William B., 175
Robertson, Pat, 182
Roe v. Wade (1973), 181
Roman Catholicism, **1–26**, 39, **171–96**, 199–200; Annual Prayer Pilgrimage for Peace, 18–19; charismatic renewal, 18; Diocese of Gallup, 3, 6, 16; and the Dixon case, 135–39; and environmental awareness, 19; and Native Americans, 1–6; and religious art, 13–14; and women, 15. *See also* Native Americans
"Roman Catholicism in Modern New Mexico: A Commitment to Survive" (Jensen), **1–26**
Roosevelt, Theodore, 172, 173

Sabbatarian movement, 43
St. Joseph Hospital, 184
San Felipe pueblo, 83
Sanchez, Herman, 130
Sanchez, Robert, 4, 6–7, 14, 21, 189
Sandia pueblo, 96
Sando, Joe, 90
Sandoval, Joe, 128
Santa Clara pueblo, 118
Santa Cruz de la Cañada, 14
Santo Domingo pueblo, 4, 83
Savoia (Ramah), 104, 106–7
Scherer, Jay Victor, 150–51
Schuetz, Janice E., **125–43**
Schultz, Charles, 181
Schwarzenegger, Arnold, 182
Scopes Trial (1925), 175, 186
Secular City, The (Cox), 48
Sephardic Jews (Spanish-Portuguese Jews), 64
Seventh-day Adventists, 127, 132, 136, 138
Sexuality, 7, 41, 54, 158–59, 161, 182

Sheen, Fulton J., 177
Sheldon, Charles, 174
Sherman, Roger Bennett, 133
Sikhs, 156–59
Snyder, Gary, 163
Social Gospel, 44, 184, 188
Southern Baptists, 33, 83, 179
Southwestern College, 145, 148–50
Spiegelberg, Levi, 65
Springsteen, Bruce, 181
Stadtmueller, Frederick A., 4
Surat Shabda, 149
Swedenborg, Samuel, 146
Syncretism, 82, 93
Szasz, Ferenc M., vii–ix, 94, **171–96**

Taos pueblo, 85, 93; Blue Lake controversy, 87–90, 180
Tekakwitha Conference, 5
Tesuque pueblo, 157
Theology for the Social Gospel, A (Rauschenbusch), 173
Third Great Awakening, 133
Thoreau, Henry David, 146
Three Pillars of Zen (Kapleau), 162
Tibetan Buddhism, 160–61
Tillich, Paul, 171
Tobias, Henry J., **63–79**
Treaty of Guadalupe Hidalgo, 82–83
Tricycle: The Buddhist Review, 160

Udall, Stewart, 159
Udall, Tom, 159
United Church of Christ, 37, 48
United Methodists, 37, 49. *See also* Methodists
"United States and New Mexico: A Twentieth-Century Comparative Religious History, The" (Szasz), **171–96**
University of Albuquerque. *See* College of St. Joseph
University of New Mexico, 185, 189

INDEX

Vahanian, Gabriel, 48
Vatican II, 179
Victory Love Fellowship, 179, 188
Vivekananda, Swami, 174

Walker, Randi Jones, **27–62**
Waterman, Robert, 149
We Hold These Truths (Murray), 176
West Mesa Christian Church, 55
White Mountain Apaches, 93
White Sands, New Mexico, 149
Whole Earth Catalog, 152, 153
Wills, Garry, 178–179
Wilson, Woodrow, 173
Women's National Indian Association, 84
Women's Relief Society, 108–9
Woodstock, 157, 165
World War I, 44, 175; and Jews, 72
World War II, 46–47, 176; and Jews, 68
World's Parliament of Religions, 174, 179
Wuthnow, Robert, 182
Wycliffe Bible Translators, 94

Yakima Nation, 180
Yogi Bhajan, 145, 151, 156–59
Yogi Maharishi Mahesh, 154
Young, Brigham, 101, 104

Zah, Peterson, 90
Zellers v. Raymond Hutt (1948), 136–38, 187
Zen Buddhism, 162–63, 179
Zionism, 72
Zuni pueblo, 104–6, 111, 118, 184

Contributors

LEONARD J. ARRINGTON is Lemuel Redd Professor of Western History Emeritus at Brigham Young University. He served as Church Historian, The Church of Jesus Christ of Latter-day Saints, 1972–82. His publications include *Great Basin Kingdom: An Economic History of the Latter-day Saints, 1830–1900* (2d ed., 1993); *The Mormon Experience: A History of the Latter-day Saints*, coauthored with Davis Bitton (2d ed., 1992); *Brigham Young: American Moses* (1986); and his two-volume *History of Idaho* (1994). Dr. Arrington has served as president of the Western History Association, the Mormon History Association, and the Pacific Coast Branch of the American Historical Association.

DANIEL R. CARNETT is a doctoral candidate at the University of New Mexico specializing in the history of the American West and modern United States, with an M.A. from Arkansas State University. His research interests include the religious cultures in New Mexico.

KATHLEEN EGAN CHAMBERLAIN is a doctoral student at the University of New Mexico majoring in recent U.S. and American western history, with an M.A. from the University of Colorado at Denver. Her area of specialization is Native American history. She has published articles on Colorado history and book reviews in the *New Mexico Historical Review*.

RICHARD W. ETULAIN is Professor of History and Director of the Center for the American West at the University of New Mexico. A specialist in cultural history and historiography, he has authored or edited several books, including *The American West: A Twentieth-Century History* (with Michael P. Malone, 1989, coauthor), *Writing Western History* (1991, editor), *The American West in the Twentieth Century: A Bibliography* (1994, editor), and *Contemporary New Mexico, 1940–1990* (1994, editor). His most recent book is *Re-imagining the Modern American West: A Century of Fiction, History, and Art* (1996).

STEPHEN FOX has taught in the departments of American Studies and Sociology and in the General Honors Program at the University of New Mexico. He concentrates on the relationships between minorities and countercultures and mass culture. His publications include *Toxic Work; Women Workers at GTE Lenkurt* (1991); book chapters about the impact of the Cold War on countercultures in the West and about the use of American images in German popular culture; and journal articles on pilgrimage in the Southwest and the effects of U.S. mass culture on East Germans since German unification.

JOHN J. GRIFFIN is currently a doctoral candidate in American Studies at the University of New Mexico. He holds a B.A. in English and a M.A. in Communication from the University of New Mexico. His doctoral studies focus on religion and American culture. He has published book reviews in *Journal of the West*.

CAROL JENSEN is the Assistant Director of the Honors Program at the University of Nevada, Las Vegas. She specializes in the religious history of the American Southwest and has written several articles in this subject area. Her most recent publication is the Intermountain segment of *The American Catholic Parish: A History from 1850 to the Present* (1987).

JANICE E. SCHUETZ is Professor of Communication at the University of New Mexico. She specializes in rhetorical studies of religious, political, and legal communication. She has authored or coauthored five books: *Rhetorical Perspectives on Communication and Mass Media* (1982), *Participating in the Communication Process* (1984), *Communication and Litigation* (1988), *Perspectives on Argumentation Theory* (1990), and *The Logic of Women on Trial* (1994). She is the editor of the *Journal of Communication and Religion*.

FERENC M. SZASZ is Professor of History at the University of New Mexico. He specializes in American intellectual, cultural, and religious history and has written a number of articles and books on this theme. His latest books are *The Protestant Clergy in the Great Plains and Mountain West, 1865–1915* (1988) and *The British Scientists and the Manhattan Project: The Los Alamos Years* (1991), and he has edited *Great Mysteries of the West* (1993). He is currently working on a study of religion in the modern American West.

HENRY J. TOBIAS is Professor Emeritus of History at the University of Oklahoma. Although originally a specialist in Russian history, in recent years he has published *The Jews in Oklahoma* (1980) and *A History of the Jews in New Mexico* (1990). He has also published articles and book reviews on New Mexico in the *New Mexico Historical Review*. He is currently writing a history of Santa Fe since 1880 with Charles E. Woodhouse.

RANDI JONES WALKER is Assistant Professor of Church History at the Pacific School of Religion and on the Core Doctoral Faculty of the Graduate Theological Union in Berkeley, California. She is author of *Protestantism in the Sangre de Cristos, 1850–1920* (1991) and is currently working on a biography of Emma Newman, a Congregational minister in nineteenth-century Illinois, Kansas, and California.